Building a Better Busines[s]

'One of the most stimulatin[g] [...]
for a very long time.'

> Sir Digby Jones, director-general, Confederation of British Industry

'A really helpful guide to success. Essential reading for anyone
running a business.'

> Brent Hoberman, co-founder and CEO, Last-Minute.com

'Excellent management books should spur you into action. This
one does! A thoroughly enjoyable and refreshing read.'

> Lord Leitch, chairman of the Employment Panel; former
> CEO of Zurich Financial Services in UK and Asia; former
> chairman of the Association of British Insurers

'Patrick Dixon is first among equals in "how-to" business writings.
This brilliant book reveals how passion for your customers and
your mission is vital in developing strong brands.'

> Professor Liping Cai, director, Purdue Tourism &
> Hospitality Research Center, Purdue University, USA

'A perfect summary of all important factors that contribute to
success in business and private life. What a potential for better
results – and ultimately success!'

> Robert Salzl, CEO, Arabella Hotel Holding International GmbH and Co.

'Reading a book like *Building a Better Business* can be a little scary.
So much of it resonates instantly with one's own personal and
business circumstances and experience. It is also comforting to
realise that none of us is alone in trying to build better businesses
and more particularly, as Patrick Dixon says, a better world.'

> Paul O'Toole, chief executive, Tourism Ireland

'If you want to be a great leader, you need to read this book. A
vital guide to management and business success.'

> Professor Prabhu Guptara, Director of Executive
> Learning, Wolfsburg, subsidiary of UBS

'A message that every business leader needs to listen to and turn into action.'

Professor Derek Abell, president, European School of Management and Technology, Berlin

THE
FUTURE
OF (ALMOST)
EVERYTHING

The global changes that will affect every
business and all of our lives

PATRICK DIXON

P

PROFILE BOOKS

First published in Great Britain in 2015 by
Profile Books Ltd
3 Holford Yard
Bevin Way
London WC1X 9HD
www.profilebooks.com

A CIP catalogue record for this book is available from
the British Library.

ISBN 978 1 78125 497 4
eISBN 978 1 78283 181 5

Text design by *sue@lambledesign.demon.co.uk*

Typeset in Dante by MacGuru Ltd
info@macguru.org.uk

Printed and bound in Great Britain by Clays, St Ives plc

Contents

Introduction

The truth about the future

My job is to live in the future and to see tomorrow as history. Global companies use me as a guide to the *truth* about life in years to come: what to expect, how to respond, how to provoke fresh thinking. Here is what I tell them, about the future of almost everything, about the things that really matter.

We face the greatest threats to survival in human history, while new technologies will give us the greatest opportunities ever known to create a better world. Some decisions made today will affect life on earth for a thousand years.

This is an extraordinary time to be alive. Our world is being shaken by seismic events, which are overtaking governments and corporations. At the same time, many trends are developing relatively slowly, people's lives are evolving rather gradually, and history shows that the most shocking predictions are usually wrong. So we need to pay close attention to what is most likely and plan for the unexpected.

Either you see the future as something to prepare for, or as a world to shape by your own actions. This book is therefore about being *futuristic* rather than *fatalistic*. Take hold of the future or the future will take hold of you.

You may have the greatest strategy on the planet, but if the world changes unexpectedly, you just travel even faster in the wrong direction. As I learned in my first career as a cancer doctor looking after the dying, *life is too short to lose a single day* doing things that are a complete waste of time, or that we don't believe in, so we need to know where we are going.

The greatest risk is institutional blindness

Media headlines are full of sensational, confusing and nonsensical predictions, so where do true *foresight* and *insight* come from?

Over many years, I have seen time and again that the greatest risk of all to any organisation is institutional blindness. When bankers spend too much time with other bankers, the result is soon a banking crisis.

When IT people spend too much time with other IT people, the result can be a major system weakness. When military commanders spend too much time playing war games with their colleagues, the result can be...

The scariest audience I have ever addressed

I give up to sixty keynotes a year, in many nations, but the scariest audience I have ever addressed was the Pentagon. My task was to give a trends lecture to 500 senior military leaders, and suggest ways in which they could use their vast military powers to *reduce* international tension, *improve* the image of America, *prevent* future wars, and *eliminate* national security threats.

The people in my audience were commanders of a major part of the world's greatest force of warships, fighter planes, submarines, nuclear weapons, cruise missiles, drones, tanks, artillery, troops, military intelligence, and so on. Some of the most powerful people on earth.

I wandered around the exhibition hall outside the auditorium, looking for some last-minute inspiration. It was packed with impressive displays of military hardware. Sales teams of global arms companies were explaining to me how to target and kill large numbers of people even more efficiently, with even less effort and risk, using their exotic technologies.

It struck me how last century it all felt. The capability of such hardware was truly shocking, and their technologies were awesome, but owning clever weapons can never build trust, nor deal with underlying causes of conflict, nor repair the heart of broken nations.

How to trigger a major conflict in seconds

In future, the defining issue for a commander will not be as simple as how many missiles, or drones, or other forces he controls. It may be something like whether he should give an order, in the next few seconds, to shoot dead a six-year-old child who right now is walking slowly towards a US army checkpoint, who might just conceivably be carrying a bomb – and all in full view of live TV news feeds.

A child whose death could spark local outrage, widespread civil unrest, and further bloodshed, as well as global condemnation, especially if no bomb is later found. The entire might of a military superpower is completely useless in such a moment.

What worried me most of all as I paced outside that hall was that I had been strongly warned that I was the *first* non-American that had *ever* been allowed to address that regular military assembly. Their policy had been that only the voices of American citizens were worth hearing. So it was a unique privilege to be there, and as it turned out, they were very gracious in their willingness to listen to someone with a different world view.

Trapped in a narrow vision

Any organisation can be affected by a mild form of collective madness – the inability to see the wider context. Leaders lose perspective, narrow their vision, fail to understand new competitors, lack insight into how consumers or nations really feel, and become over-complacent or rigid in thinking.

Each of us reads the world around us through our own set of glasses, which distort our perception and reactions, shaped by our culture, birthplace, history and experiences. Therefore *the* most important step in accurate Futuring is to take *off* your own glasses, and create mental space to put on other people's, to see the world through very different eyes.

A personal journey

My own life journey, to try to see the future of our world in new ways, has taken me to 54 countries. I have talked with leaders of corporations and governments; engaged with every industry; met innovators and entrepreneurs; advised the super-wealthy; and worked with the poorest of the poor, whether in megacity slums, refugee camps or remote rural villages.

In this global process, I have also explored many future decades, sometimes far into the 22nd century and beyond.

Market research can't tell you the future

One of the first truths I learned is that market research is a completely useless and dangerous guide to the future. Companies and governments waste much of the $40bn they spend on it a year, asking questions about how people think they will behave in future. But moods can change in hours, in response to new products, social media, atrocities, sporting events, huge scandals or the death of a national hero.

Market research is still important, however. We do need to pay the closest attention to our customers, and how they feel. Listen carefully to what they say, and sort out any problems they see. But don't *believe* them when it comes to the future. *Study your customers well*, and then *imagine how they may change*, in a world far beyond their horizons. That is why all designers and innovators rely on genius rather than market research, and why our journey is so important.

One word will drive the future

Another truth I learned is this. One single factor will drive the future more than events, economics, innovations, technology, demographics, religion or politics.

This one thing has driven all human history and will determine the direction of humankind for the next 10,000 years. It will dominate every customer decision and government election, every relationship and every leisure activity, and is the hidden force within every major trend.

Leaders often focus on metrics, data, financials, analysis, processes, customers, competitors, investors, public opinion and regulations – but this misses the point. All these things matter but there is one central element, which is even more important in shaping tomorrow.

Markets are driven by investor *mood*. Wars are triggered by *anger*. Leadership is based on *trust*. Uptake of new technologies is linked to customer *engagement* and *pleasure*. Regulations are driven by *activism*. Elections are won by *conviction*. Team performance is driven by *motivation*. Relationships are formed by human *needs*, *passions* and *desires*.

So if we wish to explore the future, we need to look at how people are likely to FEEL, as well as what they will THINK. The single word that will drive the future is EMOTION. As we will see in every chapter of this book, emotional reactions are usually far more significant than events themselves. All leadership has to connect with emotion, which is why robots cannot lead.

How far do you need to see?

Whenever I am asked to give a lecture on the future, I always ask the same question: How far ahead do you want me to take you, and into what areas?

If you are a *share trader*, you need only to see 3 milliseconds further than the rest of the market to make billions of dollars in high-frequency trading – which accounts for 50% of all buying and selling on the American market.

If you are a *fashion house*, 6 months ahead may be far enough. If you are a *bank*, your future horizon is probably no more than 5 years. If you are a *major insurer*, your view will stretch to a decade or more.

My *pharma* clients need 25-year vision, because it takes them 15 years to bring a new drug to market, and patents expire after 25 years. So the CEO has to work out what health care will be like 25 years from now, and what government budgets will be.

Energy companies want to look even further. Not long ago I was talking to a senior executive who signed contracts a decade earlier to extract oil and gas from under the Caspian Sea. It will take at least another decade to get those fields operational, with a lifetime of 30 years or more beyond that. So at the moment of signing, she had to take a 50-year view of future energy prices.

How do you guess the future?

How on earth do you *begin* to guess the average price for a barrel of oil from 2040 to 2050? How do you take a view of what the French government will be forced to spend on prostate cancer in 2040?

I will share with you a methodology to make sense of your own future, one which has stood the test of time for more than 17 years, as a comprehensive and balanced structure, meshing together every global trend. But first we need to look at the basis of all forecasting, how all trends connect, and why so many changes are more predictable than you might have thought.

Some people tell me that it is impossible and completely pointless to try to predict the future. All we can do is prepare for uncertainty. My own experience, over three decades, shows that such a view is ignorant, dangerous, naïve, foolish and fatalistic nonsense when it comes to the longer term and the wider picture. It all depends, of course, on what you are trying to predict, and in what detail.

Yes, it is true that history proves no one can consistently predict short-term swings in market prices or exchange rates, and we can never be *certain* what tomorrow will bring, but that is not what our journey is all about. It is perfectly logical and vitally important for every decision-maker to have well-reasoned expectations of what he or she thinks is most likely to happen – while also considering the possibility of alternative scenarios, to manage their risk of being wrong.

Long-term trends are often very predictable

All reliable, long-range forecasting is based on powerful mega-trends that have been driving profound, consistent and therefore relatively predictable change over the last 30 years. Such trends are the basis of every well-constructed corporate strategy and government policy. Here are just a few of many hundreds of examples:

◆ gradually falling rates of growth in world population
◆ people choosing to marry later, or not at all, leading to fewer children
◆ fall in price of digital technology, telecoms and networking
◆ rapid growth of all kinds of wireless / mobile devices
◆ connectivity between people, companies and machines
◆ rapid growth of emerging market economies
◆ rapid growth of emerging market middle-class consumers
◆ hundreds of millions of people moving to cities
◆ large migrations from poor nations to wealthier ones
◆ better global literacy and more university graduates
◆ fall in costs of production of most mass-produced items
◆ rapid increase in global trade and intense hunger for travel
◆ formation of trading blocs, free trade areas, currency zones
◆ ever-larger global corporations, mergers, consolidations
◆ rapid growth of gene screening to predict future health
◆ growth of biotech therapies including stem cells
◆ ageing of many populations e.g. EU, Japan, South Korea, China
◆ baby booms in emerging nations such as India and Nigeria
◆ feminisation of many societies, with more women at work
◆ better life expectancy with improved diet and health
◆ increased concern about environment / sustainability
◆ destabilisation of nations with mineral or energy wealth
◆ shift from wars between nations to civil conflicts
◆ wider acceptance of democracy (but mistrust of politicians)
◆ wider adoption of civil rights, protecting the vulnerable
◆ higher customer expectations for convenience, comfort, value, service, honesty, reliability, speed – and more complaints when standards fall
◆ more automation of routine tasks, in homes, offices, factories.

I could list hundreds more for your own specific industry or nation. These wider trends have been obvious to most trend analysts like myself for a while, and have been well described over the last 20–30 years. They have evolved much more slowly than booms and busts, or social fads.

And even in other trends where changes were expected to happen very rapidly, the reality has often been much slower than many forecast – for example the death of traditional bank branches, or fall in volumes of cash in circulation.

All trends connect to all other trends

All major trends will interact to shape our future world. While a few will be disrupted by wild card events, as we will see in Chapter 1, most are unlikely to be.

What is more, your own *personal* future is being shaped by over 7 billion other people's futures. All personal worlds link together to form what our wider world will be. That is why it is so illogical and dangerous to focus on a single trend without the full picture. But sadly, that is what so many economists, biologists, techno-gurus, military advisors and other specialist 'experts' tend to do, each blindly micro-forecasting within their own speciality, in isolation from the *true* macro-picture. Hardly a surprise, then, that so many have fared so disastrously in their Future-Casting over the past two decades.

I am not saying that I haven't also got some things wrong. Anticipating future trends is always a risky and potentially humbling process. If you want to judge for yourself, you will find over 600 YouTube videos, hundreds of presentations and articles and the text of 6 entire books posted since 1997 on my website, visited by over 16 million different people.*

Just to be absolutely clear about this, each trend only makes complete sense in the context of every other trend – which means that this book really needs to be read through more than once. As we will see, the moment we talk about, say, digital tech, we are

* http://www.globalchange.com

also talking about e-commerce and retail. But as soon as we look at retail, we are touching on demographics, emerging markets, manufacturing and global trade. And as soon as we discuss global trade, we are into a debate about future fuel costs for shipping and trade barriers, and so on.

2030 is closer than we think

We are going to look mainly at the 'future of almost everything' over the next 15 years. But before we do so, as a reality check, we need to be really honest with ourselves about the answer to a very important question. You may think this a strange one for a Futurist to ask, someone whose career has been built on making sense of rapid change, but nevertheless the question is:

How much has really changed in the past 15 years?

The truth is, that despite all the hype about the speed of change, it would not take long to update a business leader who recently woke up from a coma that lasted 15 years. Probably less than a couple of hours, to cover the most important global and social changes. Let us call him Tom…

Little would really surprise Tom. What would we tell him about? The dotcom crash and 9/11 attack; wars in Iraq, Afghanistan and Syria linked to Islamic militants; cheaper and more mobile computing; faster web, more e-commerce and rapid growth of social media; cheaper technology; Asia rising fast; more worries about global warming and wind farms everywhere; big market crash following a long boom, triggered by a bank lending crisis; corporate banking scandals; rising retirement age and worries about pensions; Russia flexing muscles again… and some worries about viral epidemics.

Pushed to see radical change?

But walk Tom down the streets of any capital city in Europe and I suggest that he would struggle to see much *radical* change. Perhaps that seems surprising – but, for example, in fashion, music, day-to-day culture, politics, hopes and dreams of young people I would say things look pretty much the same, apart from more people looking at smartphone screens more of the time, and buying more online.

Indeed, Tom would doubtless point out that many people, like him, were already using smartphones such as the Nokia 9000 in 1996, with full web browser, email, camera, word processing, notepads and prices halving every 12 months. And he might well tell me that his daughter used to run up to 16 chat screens simultaneously back in 1997. Most of the other things above were also signposted in the 1990s in some way. So what would really feel so radically new to Tom today?

Young and old share very similar lives

There is also far less of a 'generation gap' today, compared with what we saw in many developed nations back in the 1950s to 1970s. Younger and older people are listening to similar music. They watch the same films, wear similar clothes, travel to similar places, share most of the same values.

People eat out more, and in general standards of living have risen. Technology is cheaper. Kitchens tend to be more open plan but most homes in Europe and America look similar to what they did in 2000 – after all, most are more than 30 years old. Offices are more open plan, and people carry computers or mobile devices rather than sit at work-stations. But most still commute to work. And TV news looks and sounds the same. Familiar Hollywood film plots keep being recycled, albeit with better computer graphics, and major sporting events still attract huge crowds.

Of course, while Tom was in a coma, hundreds of books and web pages were written alleging the opposite, hyping up the revolutionary impact of, say, social media or recent events, but our own experience and common sense tells us something different, unless you happen to be a mobile marketing executive, or live in some parts of the Middle East.

Many things in 2030 will also be remarkably similar

We will see in the chapters of this book how profound many changes *will* be. However, to place those disruptions in proportion, the *truth* is that *daily life* for most people on earth will be very similar in many ways in 2030 to what it is today. A three-year-old child will have a life that is very familiar, when they are 18, to people who are 18 today. They will have recently attended high school, taken exams, and be heading for their first jobs or university. Their hopes, thoughts and dreams will be similar in many ways to yours at the same age.

They too will look in the mirror and wonder about self-image. They too will hope one day to meet the right person and settle into a wonderful long-term relationship. They too will think a lot about ways to have a happy, comfortable life, and also from time to time about 'making a difference', or what government they want, or about a more sustainable world. They too will feel worried about the future.

And when that new generation become parents themselves, they will have similar worries to previous generations about the well-being of their own children. So please don't make the mistake of thinking that their basic human nature will be any different because of next-generation digital, mobile, robotics, virtual life, wearable devices, gene programming, social connectivity or anything else.

The M generation is more concerned about the long-term future

Yet at the same time, as I say, fundamental shifts *are* taking place, which will transform entire societies, wipe out many multinationals, destroy many governments. And the M generation – those whose entire adult lives are being lived in the third millennium – is far more concerned about long-range issues such as sustainability.

History will record a very different kind of world by 2050, with a totally new balance of power, new global cultures, new industrial giants, new forms of government and new social habits. The generation born in 2030 will all be adults in 2050, and most of those who are born to middle-class families will expect to be alive in 2130.

Most debates are about short-term timing

I have found that most short-term debates about the future in boardrooms are NOT about what is going to happen, which is often fairly obvious, but about *when*. Timing is often the most important issue for companies.

For example:

◆ When will most e-commerce transactions take place on a mobile device, globally?

◆ When will the amount of cash in circulation in Europe stop growing?

◆ When will China become the world's largest economy?

◆ When will our current website feel completely out of date?

◆ When will we have a vaccine against AIDS?

Six Faces of the Future

So let's move onto the futuring method that I have used over much of the last two decades. The **Six Faces of the Future** mesh together as a forecasting tool, to stretch our world view and challenge the way we normally think. Each face is important and is a chapter of this book, but the relative strength of each face will depend on who you are and where you live.

It is impossible to keep all six faces in view at once: some are related, others are opposites. Together they form the faces of a cube, which we need to constantly keep turning. Emotion is the force that makes the cube spin. The faces spell the word 'FUTURE'.

Fast – speed of change, Wild Cards, future of digital technology

Urban – future urbanisation, demography, health, fashions, fads

Tribal – future nations, cultures, social networks, brands, teams

Universal – future globalisation, retail, trade, manufacturing

Radical – death of politics, rise of radical activism, sustainability

Ethical – values, motivation, leadership, aspiration, spirituality

You will see that Fast and Urban are closely related and sit together on one side, while Radical and Ethical are also together on the other. On top is Universal, and beneath, pulling in the opposite direction, is Tribal.

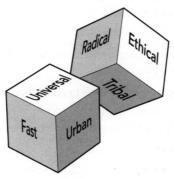

Here is a really important thing: most executives spend their lives looking at the cube from above, at a world that is Fast, Urban and Universal, and are almost blind to another dimension. However, one twist through 180 degrees presents us with a very different view: a world that is Tribal, Radical and Ethical.

Understanding the tension between these two dominant views is really important. As we will see, a tiny minority who are strongly Radical, Ethical and Tribal can affect the rest of us profoundly. Think of Islamic State or climate change activists or about consumers who campaign to stop child labour. Radical in thinking, driven by a strong sense of shared Ethics (you may not agree with these ethics but that is irrelevant), and very Tribal (tight, together, well organised).

For every trend, look for a counter-trend

As we will discover, every trend tends to have its counterpart, which is why media pundits are able at once to describe, for example, trends to greater liberalism and greater conservatism, in parts of the same city or nation.

Drug use soars, with growing calls for decriminalisation, at the same time as a neo-prohibitionist movement seeks to make it all but impossible to smoke a cigarette in a public place. Hyper-sexual-isation of children is promoted every day in Western media, at the same time as outrage grows over child abuse.

Expect to see powerful culture clashes between opposing trends, a world increasingly of extremes over the next 100 years, with tendencies to intolerance as groups fight to dominate the future – as we are seeing not only in culture clashes between Islam and liberal 'Western' culture, but also within Islam itself. The greatest forces will be unleashed by clashes of *conscience* rather than *culture*, influenced by religious conviction, or lack of it.

The big question is this: if trend and counter-trend coexist, which will be dominant? The truth is that in a pluralistic, multi-track society there are a number of pendulums operating in every city and nation, which is why trend-watching is so fascinating.

All leaders must be Futurists

People often ask me what a Futurist is. But in a sense, all thinking people are Futurists. It is part of the human condition to think about tomorrow and plan ahead. Futurists are just professional future-thinkers, with a span that reaches across many industries and nations.

All leaders have to be Futurists. People only follow leaders when they believe in their vision of a better future. So where does your own vision come from? It has to be based on a deep understanding of what tomorrow could be. The stronger your vision, the greater your leadership will be.

Vision has to be founded on stark reality, based on what we know today – where we are likely to end up if no action is taken. And built on practical hope – what we could achieve if we all work together.

Look back from the future of 2500

A useful Futuring tool is to imagine that you are in some future time, looking back. For example, a great exercise is to sit down and write last year's Annual Report of the company you work for, as if you were the chairman, living in the year 2020 or even 2025. It really sharpens your thinking about what could happen. Now let us jump further forward, in the same spirit, to the year 2500.

If we look back in the year 2500, reflecting on over 25,000 years of history, we will note the exponential rise from 1750 to 2050 in population and cities, scientific discovery, health, trade, innovation, wealth, consumption and capacity for global war – all traced back to the industrial revolution that began with the invention of steam power in the UK, and discovery of electricity.

Perhaps we will also remind ourselves how population growth collapsed in the 21st century, despite giant leaps in life expectancy in every nation. We will probably reflect that the greatest challenges to survival of humankind over the last 500 years (apart from global wars) have been solved by inventions and technologies that were totally unknown in the year 2000.

We will also acknowledge how much the quality of personal life improved, for almost all of humankind – education, health, wealth, contentment and sense of well-being.

And I am sure we will also be struck by the fact that the biggest questions in our year of 2500 are *still* related to 'very old' issues like *sustainability* and *ethics*. How many people can we provide for in centuries to come? How much consumption? What kind of world do we want to live in? How can we all live at peace on a small planet? What is the right action for us to take?

We will probably agree that the most complex problems that humankind has seen over the previous 500 years were caused by the darker sides of human nature: emotional reactions to history, resistance to change, struggles for power, tribalism that led to conflict, greed, envy and a constant desire for more.

Why I am optimistic and not apocalyptic

I am often asked at the end of keynotes on the future if I am an optimist or a pessimist? As you can see from the above, I am probably an optimist, despite the many genuine future threats and challenges we face, and despite being very realistic about the horrors that small numbers of human beings are capable of.

Over the years, many so-called Futurists and trend-spotters have given dire, apocalyptic and spectacular warnings about our world running out of food, or water, or space, or about all of humankind being wiped out by major events, or being taken over by robots. For reasons I will explain, the vast majority of such forecasts are alarmist nonsense, although of course they do make eye-catching headlines.

The truth, as we will see, is that our world is far more resilient than many fear. Humankind has an astonishing and accelerating capacity for genius and innovation, and this will solve many of the world's greatest challenges in ways that are very hard to imagine today. In addition, there are many natural balancing forces within global systems, including the oceans and the global economy.

So then, let us turn to the first Face of the Future, which is all about the speed of change, and what that may mean for you.

Chapter 1

FAST

HISTORY IS CHANGING FASTER than you can calculate a risk or exploit an opportunity, whether you look at the economy, global events, industry, social factors or politics. The interval between early signs and a full-blown new trend is shorter than ever, and long-range forecasting is becoming more complex.

The developed world is cash-rich, time-poor and feels intensely impatient. Chapters of personal lives are measured in minutes, major events in seconds. Five billion people are communicating digitally, usually many times an hour on mobiles, unless asleep. There is a widespread obsession with instant information, answers, new products and new friends.

Digital pressure or addiction will become one of the commonest causes of anxiety, depression and mental breakdown, particularly among young people. A recent study in the UK found 13% of smart-phone users were psychologically addicted to their devices, with the average user spending around 4 hours on their device a day, often to the neglect of their jobs, family and other aspects of life.

Expect huge growth in ways to instantly de-stress, wind down, regenerate.

Some say that daily life for most people has never changed so fast, and we must be close to the limits of human endurance, but this is untrue. Large populations have coped surprisingly well with far more dramatic, rapid and convulsive changes at times of natural disaster or regional wars.

Strategies overtaken by events

Speed of change will be a huge challenge for every leader. All strategies of large corporations will be at risk of being overtaken by events. Your world can change faster than you can hold a board meeting. Expect growing emphasis on leadership agility, dynamic strategy, adaptive organisations, contingencies and risk management.

Most managers struggle even to keep up with the few technologies they have today. They stumble from one new App or online tool to the next, feeling the pressure of information overload. Success will mean faster integration of next-generation tools, finding better ways to make sense of the constant barrage of information.

Most medium-sized or large companies will fail to cross the bridge from old to new: they will shrivel and die over the next two to three decades, driven out of business by leaders who are techno-blind, and uncomfortable with the speed of radical change. It is confusing for people who have spent an entire decade or more in the same industry.

Reaction against constant change

In a constantly changing world, things that do not change will gain value. Expect more listed buildings and preservation orders on bits of towns, government buildings, churches, mosques, temples and monuments. Expect growth of traditions that remind us of a familiar past to grow in popularity.

Ancient trees will be even more respected, together with unspoiled moorlands and forests. Old houses will continue to be popular, for those who can afford to live in them, and convert them to comply with energy saving regulations.

Wild Cards: 40-year impact in 20 seconds

Our world is now so joined up, interconnected, and interdependent that small events can rapidly trigger giant convulsions.

Single events can become defining moments – such as the collapse of communism and the end of the Cold War 25 years ago.

We can still feel the follow-on impact today across the world, in hundreds of different ways.

A few seconds can be long enough to change history. An earthquake lasting less than a minute triggered a crack in a Japanese nuclear reactor in Fukushima Daiichi district. As a result of intense public anxiety, Germany and Japan abandoned nuclear energy, which will impact global energy markets for more than 40 years. Yet, at the same time, the UK and China embarked on a nuclear boom. As I have said, emotional reactions to events are often far more important than events themselves.

The sudden retaking of Crimea by Russia (granted to Ukraine in 1957) was triggered by anxiety that their naval port would be lost to NATO, following chaotic scenes during the 2014 Ukraine revolution that toppled an elected president. The invasion led to immediate steps across the EU to reduce dependence on Russian gas supplies over the next 50 years. It inflamed conflicts elsewhere in Ukraine, and started what many feared could become a new Cold War, while sanctions damaged both Russia and the EU.

The global alliance against terrorism that was formed after the World Trade Center attacks in New York in 2001 led to two international wars and continues to feed bitter anti-American anger across parts of the Middle East, Afghanistan and Pakistan.

Hundreds of risks

In every large business there are many low probability but potentially high impact risks or Wild Cards. And if you have a list of 400 risks, each of which has only a 1% chance of actually happening in any year, then by the law of averages, you will see 4 major events each year. In some years there will be none, and at other times you may see several in the same month.

But in our globalised, ultra-connected world, every risk can connect to many other risks in ways that may not be obvious, and so it is even more important to prepare for combinations of risks.

Consider this before turning the page for the answers:

What do you think is the risk of 2 people in 10 having the same birthday? Or the risk of 2 people in 70?

The answer is: Risk of 2 in 10 people having same birthday is 10%; 2 in 23 is 50%; 2 in 70 is 100%. Far higher than most people would guess. I call it coincidental risk, and the figures are based on a well-researched statistical challenge called the Birthday Paradox.

Why benchmarking is so dangerous

Every large corporation is required to manage risks and report on them to shareholders. Unfortunately, as we saw in the economic crisis of 2008, banks can employ hundreds of risk managers, and still be destroyed. Why is this?

For years, many companies relied on 'benchmarking' – how we are doing when measured against the competition or our industry as a whole. Profitability, growth rates, rates of pay, terms of employment, staff turnover, customer satisfaction, appetite for risk-taking, and so on. However, the whole approach is often a fast-track to disaster, leading an entire industry to march blindly in step together, lemming-like, over the same cliff.

Risks of following the crowd

A year or two before the sub-prime crisis, I gave a lecture to several hundred senior risk managers from the world's largest banks. I explained how worried I was that major risks in banking were not being properly addressed.

Afterwards, I was approached by several risk managers. They said that I was right to be worried, and explained why they were unable to act. If they advised their boards, for example, that they needed to be more cautious about certain types of packaged loan products, the answer invariably would be something like:

'But as benchmarking shows, we are taking similar risks to the entire industry, and regulators are not objecting. If we take a more cautious line, our financial returns will be lower next year, analysts will criticise us, and our share price will fall.'

Risk managers have to be independently minded, with a broad, rigorous view, informed by trends outside their industry,

Examples of major Wild Cards

◆ viral plague – rapidly spreading, cases in every continent

◆ Chinese unrest – political/economic instability or meltdown

◆ North Korean collapse – huge migration and social chaos

◆ eurozone breakup – after another huge global economic crisis

◆ sustained cyber-attack – paralysing government, telecom, utilities, transport, banks for several weeks

◆ major, sustained military action against Israel

◆ threat to a major city from terrorists with likely nuclear capability or some kind of 'dirty weapon'

◆ series of attacks similar in impact to 9/11

◆ solar geomagnetic storms that knock out telecoms/IT

◆ huge volcanic eruption that affects earth temperature

◆ massive failure of an investment institution, affecting over $4 trillion in assets

◆ miscalculation by a powerful nation leading to sustained regional conflict

◆ large meteor strike on a major city – like that which flattened 830 square miles of Russia in 1908, or the one which hit Russia again in 2013, with kinetic energy greater than the atomic bomb dropped on Hiroshima.

not institutionally blinded, and with the courage to be literally 'eccentric', to stick out from the crowd, take a different view.

Short-termism will destroy corporations

Many global corporations are run from one 12-week period to the next with very little regard to the longer term. Business leaders are drawn down this route by legal requirements to report profitability every quarter, and are expected to provide profit warnings if any significant adverse event should occur.

So, as we have seen in many recent scandals, decisions are

inevitably linked to issues of timing: how to delay investment into another quarter so as not to damage analyst ratings, or other ways to massage the figures. It can be almost impossible to make large-scale strategic moves, which may deliver profits only in 5–10 years' time.

This problem of short-termism has been made even worse by huge annual bonuses paid on the previous year's results. And when you add in all kinds of other linked incentives such as share options that may be about to be cashed in, the result is a toxic mix. Expect more interference by regulators, forcing listed companies to pay bonuses based on performance over several years.

And of course, CEOs can be forced rapidly into the wilderness. The average length of tenure in America for a CEO of a large corporation is only 5 years, or 7 years across the EU.

In stark contrast, I have also worked with many family-owned corporations – or ones where the family has a controlling interest even though the company is listed on the stock exchange – and the conversations are often shockingly different. 'Our company was started by my grandfather over 80 years ago, and every day I worry about what kind of company I will hand over to my grandchildren.' You see decisions made with a 30–50 year time-horizon, by family leaders who have been at the helm for a decade or two.

Such companies often have a strong sense of direction and purpose, command loyalty from staff, and stay in business for many decades. And yes, of course, there are downsides to family ownership, including time-expired leaders who refuse to step aside for the next generation, and lack of talent, ambition or even vague interest among younger family members.

I have talked to a number of senior leaders of publicly listed companies who wish that they also were 'privately owned', and who have considered ways to delist. Expect more such conversations, looking to different models of ownership, including private equity – although I know that such a route can also bring ruthless and soul-destroying time pressures, depending on the investors. Some companies such as Unilever have already stopped producing detailed quarterly reports, in a bid to restore sense and sanity.

Future of the global economy

The first decade and a half of the third millennium was a highly embarrassing time for the academic discipline of economics, and for economists generally. So many economics professors failed to see the gathering crisis, or to predict accurately how long it would last.

Old-school economics is dead

Before the crash I lectured widely on, and wrote about, huge and growing risks from poorly understood global trades in complex financial instruments such as derivatives, and risks from ever more powerful yet lightly regulated hedge funds, in the context of wide-ranging global trends. I also warned of instabilities in global markets to come, severe runs on currencies in some emerging markets, and of deflationary shocks, which I predicted would be so powerful that inflation targets of 2% would look dangerously low at times, with no cushion in severe downturns.*

We saw many of these things unfold following the collapse of Lehman Brothers in September 2008, as part of the sub-prime lending crisis. However, I failed to see how deep the global crisis would turn out to be, wiping out government solvency as well as banks, and how long the crisis would last.

Here are the major factors that are likely to shape the global economy over the next decade:

1. **Global economy survived better than many thought.** Thanks to emerging markets, the global economy grew in every year of the crisis except 2009. Growth in China slowed but never below 7% a year. A short-term fall in oil prices will also help growth.

2. **Global corporations with trillions to spend.** Throughout the crisis, the world's multinationals saved huge amounts of cash. By 2014, the largest were holding total balances of more than $2.8 trillion, of which over $450bn were in international accounts

---

* See, for example, *Futurewise* (3rd edition 2003, 4th edition 2007, Profile Books), plus numerous lectures.

of six large West Coast American companies like Google and Apple. Expect large-scale spending of cash mountains over the next 5–10 years.

3. **Growth in Sovereign Wealth Funds – ready to invest.** By 2014, Sovereign Wealth Funds of countries like China, Norway, United Arab Emirates, Saudi Arabia and Singapore were worth more than \$6 trillion. China alone owned more than \$4 trillion, much of which was in US government bonds. Expect rapid diversification into real estate, commodities, mining, infrastructure, health care, logistics, technology companies and a wide range of other sectors, to secure China's future.

4. **Growth in value of privately owned property.** In the UK alone, private real estate was worth over \$6 trillion by 2014, with rising house prices, and low interest rates. People aged over 65 are sitting on more than \$2 trillion of tax-free capital gains made since 1980. A significant amount will pass down generations, or become available using equity release products, over the next 10–15 years. Expect the same in a number of other countries.

5. **Central banks will take a more relaxed view of inflation.** Fears of deflation will mean banks will err more towards stimulation until they are certain that a robust recovery is underway. This is despite fears in countries like Germany of hyper-inflation, because of its own history in the 1920s. Inflation rates in some developed nations will fall almost to zero, or slip into deflation, at some point by 2020. Europe is badly prepared for further shocks, such as more extreme Russian sanctions, major conflict in the Middle East, or rapid slowdown in China. Countries like the UK are particularly likely to encourage higher inflation – helpful in reducing national debt, as many bonds are fixed at low interest. In contrast, inflation will be a significant worry in many emerging nations, as shortages emerge of skills and local resources, and as middle-class demand rises.

6. **Over 500 million new middle-class consumers** have been created by economic growth since the new millennium, and will drive demand.

7. **Booms and busts in huge cycles.** The world's biggest and longest bust in generations will most likely be followed at some point in 5–10 years (after trillions spent in stimulus) by one of the world's greatest booms, unless there is a major event, such as viral pandemic, or regional conflict, or a further economic crisis, which postpones the eventual mega-boom and mega-bust. Expect larger and longer economic cycles until well beyond 2035.

8. **Further risks of mass defaults on debt.** Despite new regulations, risky financial deals are already growing rapidly again, exploiting gaps in laws, with ever more complex and cunning financial products, sold mainly by shadow banking (clusters of companies carrying out bank-like activities, without being regulated as banks). These are likely to create future economic shocks. In 2014, global debt was more than twice the size of the entire global economy. Among many nations, China will be vulnerable, with over-stimulation of the economy, low borrowing costs, and unsustainable debt – even though government debt is very low compared to many developed nations.

   Total debt in China jumped from 140% to 220% of GDP in 6 years, to around $25 trillion, if we include debts of private companies, state-owned enterprises, and individuals as well as central and regional government debts. That total is more than the size of the entire US and Japanese banking sectors combined. The UK, Japan, Sweden, Canada and America had total national debts from all sources amounting to over 250% of their GDPs. In the past, debts on this scale have usually been dealt with by encouraging inflation and allowing currencies to slide.

9. **Economic stimulation from next-generation technologies** such as the Internet of Things, Smart Homes, Smart Grids, Green Tech, Biotech, Robotics and Nanotech are likely to boost the global economy by $70 trillion by 2040. Spending on everything related to green tech and energy saving will itself exceed $40 trillion during the same period. This will be encouraged by oil prices, likely to be above $125 for much of the period, despite

falls to below $70 from time to time in response to overproduction in global downturns, and to growth in green tech.

10. **By 2030, Asia's combined economic output will be greater than that of Europe and America combined.** This single fact will dominate most other trends in this book. Asian growth will be accelerated by aggressive and ambitious government policies, mobilising nations for innovation in key sectors. For example, China will dominate global wind turbine production, and South Korea will invest heavily in digital and biotech.

Correcting a 1000-year cycle

We are witnessing a fundamental re-balancing of wealth across global populations. In the year 1500, India and China represented more than 50% of all global output. By 1900 this had dropped to only 17%, outpaced by industrial revolution in Europe. So the process we are seeing today is part of a 500-year correction in a 1000-year cycle.

However, here is a short-term reality check: the EU and US still account for 60% of global GDP, 33% of global trade, and 42% of global sales of services.

During this period of re-adjustment globally, North–South tension is likely to increase as more emerging economies find that abolishing all trade and currency restrictions in a rush for growth also places their countries at the mercy of rumours, moods, hunches and opinion in the chaotic, global, gambling den of market traders.

I have sat in UN-related and World Economic Forum meetings where the most senior leaders of emerging nations have been systematically bullied into scrapping regulations, in order to become more globalised. But they have been rewarded sometimes by what some in their nations would regard as the rape of their own economies.

Unstable and chaotic markets

Expect an even greater backlash against globalisation in some nations, who may feel that they are being reduced to 'economic slavery' by massive, destabilising currency flows, and by other market forces. Over $5.3 trillion of currencies are traded every day, yet nations like the Philippines, Peru, Poland or the UK hold less than $80bn in reserves to defend against speculators. Enough to last only a few days.

I remember lecturing in Turkey one day in February 2001, during which the currency fell more than 10%, interest rates soared to 3,000%, and the central bank lost $5bn. The Bank of England was also hammered in a single day in September 1992. At one stage the Bank was buying £2bn an hour to prevent devaluation, and lost £3.4bn before conceding defeat. Meanwhile George Soros made £1bn selling pounds to the Bank that he did not even own. We have seen similar events in Russia more recently.

More attacks on central banks and currencies

Expect more such attacks as large investors continue to make (and lose) huge fortunes trying to outguess volatile markets, at times hoping to undermine one central bank after another. We will see similar speculative attacks on commodity prices, short-selling stocks of companies, and attacks on the stability of entire stock exchanges. Expect new regulations to try to contain some of this, for example forcing investors to disclose major positions in the market, or trying to slow down the velocity of hyper-trading linked to computers.

Many Asian countries are better protected from currency attack than they were a decade or more ago, with stronger reserves and alliances, but market power will continue to grow as the process of globalisation steps up a gear, with even greater connectedness.

Future of telecoms and IT

A lot of *nonsense* is talked in telecom and IT forecasting. The truth is that *we are still in the first hour of the first day of the mobile digital universe.* In generations to come, it will be said that the real impact of these technologies only came after 2030.

Here is a common-sense view. There are already more mobile phone subscriptions than people on the planet. Over 30% of the world will soon own at least one smartphone – many costing less than $100, with relatively unknown brand names. By 2025, over half of all new smartphones are likely to cost less than $70, with prices dropping rapidly. As outlined later, banks and telcos will be giving smartphones away with free contracts (p. 192).

Vietnam is typical of the next wave of mobile. Wage costs are half those of China, yet 90 million people own over 110 million SIM cards. Millions of people are jumping directly into mobile web without ever owning a land line or having heard of broadband.

Phone calls are so 'last-century'

The average young person in the UK rarely uses voice calls or email, as old patterns give way rapidly to social media.

The future of telecom and IT will be smaller, more mobile, more powerful, cheaper, faster, and cloud based. By 2025 we can expect total fusion of online and offline life in many parts of the world, with radical changes in consumer behaviour, in retail, personal banking, social relationships, decision-making, learning and entertainment. (See 'Future of retail banking' in Chapter 4, p. 188).

How the web will redefine time

The web has made us very impatient – most people in my audiences around the world tell me that they press the back button on a web browser in less than 4 seconds if a web page is slow. That means losing up to 90% of customers in 4 seconds. Even if you don't lose them, it means that they are irritated. And it follows that 90% of younger web users in developed nations may press that back button in less than 1.5 seconds by 2025. Impatience will be a factor in every business relationship.

The same applies to call centres. Most people hate having to press loads of buttons. Every second matters. Business leaders tell me they consider it a form of personal theft when their time is wasted, and a social crime to install such systems.

Yet in a strange double-think, most of them also tell me that they have installed exactly the same awful systems for their own customers. It is of course a classic case of institutional blindness, and also an act of near insanity, since cheap technology now allows us to detect an incoming mobile number, work out from Big Data who the person is, and why they are likely to be calling, so that the call can be automatically directed to the right person.

Five seconds to double your sales

We need to completely rethink our business relationships in terms of minutes and seconds. Companies that do so will win huge competitive advantages.

So how long does it take to find a shop assistant to help with a question you have? How long to wait in the checkout? How long for the ATM to give you money? How long to complete an online transaction? How long to respond to an email? How long to wait for a written estimate of costs? How long to return a contract?

Expect huge efforts to speed up and simplify the customer experience. Every web page click loses sales. Every second counts. Every additional choice means fewer sales. Instant ID checks will be universal, using biometric sensors on mobile devices, pre-authorised spending limits and instant confirmations.

Voice-to-text will be a standard feature of all business mobile contracts by 2025. Voice messages sent instantly as SMS to mobiles, email accounts, and so on. SMS-type short-length messages will overtake email for personal communications. If you want a lead over your competitors, use SMS more often. Written e-messages of all kinds can have intense emotional power, more than voice or video, which is one reason why we can expect rapid messaging growth.

Telco business models are completely broken

Over 90% of all web traffic will be video by 2025 in many developed nations. It is already the case in the UK that BBC iPlayer, NetFlix and YouTube alone account for more than 50% of the nation's web traffic.

A single 2-hour video in HD is equivalent to a hundred million emails, tens of thousands of photos or many days of constant voice calls. So forget charging for voice, SMS, web browsing or anything else – the costs of providing such services are dwarfed by streaming video. *Therefore today's telco business models are completely broken. Telcos are becoming one thing: video providers.*

Data traffic on mobiles will increase 1000 fold in the next 5 years, on 50 billion mobile devices connected to 5G, running at 10gps. That means an entire high-definition movie will download in less than 3 seconds.

So telcos are making every effort to develop new kinds of business, for example, helping corporations run IT services, providing comprehensive data storage, becoming banks, and so on.

Mobile payments will hit telcos and banks

We are seeing a huge explosion in the number of mobile payments, particularly in emerging markets. One in four adults across Africa are already using mobile money accounts. Africa is re-inventing retail mass-market banking, and Asia is following fast.

The trouble is that a telco may be handling 100 million payments a month on its network yet making virtually no money from it all. Who is *really* handling those payments? Who is providing the financial statements to customers? Who gets the Big Data? Who owns the customer relationship?

In the UK, over 25 million people will be making mobile payments by 2020. However, these innovations will be held back by customer confusion, caution and habit. Look, for example at the very slow take-up of contactless card payments. Watch out for new mobile payment platforms to rival PayM, which could be used by 90% of all bank account owners by 2017. (See 'Future of retail banking', p. 188.)

A billion wearable devices

As I predicted years ago, mobile screens are becoming larger and smaller – with huge debate about optimum size.

Wearable devices have taken off more slowly than I expected, because we have lacked a 'killer' application: a really compelling reason to make your shirt, belt, trousers or shoes go digital. Yes of course we have seen Apps to measure things like heart rate, or distance walked, but for most people these are just gimmicks – which is why, for example, Google Glass flopped.

Despite that, more than 250 million people by 2023 are likely to be wearing smart devices such as wristbands recording motion, or smart watches that integrate with mobiles. In many people with serious chronic illness, the balance will soon shift in favour of home-based medical monitoring, whether blood oxygen, sugar levels, heart rhythm, and so on. But this will not be the case for normal, healthy people for a while.

The challenge is in creating huge numbers of low-cost sensors for smartphones and other devices. Hence the research by Google into smart contact lenses that detect blood sugar levels, and transmit results using an aerial of very thin coiled wire. Home health monitoring will be App based (modular), connected to other things like home security. (For more on medical technology, see p. 88.)

Convergence is the enemy of innovation

Convergence is a terrible game for telcos to play: it means that every device converges in price and features. Every phone looks and feels almost the same. Every operating system works in a similar way. It also means that every device is packed with hundreds of features that no one uses.

Convergence is the *opposite* of innovation. All *true* innovation is by definition about doing things differently to serve customers better. The lesson of history is that all successful innovations are copied rapidly, as competitors converge onto the same things.

Convergence means that the only way to make your product stand out is on price, since everything else is so similar, and that means a desperate spiral to the bottom on profitability.

So expect hundreds of new entrants into the world of telcos over the next few years, all copying things that work well already, and few survivors. Expect one or two to become household names, growing from almost nothing in less than 5–10 years, winning almost entirely on price alone. Expect huge pressures on profits of today's telco giants as a result.

Expect the pace of true innovation to slow down in mobile

devices, as each becomes more perfectly optimised, within natural limits imposed by the size of fingers, pockets, and resolution of the human eye or ear.

Simplicity will be a survival issue

Most devices are still over-delivering on features that are rarely used by most people, making life far too complicated. A huge reason behind the success of touch-sensitive tablets has been simplicity, which is why one of the fastest-growing groups of users of the iPad has been those aged over 65.

It is a scandal that many IT systems are still sold with software full of bugs, with incompatibilities and failures that would put manufacturers in prison if they were making cars or planes.

I am often asked by IT companies or telcos to gaze into the future for them – but often my message is very different. Go away urgently and sort out the mess you have today in your existing products, make them work properly, and support your customers better, before you embark on yet another series of half-perfected innovations.

Customers will become increasingly intolerant of complex products, and simplicity will be a core value for every successful IT and telco company.

The truth is that despite all the above, the pace of real techno-innovation remains painfully slow. For some years I have subscribed to a large-circulation European magazine called *T3*. Every issue is supposed to be packed with the latest gadgets and Apps and games and other techno-breakthroughs.

But the fact is that there is hardly enough real news to fill an issue every 3 months, let alone every 4 weeks. Yet another retina-quality screen for a smartphone. Yet another App to help navigate busy streets. Yet another music streaming service. Yet another way to measure the quality of your sleep. Yet another camera with a few more megapixels.

Most so-called innovation is merely copying features on some other manufacturer's product, or tinkering with the spec of the basic design.

New ways to feed your brain

Many smartphone users already take their phones out to check their screens over 200 times every day, including last thing before falling asleep and first thing on waking. What about tomorrow?

The fact is that the connection between brain and device is far too clumsy and slow. For example, our reading speeds are no faster than they were – actually in many cases they have fallen, since it is faster to speed-read a printed page than one on-screen. And typing speeds are also slower on mobile devices.

Expect intense efforts to find ways to get instant knowledge without having to look at a screen in your pocket or on your wrist. Many people (including me) have been very sceptical about clunky prototypes like Google Glass, but we do need to completely rethink interfaces.

Expect many more types of head-based displays, gesture controls – all of which will ultimately be threatened by direct digital-brain interfaces. The first such devices are helmets for gamers, which use brain waves to control the action.

Many people already have biodigital brains

As I predicted 15 years ago, we have seen rapid advances in the creation of biodigital brains, where brain cells are fused into the surface of chips, and connected to mobile Apps. The first experiments were carried out in 1993, implanting small chips into brains of mice and rats, which were then able to transmit basic thoughts to each other at the speed of light – such as requests for food or drink.

More recently, rats have sent each other mental messages over thousands of miles between cages in North Carolina and Brazil. Several rats were connected at once in a 'brain net' so that they could collaborate on problem solving, mind reading each other.

Doctors have already implanted similar chips inside the heads of more than 450,000 human beings, and are implanting chips into 50,000 more people every year. These cochlear implants connect with the auditory nerve inside the inner ear, and are very successful in restoring some kinds of severe hearing loss, without any risks of brain damage, epilepsy or other problems.

Send an email (or possibly an image) by thinking alone

Other experiments have given blind people primitive sight – with chips implanted into the visual cortex of the brain, or connected to the optic nerve inside their eyes. I have met a paralysed man who controls his arm, hand and fingers by thinking alone, not by chips in his brain, but by chips in his upper arm that sense nerve activation.

Scientists at Harvard Medical School have already enabled people to send simple messages to each other over several thousand miles, by thought alone, using a helmet to detect brain waves, and another head-mounted device to create sensations of light flashes in brain tissue.

On current trends, biodigital brains will be a relatively normal part of life for over 25 million people by 2050, mainly to restore hearing or sight, as well as to overcome brain or spinal cord injuries, or, more rarely (for those who are wealthy and curious enough), to try to extend mental horizons, memory, intelligence, thinking speed and powers of concentration. One challenge to overcome is that chips planted directly into brain tissue can increase the risk of epilepsy, by irritating the brain.

Digital insights will become common but strange

How will such digital insights feel? Imagine walking down the street and just sensing, by instinct in a way very hard to describe, that the shop you need is further to the right, or having a 'gut feeling' that your heart rate has increased to around 80 beats a minute, or 'just knowing' that the person walking by is a relative of someone you know very well.

We will also see other strange inventions – for example, scientists have already created devices that allow genes inside the brain to be activated by the power of thought. Thinking activates a small light, which then activates light-sensitive pathways inside cells.

Most people feel very uncomfortable about chips being implanted into their brains, or the brains of their children. What about health risks or being hacked? Here is yet another example of how the future is not just about innovation, but also about emotion. You can have the smartest invention in the world, but if it fails to connect with passion, it is likely to fail as a successful product.

Worries about electromagnetic radiation

Expect growing concerns about the lifetime effect of low-dose exposure to electromagnetic radiation from overhead power lines, mobile phones, implanted chips and other devices. There have already been suggestions that there may be a weak link between cancer and intensive use of mobile phones. Some studies have suggested that tumours are slightly more common on the side of the head that a person usually uses for mobile phone calls.

Expect further evidence that mobile phone radiation affects brain function, as well as affecting the function of other cells. Expect legal action too, even though risks to an individual from normal use seem to be extremely low, and will become lower still, as phone calls become less popular, replaced by SMS, mobile web, and so on.

Ongoing boom of recorded video moments

I predicted years ago that personal video would be really important, but I was wrong about the speed of uptake of *live* video.

People love uploading recorded video – carefully checked, edited, selected – to match their personal image. YouTube users are uploading more than 100 hours of video every minute, and 1 billion different people use YouTube each month, watching an average of 6 hours each, of which 40% is already watched on mobile. At present 80% of traffic is outside the US, but YouTube reaches more American 18–25-year-olds than any cable TV network.

Why people still hate live video at work

Despite what I expected, live video links will I think continue to be relatively unpopular in most workplaces, compared to video calls between close family and friends. The reason is data leakage.

Just look at the number of people who have video cameras built into their phones, and ask how many times they are used for video calls. Or the number of people who would prefer a voice confer-ence call to a video conference call at work.

Video calls reveal far more than you may realise at the time. Did you brush your hair before the call? Do you look like you have a hangover? For a home-worker – did you remember to shave? Can they see the washing up in the sink? Can they see the dog and one of your children wandering around? Can they see the laundry basket?

For family calls, such data leakage is enchanting and delightful – a feeling of being there, of actuality, a touch of authentic daily life – seeing the grandchildren wandering around or playing with a friend, being given a video tour of the garden, and noticing lots of things, capturing atmosphere, sharing experiences, treasured moments.

What is the future of the web?

The online world will influence even more of our daily activities over the next five decades, and most aspects of civilised life will be deeply linked to it, in one way or another.

Most people's online worlds will be completely dominated over the next decade by no more than 10–20 global brands. Today those might be companies like Amazon, Google, YouTube, Facebook, Twitter, eBay, Alibaba and LinkedIn. Their real value is brand recognition, and each will come under threat from next-generation competitors.

China will soon dominate the web

Mandarin has recently overtaken English as the most common first language spoken by web users, with over half a billion Mandarin speakers online. If you walk the streets of Beijing, Shanghai or Kunming, you will see the revolution yourself. Most younger people are deep into their smartphones, hurrying along or crossing the street. And the rest are clutching them tightly at all times.

China is already the world's largest e-commerce market, worth $540bn in 2015, and as the world's largest maker of smartphones, is also about to become the world's largest mobile commerce market.

Alibaba is the largest online retailer in China, with revenues growing by around 50% a year to around $80bn in 2014, compared to $100bn for Amazon. Alibaba sales were then greater than the global sales of eBay and Amazon combined, around 2% of China's entire GDP. The shares of the company were worth over $150bn, with 600 million registered accounts and 100 million e-commerce shoppers every day, representing 80% of all China's e-commerce.

Alibaba has seen a 10-fold increase in mobile revenues in 12 months to a third of all sales, up from 12% the year before, as the number of smartphone shoppers rose from 136 million to over 188 million in just 6 months. But watch out for new, very smart e-commerce competitors in China such as Tencent Holdings, and Xiaomi phones.

Expect new competitors to secure large enough market share to survive as credible threats, with extremely attractive, simple, clever innovations – things that capture the imagination of hundreds of millions of people within days or weeks, making existing huge players look like 'uncool' dinosaurs. Expect most new players to be absorbed by acquisition into ever larger familiar brands.

Google will try hard to manage your entire life

Google will set the pace for innovation across many new sectors over the next two decades, ranging from driverless cars, to next-generation biotech, and smart homes. To achieve this, Google will acquire a very wide range of much smaller companies. Take the $550m purchase of Deep Mind for example, which teaches computers to think like humans. Or the move to buy Nest Labs for $3.2bn, which is a leader in WiFi-linked smart devices for use in your home.

By 2014, Google Android had 72% of the mobile market for operating systems, compared to only 14% for Apple. Google will come under increasing scrutiny – particularly in Europe where there are worries about abuse of monopoly, given Google's more than 90% share of search queries, compared to 68% in America, and in nations like Russia that seek more web censorship (worries about antisocial behaviour). Google will continue to feel a cool wind, along with other large American IT companies, following revelations of deep co-operation with American spy agencies. The EU will continue to try to break up Google's extending powers.

More web-based billionaires with a touch of genius

Expect many new web billionaires with typical time from startup to buyout or stock market flotation of 4–5 years. Most will make their money with genius innovations that add significantly to the scope of established giants like Google, Amazon, eBay, Facebook, Alibaba. In most cases, at least half the value will be locked up in their loyal user-base that enables the buyer of the company to reach a new community.

Expect such inventions to revolutionise customer experience in personal banking and online payments, wealth management, personal messaging, photo handling, archiving people's 'libraries of life', music handling, note taking/thought capture, speech recognition, document creation, health monitoring and automated homes. Some of the most successful will be in very well-defined areas, as we have seen with taxi-ordering Apps like Uber or holiday rental sites like Airbnb. The secret of success will usually be a really smart, elegant and 'cool' site or user interface. YouTube was not the first video streaming site – but it was by far the easiest and most fun to use.

The future of entertainment

So what about the future of video, film, music, theatre, live TV and other entertainment? Mobile is already totally transforming video and TV consumption, while music has been hit by the greatest transformation of them all because of online streaming and digital downloads.

The music industry will face meltdown and chaos

Music is still a $65bn a year industry, and spends $15bn a year on new recordings, but big labels are in crisis. Over 40% of their global revenues already come from digital sales, more than half in some nations, but not enough to make up for loss of revenue from physical albums.

Many big music labels will be wiped out by social media music. Young listeners expect all music to be free – or nearly so. The music market is being flooded by highly talented home-based musicians, churning out millions of hours of free entertainment, in the hope of being 'signed' by a label.

In the past, big labels used to invest in lots of small bands, hoping one or two would really take off, but in future they will sign very few, after early success online. Labels will continue to dominate global album sales well into 2020, but 85% of their revenues will come from a handful of ultra-successful bands. Most up-and coming artists will be forced to bypass labels altogether, and sell direct, working with promoters and event organisers.

Expect 80–100 million people to be paying for unlimited streaming via services like Spotify by 2020 – but most musicians will earn less than $0.002 per play.

Radio music will survive

Traditional music streaming was of course radio, and radio will continue to enjoy huge audiences, because it is convenient as background entertainment at home or in the car. Another reason is the feeling of companionship, with tens of thousands of others sharing the same songs.

Live music is a $25bn a year industry. In 2013, concert attendance worldwide grew by 26%. Expect more blockbuster tours – like U2's 360 tour from 2009–2011, grossing $736 million, playing to 7.2 million people around the world.

Most successful artists will generate the bulk of their income from live events, sponsorships, commercials, celebrity appearances, and so on. More top artists will give away their music, aiming to use it as a way to grow income from these other sources.

Future of the film industry and gaming

Compared to the drastic transformation in the music industry, the film industry will change rather slowly, with more mega-budget films, and astonishingly realistic imaging of imaginary creatures, worlds and events. The industry will struggle to generate enough quality output to satisfy ultra-high resolution home-based cinema, just as TV and cable companies will struggle.

Most film-making will continue to be directed at the US market – responsible for 31% of around $100bn global film revenues. America generates 29% of global entertainment and media sales, followed by China. The global market will be worth $2 trillion by 2017.

Boom for live cinema

Piracy will remain a constant and annoying issue, but will not prevent rapid growth in cinema audiences across the world, attracted not only by breathtaking visual immersion but also by excitement in sharing the experience.

As with music, most videos in developed nations and emerging market cities will be downloaded or streamed for personal viewing by 2025, with collapse in both DVD and Blu-ray sales.

Films in 3D will continue to impress and disappoint, depending on audience and genre. Expect wide ownership of home video screens that allow small groups a reasonable 3D experience without wearing glasses. The first curved ultra-high resolution screens are an early indicator of what will be possible.

Expect huge growth in on-demand watching, while big live TV shows and sporting events will continue to command huge viewing figures (people like to be virtually joined in a communal watching experience – we used to call it watching TV).

Augmented reality and total immersion gaming

The film industry will continue to merge with gaming, with inter-active HD animations and sequences by 'real' actors. Headsets will be more widely used, with higher resolution screens and smoother response to head movement. However, headsets will be rejected by most gamers for day-to-day use before 2025, because of eye strain, weight, lack of comfort, cost, being uncool, short battery life. That will not stop expensive experiments, as we have seen with the $2bn spent by Facebook on Oculus. Expect worries about heavy use of 3D glasses in young children.

Augmented reality glasses will be used in a wide range of specialist applications ranging from those aimed at surgeons (to enable them to see extra data), and tourists (to wear when visiting museums or galleries or monuments), to the military.

Future of infotech

The digital revolution has hardly begun. You will see more changes in the next 15 years than since the start of personal computing in 1975.

Microsoft and Apple will both face a similar challenge over the next decade: how to find radical innovations to drive business growth, when both companies are burdened by a range of well-optimised but ageing products, and when the market for computers continues to be wiped out by that for larger mobile devices.

Microsoft will still be addicted to revenues from Windows and Office software, well beyond 2023, plus a growing range of business enterprise products. Microsoft will struggle (and possibly fail) as a global mobile company. Most new investment and revenue growth by 2025–2030 is likely to be from cloud-based services.

Apple will need to reinvent itself

Apple led the way with a generation of simple, usable, elegant products, which transformed consumer expectations. However, Apple will need at least two more breakthrough products between 2017 and 2020, each equivalent to the first iPhone and iPad, totally different to anything seen before.

Apple will be threatened by giants like Samsung Electronics, which is likely to dwarf it by 2020. Apple computers, iPads, iPhones and TVs are history – innovations will be incremental, blurring the differences between these items. The next range of i-devices will be much smaller and larger. Apple will invest heavily in a rapidly growing range of wearable tech, going far beyond the i-Watch.

Apple will also make larger smart TV hubs, with total entertainment, web, mobile, home integration, as part of deep investment in home automation.

Expect big investment to integrate all channel activities into a joined-up experience. So the iPhone knows you are watching a TV quiz show, and the iPad knows you are also on the phone to a call centre while searching for better online offers. Every other manufacturer will follow.

Quantum computing means a million times faster

We will see huge investments by government secret services and military into quantum computing (QC), mainly to crack strong encryption. QC will also be used for complex tasks like long-range weather forecasting and simulations of nuclear weapons. In addition, QC will transform personal computing, because we will all be able to access QC power in the Cloud, as we will see later.

For ordinary computers, Moore's Law will continue for the next 25–30 years, that is, computing or storage capacity will halve in price for the same capacity every 18 months. But traditional computing will eventually be limited by binary electronics. Each bit of data is stored in an on or off state. And there will be limits to size and speed of on/off memory stores – whether magnetic, or on chips.

Quantum computers use qubits, not bits. Each qubit can have many different forms, based on varying properties of atoms, ions, photons or electrons. Imagine writing a book in Morse code using just dots and dashes, and then writing the same book using an alphabet or Chinese characters. That is why a single event in a quantum computer has a million times more processing power than in a normal computer. So a secret military code that takes two years to crack will be decoded in minutes or seconds.

The next great digital revolution

We need to take a close look at three areas that will really matter to our future: the *Internet of Things, Big Data* and *Cloud Computing*. Each has been around for a while, but it is the *combination* of all three in new ways that will create the revolution. If you are not technically minded, you may be tempted for a moment to skim-read the next few pages, but your entire future may depend on what is described here, explained, hopefully, in a clear way. Indeed, the whole of our national security, personal privacy and freedom could be at stake.

These three factors will merge to create immense and lasting opportunities for good, but also for serious abuse on a gigantic scale. We will see huge benefits for all manufacturers, marketers, managers and customers – but also huge benefits for all hackers, terrorists and spies. The latent power of what we are talking about cannot be overstated.

The truth about the Internet of Things

The Internet of Things will be the biggest single advance in manufacturing, wholesale, distribution and systems control for 20 years. It's all about tracking, monitoring and management of billions of different things.

At least 30 billion different items will be communicating with each other online by 2022, rising to 100 billion by 2030 – hard-wired into the web, or using radio-frequency identification devices (RFIDs). These are tiny chips, the size of a grain of sand, plus a small aerial, which is used to power the device and receive or transmit as needed – so-called near-field communication.

More than 6 billion new RFIDs are already entering the environment every year, attached to clothes in shops (1.5 billion), food packaging, airline baggage, supply chain components, farm animals and pets, tickets and passports. Airbus has tagged 1.5 million different components used in its latest planes. RFIDs are already a $20bn a year market. It all adds up to greater efficiency, fewer production line faults, automated supply chains, fewer stolen goods and reduced human error.

RFIDs have limitations: it is hard to read them in general groceries because water, foil and steel can interfere with radio signals, and transmission distance is usually only a metre or two. More reliable is a permanent web connection, using a fully powered wireless device such as a watch or a light.

Expect your fridge to be able to sense changes in outside weather for example, making extra ice on a very hot day. Expect your gas boiler to send an alert if it breaks down. Expect your alarm clock to wake you up earlier if it is snowing.

Human bodies linked to Internet of Things

Human beings are already part of the Internet of Things, despite health risks. Some people have already injected themselves under their skin, with the same RFID devices as vets use in animals. In 2002 VeriChip gained a US licence to implant RFIDs into humans but in 2007 it was revealed that hundreds of animals with RFID implants had developed cancer, and the company collapsed.

People have injected RFIDs under their skin as keys to gain access to secure facilities. The Baja Beach Club, a nightclub in Rotterdam, has used VeriChip implants to identify VIPs and to enable them to pay for drinks.

In the meantime, much larger GPS devices are being widely used by police services in countries like the UK to tag convicted criminals and others who are under house arrest. They are also being used by worried parents to track children. Expect rapid growth of all kinds of people tracking, mainly using hidden Apps on mobiles. Expect abuse by oppressive regimes to control large numbers of dissenters, as well as by family members to spy on each other.

However, the Internet of Things also includes wearable devices implanted inside your body: monitoring or controlling your health, sensing blood sugar, heart rate or a host of other things, connected at all times to health services.

Expect many new hacking threats, and added worries about privacy. What happens, for example, if a terrorist hacks into 100,000 driverless cars while they are on the road (the average car already contains 60 processors and 10 million lines of software coding). What happens if hackers threaten to take over the controls of 35,000 pacemakers?

Big Data – why it really matters

The Internet of Things is generating an even greater explosion of so-called Big Data (vast stores of information about people, systems, and activities). The big question is what will we do with it all? Around 90% of all the data we have ever created has been generated in the last two years – 2.5 million trillion bytes a day. Past data will be one of the world's most important assets, but how will it be protected from attack? The people most excited about Big Data are in marketing departments of large companies. However, most companies will struggle to get a return on their investment in this area, and losing data to criminals will be a constant nightmare.

On the world's busiest websites, up to 1,300 companies are watching everything you do. Even if that data is anonymised, it is often very easy to work out who you are from clues.

More than 40 trillion gigabytes of data will be produced a year by 2020 – over 5 gigabytes for every human being. The volume of data collected each year by US companies alone is large enough to fill the Library of Congress around 20 times over. New generators of data will include networked cars, smart grids and smart electric metering, and smart buildings.

Big Data will take many forms, including:

- ◆ your phone location – second by second for the past 5 years
- ◆ all your shopping and online habits – every payment made / page searched / time per page
- ◆ social media – every friend you have and what you talk about
- ◆ global product tracking – every component, every moment
- ◆ public transport times – every bus, every train tracked
- ◆ medical statistics – every one of your own test results, diagnosis, treatment; continuous health monitoring using mobile Apps
- ◆ bike accident locations – every street, time, date, age, driver.

Big Data already reveals the truth about YOU

What happens when data is used to build a complete picture of your daily life? Many companies sell your data without permission. One data firm has already built a billion personal profiles, each containing an average of fifty different pieces of information. These are used to target online ads that already account for 25% of the $500 billion global marketing spend.

As we saw when Snowden leaked secret US documents in 2013, every intelligence agency is also using Big Data to track people, detect patterns, prevent or solve crimes, and for political surveillance.

Big Data will save money and lives – but over-reliance will be lethal

Expect fortunes to be won (and lost) investing into Big Data companies, and huge demand for experts in pattern recognition. Here are some examples of the value of Big Data:

◆ At the Hospital for Sick Children in Toronto, all data is analysed about babies leaving the neonatal ward. As a result, doctors discovered how to predict blood infection 24 hours before a baby becomes ill, by spotting newborns whose heart rates vary less than normal.

◆ Your bank sees an unusual pattern of purchases from strange locations – and creates a Fraud Alert.

◆ Amazon predicts which products to stock in warehouses close to your home, before you order them. This is somewhat similar to a supermarket tailoring the product ranges in each store according to the previous buying habits of that community. Amazon's calculations are based on your shopping habits, age, income, even on how long your screen cursor lingers over a button.

◆ Tesco led consumer marketing using Big Data, with its loyalty card in the UK. From the data it collects, it is able to come up with tailored, eye-catching offers for a specific customer.

◆ A political party tracks public opinion on social media.

Corporations also track reputation in the same way.

◆ Los Angeles police use past crime data to predict areas where new crimes are most likely – sending in extra officers. Result: 26% fall in local burglaries.

◆ The Pentagon looks for hidden patterns in aerial footage from drones, links between regular events on the ground, and local explosions or attacks.

◆ Big Data cracked open the Enron scandal, when pattern recognition revealed that dodgy deals were all given the names of exotic birds.

◆ The World Health Organisation and Google monitor the spread of viral epidemics such as ebola by looking for new patterns in Search requests in different towns and cities.

◆ Weather agencies look for patterns in readings from tens of thousands of sensors around the world, going back over decades, to improve long-range forecasts.

Employers look for patterns in what people do at work – to detect fraud in banks, for example, or to monitor use of office space; or as part of knowledge-management systems, to build up a picture of who knows what, and where expertise is in particular areas.

Location-based marketing is the next big thing

In a mobile world, the most important thing to know about any customer is where they are right now, and where they have been. That tells you a huge amount about how they are likely to be feeling and acting, especially when combined with other data we have.

Here's an example of location-based marketing. Coca-Cola has an app that records your favourite drink, and a vending machine that can produce infinite variations to create a customised drink for you. As you walk around, Coca-Cola can (with permission) see where you are. If you are close to a machine, it tells you. As you approach, it makes the drink, and as you pick it up, the machine charges your phone.

Leaking personal data in every taxi ride

Here is another example. I step into a London taxi where a screen is running a news item. The taxi detects the RFID in my glasses. So the taxi now knows:

◆ I am wearing variable lenses – so I need reading glasses. That means I am probably over 50 years old.

◆ I am wearing male designer glasses – so I am a man who also likes premium brands.

◆ I am on a journey from A to B in the centre of London on a Tuesday afternoon.

The taxi monitor then starts running a customised advert: 'Have you thought about laser correcting eye surgery? We are offering a 25% discount at our London clinic if you call us in the next ten minutes.'

My mobile phone company can also see that I am on the move, after making my way slowly down the street. A logical deduction is that I have just stepped into a taxi or bus. Pattern recognition shows that this usually happens at around this time of day, on Tuesdays and Thursdays. So now the telco can make a good guess about my destination, based on my usual habit. The company may also be seeing most of my online purchases and web searches. Some may think this kind of customer monitoring is frightening, but it is already happening, in subtle ways that few are fully aware of.

A personal guide on your journey of life

In a digital, multichannel, social media world, the key to marketing will not be shouting the same message at millions of people, but becoming an expert advisor or friend to each customer along their own journey of life.

Half of all 16–24-year-olds in the UK already use social networks or mobiles to send messages while watching TV, for example – undermining the impact of advertising breaks. Second screens are used to *talk* about programmes, not interact with them. The same is happening across the world from South Korea to Russia, Mexico to Nigeria.

As I say, marketers already see far more data than most customers realise, and it is easy to make customers feel very uncomfortable, if they reveal too much of what they know.

Who is watching you right now?

I have sat at a screen in front of a web page and watched individual letters and numbers appearing in a web form, in real time, as they were being entered by a customer living in another city. The customer was totally unaware that they were being closely monitored, second by second.

Imagine you are following someone online who is trying to buy a very expensive holiday. You see that she has entered her passport number three times incorrectly, her mouse is hovering, you sense her frustration, and fear she is about to give up. Do you phone the mobile number she entered earlier and say: 'Hello, is that Mary Jones? I see you are having trouble with entering your passport number on our web page. Would you like me to take it from you over the phone?' Or do you wait 20 minutes and pretend to be making a random sales call from the company? Answer: don't interrupt her. Use the data to learn how to improve your web form, and phone her in a couple of hours.

Little Data will matter even more than Big Data

Big Data is about spotting a pattern, but *Little Data* is all about spotting a person. Most large companies need to take very small elements of their Big Data, and focus on little things to make a practical difference to customers – or they will get buried in analysis. Billions of dollars will be wasted over the next decade by companies on useless Big Data systems that produce nothing except frustration.

Let us imagine a wealthy telco customer. He likes sailing, and is about to buy a yacht. Here is the *Little Data* picture and how it develops towards the sale:

◆ web page searches on his smartphone for yachts and marinas – over months

- ◆ visits to marinas, many of them
- ◆ purchases of yachting magazines
- ◆ several holidays over 18 months, payments to yacht charter companies
- ◆ web searches for yacht finance, yacht insurance, yacht ownership
- ◆ smartphone sees the person arriving at national Boat Show, the largest selling event in the calendar for yacht manufacturers.

Smarter marketing messages

Many months before the boat show, the phone company or bank should have been sending apparently fairly random messages from time to time about boats, or displaying them in Facebook ads, on YouTube video clips, next to web pages, and so on, for example:

'Tips for a great sailing holiday'

'Taking the family – sailing in Greece'

'Owning a boat is very affordable'

'You will be pleased to know that we have reviewed your account and pre-cleared you for a low-interest loan of up to €50,000 if you want to buy a new car, yacht, motorboat. Click here if you are interested.'

And the genius about such online marketing is that the company pays nothing for all these ads to appear on all those screens, and is only spending money if the targeted customer actually gets as far as clicking on one of them to take things further. 'Pay per click' campaigns have completely revolutionised the way marketing budgets work.

Next-generation Cloud Computing

Let us turn now to the third element in the next digital revolution, Cloud Computing, which already affects us all, and will impact every corporation in radical ways. This too offers huge benefits, and creates huge risks.

Back in the early 1970s, all computer power was centralised, was accessed by terminals and long computer cables. Then in 1975 came personal computing, where each person had their own intelligent machine. My first company was an IT startup using the world's first desktops with a maximum memory of 32,000 characters, to run medical records, payroll, word processing and health diagnosis. By 1980 desktops were more powerful than supercomputers a decade earlier.

Now we are going full circle and once again (almost) all computer power is being centralised, accessed by mobiles connected via wireless networks. The 'cloud' power used by your mobile device will be infinitely powerful.

An early example of cloud power was speech recognition. The best systems need huge memory and speed, way beyond the capability of any small device. Far more efficient to send speech by phone to some distant site and have it instantly decoded.

All humanity will be found in the Cloud

More than 90% of all web users globally are already using cloud-based email, or sites such as Facebook, LinkedIn, YouTube, Twitter or Instagram. Cloud computing will also grow rapidly as a means of preventing data loss – backing up automatically the contents of every computer or mobile.

But the real power of the Cloud has yet to be seen. 'Software as a service' will be rented by the day, week or month or year, running in the Cloud, rather than on your own machine. The savings can be colossal, not only in development, but also in keeping software updated.

SalesForce is a prime example of the new cloud world – designed to set up and run call centres almost instantly and manage customer relationships. SalesForce has capabilities that very few global corporations could possibly afford to develop on their own, with 12,000 employees and a budget of over $3bn a year.

Corporations will shift many different elements of their existing IT infrastructure into the Cloud – in many cases by setting up private clouds. At the same time, boardroom debates about risks from cloud attacks and loss of critical data to criminal gangs or competitors will intensify, especially in banking and financial services. And the larger clouds become, the more they will attract hackers.

Cyber-crime – one of world's greatest threats

Add the trio of Internet of Things, Big Data and Cloud Computing to the world of telcos, mobile devices and personal computers, and we can begin to see what a cluster of mega-risks we have created, almost by accident.

Never in human history has it been possible for one person, sitting in a bedroom at home in a distant land, to create such havoc and chaos, to seize such power. Cyber-crime will therefore be one of the greatest threats to our world over the next 50 years, and far beyond, into centuries to come. There is no way back from such a future, except by dismantling all the global e-systems that link us increasingly together.

As I predicted, every large company in the world is now experiencing frequent cyber-attacks, on their own systems or in the Cloud, whether they realise it or not. The Centre for Strategic and International Studies has estimated total cost to business to be around $300bn a year.

Losses are likely to be more than $1 trillion a year by 2025, especially if we see wide-scale attacks, sponsored by hostile governments. We are not just talking about attacks on traditional targets like bank websites, but also commercial aggression like the blackmail of Sony, after the company released a controversial film about North Korea.

There is nothing new about web abuse. At least 80% of the *247 billion emails sent every day* are spam, many of them so-called phishing attacks, pretending to be from a bank, encouraging people to enter passwords.

Expect 10 billion separate attacks a year

McAfee is already detecting over 600 million new and different computer viruses, malware or Trojan horses every year – several per second. Pharma, chemicals, mining, electronics and agricultural companies are seeing increases of 600% a year in malware attacks. Energy, oil and gas attacks are growing by 400%. Attempts to steal data from retailers are doubling every 12 months.

In many cases, tens of millions of credit card details have been stolen. A company called Target lost data on 70 million people in a single attack. A single contractor in South Korea managed to steal personal information on 20 million credit card users, more than half the country's working population. Two years previously, personal data on 35 million South Koreans was stolen from Cyworld, a popular social network.

A billion people's personal details will be stolen

Similar attacks have happened across the world. Hackers recently stole personal details of 213 million eBay users. Sony lost the details of 100 million clients to a hacker. The Heartbleed bug caused huge damage in 2014 as it swept globally, invading the websites of many multinationals, retailers, banks and email companies.

Another example was a major attack on JP Morgan Chase – following a sustained assault with tens of thousands of separate attacks each day over many months, mostly traced to Russia. In these attacks 76 million names, addresses, telephone numbers and email addresses were stolen – affecting two thirds of all households in America.

Why hackers will often escape prosecution if caught

I have met bankers who don't prosecute or even sack staff who hack into their own bank systems. 'Just thought you should know... Of course I should probably leak the news or publish the account names.' Terrified of bad publicity, they pay them off, give them a wonderful reference, and let them go and work for a competitor – where exactly the same thing is likely to happen again. There is no legal requirement in most countries for any bank to report when they have been hacked and lost data, which means that most attacks will never be known, and the true scale is far larger than most people think.

Even the most basic bank security can be pitifully weak. I remember when, shortly before spending a day advising the board of a Swiss bank, I decided to carry out a test of my own. Without being challenged, I managed to walk right into a high-security area using the oldest tricks in the book: distracting reception staff, and gently pulling apart sliding security doors with my fingers.

Large corporations will be forced to encrypt stored data

All IT and smartphone companies will step up personal security with end-to-end encryption during data transmission, and encryption of all data 'at rest' stored on servers. It is really shocking that most banks still do not encrypt data on their servers, so once a hacker gains entry, which they do in every large bank several times a year, they usually have no trouble at all reading files. It was very careless of Sony to allow hackers to so easily read all their archived emails, contracts and other documents. Best practice will mean universal encryption, which makes a large attack significantly more difficult for hackers.

Customers will be urged to set up two-step authentication, with confirmation of passwords using codes sent to mobile devices. As a result, expect dramatic growth in attacks on telco companies and all mobile devices, as people try to hack into SMS and intercept these codes. In 2014, such attacks grew more than a hundred times over the previous year.

Cyber-war – a new kind of Cold War

Expect many significant large-scale cyber-attacks against nations and groups of enterprises over the next two decades, often directed by criminal gangs rather than government staff, paid for by secret agents of other countries. The largest of these attacks are likely to form part of next-generation conflicts/disputes between nations, paralysing entire government agencies for days, causing major disruption to banking and telecommunications, damaging utilities such as power stations or parts of the national grid.

It is already happening: for example, a blast furnace in a steel mill was hit by hackers in Germany recently, causing parts of the plant to fail. But for understandable reasons, most successful attacks on major installations will be kept strictly secret, in the national interest. An increasingly common trick will be to hijack thousands of computers with a virus and order them to attack a corporate website, with multiple visits every second. The site then crashes – until a ransom is paid (Denial of Service).

Cyber-attacks on people, companies and nations

Cyber-attacks are easy to carry out on physical web infrastructure too. For example, most bandwidth in the world is carried on a few, very vulnerable, fibre-optic cables. Cutting them is very easy – all you have to do is drag a ship's anchor along a sea bed to snag them. And it is very hard to detect which ship did it, especially in relatively busy shipping areas. Recent cable damage reduced web access in India by 70%, Egypt by 60%, and with many other nations affected in the Middle East. In another episode, divers were arrested off the coast of Egypt in the act of sabotage.

For all these reasons, NATO includes cyber-attacks as one of the events that could trigger a joint response by the Alliance. However, it will be almost impossible to prove who is really behind such attacks, and therefore impossible to retaliate effectively. The US Navy is being hit on a routine basis by over 100,000 separate online attacks every hour, according to Hewlett Packard. But from where and by whom and for what purpose?

Sometimes debris is left by accident, which gives clues about origin – for example naming a piece of code, deeply encrypted inside a complex virus, after a popular TV comedian in a particular country. But subtle clue-dropping can also be a deliberate decoy, used by secret services or gangs to cast blame on an innocent nation.

Viruses designed to control entire countries

Energetic Bear is a cyber-espionage weapon that infected vital parts of Europe's energy infrastructure during the Ukraine–Russia–EU crisis. It targeted a wide range of industrial control systems, national grids, power stations, wind turbines, and biomass fuel plants. It was designed to monitor energy use in real time and to disable systems on command – but on whose command? Future energy viruses will target smart grids and smart homes – imagine the impact, for example, of a hacker from a hostile state or group turning on 15 million air conditioners simultaneously, causing instant power cuts.

A few weeks after the discovery of Energetic Bear, Russian telecom and health companies, utilities and government agencies discovered that they too had been hit by one of the most deadly and sophisticated clusters of viruses ever created, called Regin. The cluster was designed with multiple Apps to steal passwords, extract information on a huge range of systems, and take total control of many different types of industrial equipment.

'Digital bombs' inside large organisations

Targets were also hit in Saudi Arabia, Mexico, Ireland, India, Iran, Belgium, Australia and Pakistan. In many cases, it turned out that the viruses had been working away for up to 6 years without detection, despite every check. The viruses were constantly listening online for a single command to detonate tens of thousands of digital 'bombs' across every part of the nation. It has been reported that Russia is now so anxious about American penetration that security agencies are using printed paper for ultra-sensitive communications. The Chinese, meanwhile, are building a quantum computing link between Beijing and Shanghai, which they hope will lock out foreign surveillance.

In 2007, Estonian banks, government agencies, parliament, broadcasters and newspapers were also hit by three weeks of cyber-attacks that completely paralysed their web capabilities. These followed a disagreement with Russia, though responsibility was never proven.

So we will see huge investment in cyber-resilience, by governments, banks, stock exchanges and utility companies in particular, in the wealthiest nations, but smaller nations will remain very vulnerable. At least a quarter of all attacks will be espionage

– directed at stealing state secrets or corporate research that has yet to be patent protected.

Hackers will be recruited by spies and gangs

Expect growing numbers of full-time professional hackers, operating as independent consultants to criminal gangs and secret services, offering services in combination with others to plan major attacks. In many cases, these hacking geniuses will never realise who the end client really is. They may think they are working for MI6 in the UK, for example, when they are actually working for a Bulgarian gang, which is assisting Russian Federal Security Services, or for the CIA or Mossad.

Many attacks will be multidimensional. So a large-scale identity theft takes place a couple of hours before a vital payment channel is hacked, to create new PIN numbers. Minutes later, two hundred people with cloned cash cards start withdrawing cash from ATMs in over 50 cities.

Hackers will be turned against other hackers

Expect a radical rethink about what to do with convicted hackers: people with proven genius in cracking open systems, who may well be the best people in the world to test your own security, and help improve it. Do we really want to see those lives wasted in prison?

Some hackers will be offered rewards by governments to attack and destroy the so-called dark web. The aim will be to identify many millions of users of Tor web browsers (these are like normal web browsers, but prevent ANYONE monitoring your web activity) and other 'secret' tools: people who want to keep their activities and payments 100% secret.

Over 400 dark websites were closed in 2014 alone, including sites that sell illegal drugs, illegal arms deals, advertise professional assassins to kill spouses or politicians, and every kind of depravity. However, many dark web users in future will simply be trying to evade 'oppressive' state snooping – particularly in countries like Russia or China where web controls have become severe. Use of

Tor in Russia leapt from 60,000 to over 200,000 people in just a couple of months following the seizure of Crimea.

Future of surveillance, spies and state snooping

BIG BROTHER IS WATCHING YOU – George Orwell's 1984 gives a chilling picture of how technology could be used by a dictator to control millions. But the tools available today have advanced far beyond what Orwell saw.

Governments have never had so much power to invade privacy and spy on every citizen. Expect rapid scaling up of government budgets in most developed nations for national surveillance using publicly available data, commercial data, legally and semi-legally or illegally intercepted data. Cyber-espionage will become a crowded world with constant risks that experts are working for more than one master.

You should expect intelligence agencies in most developed countries to have complete remote access to any computer or phone they wish, able to listen using built-in microphones even when devices are 'not in use', to watch using built-in cameras, and to monitor every screen, every keystroke.

Secret back doors into every device

As we know from recent leaks by whistleblowers, all computer and mobile phone operating systems have become targets for the CIA, MI5 and so on, with the aim of being able to control devices belonging to private individuals or companies, read files, intercept passwords, turn on built-in cameras and microphones remotely, and so on.

Expect further revelations to show that secret 'back doors' were successfully coded long ago into most versions of Windows, Mac, Android, and so on, including back doors into encryption and security companies like Symantec, without any knowledge of the companies concerned. As a result, we can also expect growing numbers of worried consumers, living under oppressive regimes, to turn off all their devices whenever they wish to be 'alone'.

Companies like Google have been criticised for handing over security keys to government agencies to make spying easier. Many IT and phone companies are developing systems that are so secure that they cannot decode customer data even when ordered to by secret service agents. Apple and Google have already begun this process, creating security worries that newer smartphones could be used by terrorist groups to evade surveillance. Some media interviews about these 'security worries' are no doubt a smokescreen by intelligence services, who do not want the public to realise that they are right inside these new systems as well.

Every meeting and conversation recorded

On top of all this, individual Do-It-Yourself spying has never been easier – and will become even more so – via wireless devices hidden in standard power adapters, or pens, or ornaments, or concealed micro-cameras, each able to transmit over 1000 metres to a base station which then transmits instantly online, or using Apps installed secretly onto anyone else's phone, which can take just a few seconds, or using a drone equipped with a video camera.

It is already the case that business leaders should assume that every meeting may be recorded, or transmitted live to a wider audience outside the room – using just a voice memo on a smartphone concealed in a jacket pocket, or an open voice call set to hands-free.

Doctors, nurses and home carers are already discovering that their careless habits may end up immortalised in YouTube videos. The same applies in every other kind of workplace. And then there is secret tracking of family, friends, competitors or enemies – made so much easier by automatic trace facilities built into every mobile device, and wide availability of spying Apps.

How to become an instant 'spook'

As a test, one day I decided to plant a powerful bug on a participant sitting in the second row of a seminar of senior bankers, without any of my audience seeing what I had done, to show how vulnerable they were. I did this right in the middle of a lecture, in full view of everyone yet without them realising, in half a second. After I revealed what had happened, the participants took quite a while to locate who was carrying it, and where it was placed, even when the receiver was in their own hands.

Of course the greatest risks to all large corporations and governments will continue to be insiders – either criminals, or spies, or 'innocent' staff who have been blackmailed into co-operating.

Future of publishing, paper and news

We have looked at spying, but what about public media and government scrutiny by news agencies or book authors?

Expect continued rapid growth of e-book sales, and a gradual decline in sales of paper books and magazines, except in niche areas such as glossy travel books or 'experience books' for children. The physicality of books will become more important: touch, look, feel and smell.

Sales of e-books are likely to overtake those of paper books in the UK by 2018, when at least 50% of the population will own an e-reader of some kind – even if just a smartphone App. Sales of e-books are likely to triple in the next 5 years from £380bn to over £1bn. Sales jumped 66% in 2012 alone to 12% of UK book sales, while the paper book market share fell by 2%. Yet it is also true that in 2014 Kindle sales were flat in the UK while pre-Christmas sales of physical books leapt by 5% in one of the largest chains, children's books up by 9%. Physical books have a lot of life in them yet.

Specialist magazines will be more resilient – indeed, throughout the last few years, magazine titles in many countries have boomed in number, for ever more niche groups of readers. Magazines will continue to benefit from convenience, and from a superior look and feel to reading matter on a mobile device.

Paper will still mean a faster read

Stupid predictions have been made for years about the 'paperless office', when the truth is that more paper is printed each day per manager than ever before in most corporations: 92% of executives print something each day, 45% print 10 pages or more and 15% print more than 50. As I predicted years ago, paper will be with us for a long time yet.

Despite the huge growth of e-readers and online news channels, e-books and all electronic media will face a challenge from print for a long time to come, because of one single fact: reading speed, due to larger page size, format and resolution. Reading speed is less of a consideration when enjoying a novel on an e-reader, but it really makes a difference at work.

As every busy executive knows, the fastest way to read and mark up a set of lengthy board papers, or a long contract, is to print it out. Most people read printed pages at up to ten times their on-screen speed, using unconscious techniques such as page scanning, and are less likely to miss important sections than if they scroll through endless electronic pages of text. Their recall is usually better with paper, especially if they have a 'photographic' memory, and they are better able to reproduce important thoughts at the relevant part of the board meeting, because of their notes in the margin. And they usually find what they are looking for more quickly than by using the 'find' function in an e-version of the text.

Speed-reading will help newspapers

Set the speed-reading challenge to any group of friends and see for yourself. Most senior leaders can only read around 500 words a minute on-screen, but can easily make overall sense of an entire 40,000 word publication in less than five to ten minutes. So any corporation running a strict paperless office is wasting a huge amount of time and money.

You may think all this will change with higher resolution, larger screens, but this will not be the case for a long time. We already have large 'retina' screens, operating at the maximum resolution the eye can process, but they are hardly mobile. We will need to wait for electronic paper: flat, foldable membranes with the same contrast, resolution and convenience as large sheets of paper. Expect prototypes by 2020, but large retina-resolution sheets will be unusual and costly until well into the 2030s.

Future of news agencies, newspapers, news channels and reporting

It has often been said that 'News is what someone else does not want you to print. All the rest is advertising.' But the fastest spreading online content is heartwarming videos, funny lists, and eye-catching headlines on sites such as Buzzfeed or ViralNova. These appeal to positive, affirming emotions, and are promoted by friends.

Newspapers in crisis – but growth in emerging nations

Newspapers will rapidly decline in almost all developed nations over the next 5–10 years, while readership will grow in news-loving nations such as India, driven by expansion of the middle classes.

In 5 years, newspaper readership fell in America by 47%, but will grow by at least 15% in India in the next 5 years. One in five of the entire world's daily newspapers are published in India – more than 100 million separate titles, with 45% of all advertising spend.

In developed nations, traditional newspapers will struggle to convert readers into profitable online subscribers, losing over 60% of their previous income in many cases. Expect closures, mergers, consolidations and serious downgrading of content, as staff are laid off, offices closed, and regional and specialist reporting stopped. The number of newspaper journalists in America fell from 55,000 in 2007 to just 38,000 in 2013. Expect numbers to fall further to less than 20,000 by 2020.

At the same time, some free newspapers will do rather better, whether dailies given out in metro stations with minimal editorial teams, or local weekly papers in areas with robust local advertising, particularly from estate agents.

Future of news media

More Americans now watch news online than on cable TV, including more than half of 18–29-year-olds. Over 5,000 new full-time jobs have been created by around 500 digital news firms, including jobs for experienced journalists who have left newspapers like the *New York Times* and *Washington Post*. Digital newspapers will develop a new working model – for example, there is no cost-limit on length of an article, nor any need to make it all fit neatly in pages of a printed newspaper.

Growth in digital news will not halt the declining audience of news companies. For example, Facebook users who click on news links only spend 90 seconds a month on news sites, on average.

As I predicted, news broadcasting is now a social activity – half of all social media users already share news, and comment on news posts, while 7% of American adults have posted news videos they made themselves to a social network or news site.

Research shows that sad news stories are least likely to go viral. Positive stories get the most share-time. Expect these trends to profoundly shape our communities, and impact all news companies. The fact is that entertainment has always been a bigger business than news.

Who cares about depressing news online?

There is still no proven business model for a fee-paying online news service, because of impossibly strong competition from hundreds of well-respected, free sources such as the BBC, Guardian and the Huffington Post (a news Wiki), including news aggregator sites such as Google. In addition we can expect to see a cluster of new 'community' news sites, similar in philosophy to the Huffington Post, again all free access. Curators of content will multiply: people who gather various types of related web content, sometimes adding editorial of their own.

In 20 years' time, high-quality, in-depth investigative journalism for print media will have almost disappeared in developed nations. Aspiring journalists will be working instead for TV news, with linked (free access) web pages. But even large TV news companies will struggle in future with the cost of maintaining their own reporters across the world. The three largest news channels in America – CNN, Fox and MSNBC – lost 11% of the prime-time audience in a single year.

Expect rapid growth of freelance reporters and camera teams, without formal backing of news companies, or their protection, working alone or in packs, taking huge personal risks in the competition to get stories and sensational images. The result will be more frequent deaths among journalists, especially in war zones, together with worries about loss of professionalism and possible bias.

News fatigue will cut audiences further

In the past, most news tended to be sad or bad. Slayings, beatings, rapings, job losses, natural disasters, air crashes, bomb blasts, wars, business scandals, and so on. Editors cram all the worst and most sensational events onto the front page, or the first 60 seconds of TV headlines. The more gruesome the images, or the more sensational the event, the more it will be broadcast.

Audiences are experiencing 'news fatigue', fed an ever more sensational diet of stories, built mainly around availability of images. This matters most for TV news where it is almost impossible to report a story without video. Any citizen with a smartphone can be a news source, but quality is declining.

TV news distorts reality, even more than printed news or web pages. You could be forgiven for thinking at times that the entire world is affected every week by terrorist bombs, or by terrible murders, or by natural disasters. Whereas the truth is that on most days of the week, there is not enough real national news to fill bulletins.

Audiences will also be increasingly bored by current affairs debates and political interviews. As we will see in Chapter 5, differences between politicians are usually exaggerated in media debate. Most people in developed nations don't trust politicians anyway, so why bother to listen to what they say?

Expect democracy to be weakened as a result of all these different factors, with less media scrutiny, and greater susceptibility to being hijacked by relatively ill-informed, viral social media campaigns (see Chapter 5, 'Radical').

★

In this chapter I have shown how the speed of change is accelerating.

I've described the risk of Wild Cards, how emerging economies will grow, and the impact of digital. And also the paradox that some things are changing surprisingly slowly. We need to look next at how our world is *physically* moving, with a billion migrating to cities, huge demographic changes, rapid improvements in life expectancy, and what it all means for your future.

Chapter 2

URBAN

THE SECOND FACE OF THE FUTURE IS URBAN – radical changes in megacities, migrations, demographics, health and life expectancy. Our entire world is becoming urbanised at an astonishing speed and the demographics of any city or nation will predict its future. How big the market will be for children's toys; how many high school places will be needed in ten years; how many women will develop breast cancer; how many workers will draw state pensions.

One billion children will become consumers in the next 15 years – the biggest jump in human history. Today in Africa 350 million children see glimpses of your lifestyle and compare this to their own, surviving on less than $3 a day. Most of them will spend their entire adult lives living in cities, chasing dreams of wealth.

By 2025, most people on the planet will be in Asia. Indeed, 85% of the world's population will be living in emerging markets or today's developing countries by then, mostly in cities. Only 1 in 7 will be in today's developed nations, driving less than 10% of the world's economic growth.

Unsustainable population growth

More than 9 billion people will be living on earth by 2040, around 2 billion more than in 2014, despite the fact that the number of children born per couple globally has already fallen to only 2.4 (replacement level is around 2.2).

Many experts predicted that population would peak at just over 9 billion by 2050, but African nations like Nigeria still have far higher birth rates than those models assumed. We could see as many as 11 billion people on earth by 2100.

Many nations have young populations, that is, with up to 50% of their population under 25 years old. Even if there is not a single baby born in these communities over the next 20 years, this one age-bulge guarantees a boom in the number of parents over the same period – barring global plague or a catastrophic world war.

A huge challenge will be to feed, clothe, shelter, power up and water even 9 billion people without destroying the planet, especially with economic growth and increasing personal incomes.

Population growth cannot be slowed suddenly without creating other crises, with huge populations of elderly people that will dwarf the problems faced in Europe or Japan today. Expect 1 billion people over the age of 60 by 2025, and 1 million people over 90 in Italy alone by 2026 – enough to alter the outcomes of every election.

Vast populations are on the move

Around 1 billion people will be drawn to cities over the next three decades, in search of a better life. Over 300 million people will migrate from rural areas to cities in China alone over the next 25 years, 300 million in India, and a further 475 million across Africa. Half the world's GDP growth over the next 20 years will come from around 450 cities in emerging markets, mostly places that global executives have never heard of, often in nations they have never visited.

These cities will create the world's greatest new markets, with hundreds of millions of new city retailers – many of whom will be street traders. Tens of millions of new car repair workshops, furniture makers, air-conditioning installers, fast-food sellers.

This growth will generate clusters of new global companies. Over half of the world's largest 500 corporations will be based in emerging markets by 2035, compared to just 5% in 2000.

Wealth contrasts will drive migration

When a third of the entire human race lacks basic necessities, such as running water, basic sanitation, and adequate food, it is hardly surprising that these people want to move to where such things are taken for granted. More than half our world is living on less than $3 a day, and 22,000 children die each day from poverty. Nearly 1 billion people cannot read or write. Every day around 840 million are hungry. Almost one in three of those in the least developed countries die before the age of 40.

The wealthiest 1% in our world own 50% of the world's wealth and 20% own 75% – their income per head is 60 times that of the poorest 20%, and the gap is increasing rapidly. The richest 80 people on earth own as much wealth as the poorest 3.4 billion people. Around 1,600 billionaires own $6.4 trillion, more than the combined income of the poorest 120 countries in the world. In America, the wealth owned by the top 3% in the country rose from 51.8 to 54.4% between 2007 and 2013 while the share held by the bottom 90% fell from 33.2% to 24.7%. And the same kind of shift has taken place in most other developed nations.

The contrasts are greatest in rapidly growing cities. In Mumbai, for example, in the shadow of the most expensive real estate in the world, you will find slum dwellers in shacks of plastic and plywood, and street pavements crowded with sleeping workers at night.

If just 0.1% of low-income migrants become politically motivated and organised the result will be new protest movements that will dwarf anything our world has ever seen.

Living in cities

More than half the world already lives in cities, of which a large number are megacities of more than 10 million people. A decade or more ago, many forecasters came out with wild, idiotic statements about declining cities. They claimed that many millions of wealthier people would move to rural areas, working virtually, driven away by noise, pollution, house prices and fear of violent crime.

It was obvious to me then that this was nonsense. As we have already seen, people love being in busy communities. They love the buzz of cities, the range of opportunities, bars, cafés, clubs, restaurants, cinemas and theatres. And crime rates in many cities have fallen significantly. Cities are good for the environment: they pack people into small areas, protecting countryside from sprawling destruction. Cities are very efficient, with smaller distances from work to home, school to home, shops to home, home to hospital and major economies of scale for rail or roads.

A billion live in city slums

In most emerging market cities a taxi driver can drive you in 15–30 minutes from a smart hotel district to jam-packed slums, where makeshift homes rise precariously to three or four storeys. Take a walk down dark and narrow pot-holed streets. You will see children and animals playing in open sewers, stagnant streams blocked by piles of stinking rubbish, tangles of electric cables strung from house to house, no running water, few pit toilets, disease and deprivation.

Yet if you have the privilege to be invited as a guest into such homes you will usually find immaculately kept rooms, mobile tech, well-educated, ambitious young people, and maybe parents with professional qualifications.

Come back in a decade and most of those slums areas you visited will be steadily developing into emerging middle-class districts, with concrete homes, running water and sewage. But another million new people may have arrived, building new shacks, and so the city growth continues.

Some slum-dwellers become millionaires

Urbanisation is creating real estate millionaires in what were urban slum districts – people who built informal dwellings on land some time ago, and somehow gained land rights, surrounded gradually by high-rise blocks of smart new apartments.

More than 2 billion people will find themselves empowered by new wealth over the next 25 years, with more choices, better access to health care, online media, e-commerce, financial services, and so on. At least 1 billion will be first-generation middle class – first to go to university; first to own a car; first to take regular holidays or own property.

Many megacities are likely to plateau in size at around 20–25 million people, as infrastructure limitations start making life unpleasant. So for every million low-wage migrants that arrive, another million middle-class workers will leave for smaller cities or towns in nearby areas. And the process of rural migration will end when the great majority have already left for cities. This is already the case in Brazil, for example, where cities like Rio de Janeiro are no longer being hit to the same extent by large waves of new migration into densely packed favelas.

Mega-infrastructure

Megacities will need more mega-facilities. Expect more new investment in infrastructure from 2020 to 2055 than in all human history – schools, hospitals, power stations, national grids, water supplies, sewage treatment, roads, railways and airports.

Linked to this, we will see many booms and busts in real estate, construction and commodities.

Much of this infrastructure will last far longer than most people think. The impact of each growing city on the landscape will be clearly visible for at least 30,000–50,000 years into the future, even if that city is abandoned or destroyed for some reason. Many of our new motorways, railway cuttings, embankments, quarries, tunnels and sea ports will be used by travellers or traders for thousands of years. Consider that many Roman roads built 2000 years ago are still busy highways today. Many Stone Age earthworks are also clearly visible in rural areas, even though they were abandoned 5000 years ago.

Commodity instability

Rapid urbanisation will create instability and chaos at times in commodity markets such as steel, copper or aluminium. Expect many more large price spikes and falls as speculators try to cash in on uncertainty. Steel prices will be affected by real estate booms and busts in China, and by global overcapacity, with 1.6 trillion tons a year produced. China uses twice as much steel as India, America and the EU combined.

Mining companies will be forced to mine deeper for lower quality ores, and will need to take a 40–50-year view of prices, to recoup investment. As commodity prices rise, waste (slag) heaps will be re-mined to extract additional material. China will snap up mining rights, mining companies and mining technologies.

Countries with the greatest mining wealth will be forced to spend more on armies and internal security. They will be more likely to have ultra-wealthy leaders, see huge finance siphoned out of the nation, to have a corrupt judiciary and to experience civil wars.

They will also be more likely to have under-performing economies, because exchange rates rise as soon as commodities start to be exported. And as soon as that happens, every other exported good and service becomes less competitive, so the rest of the economy suffers.

The future of Africa will be driven by cities

Africa will continue to be the world's fastest growing continent in industrial output, barring a regional disaster such as a new, very widespread pandemic. Despite a bloody history of tribal conflict, sub-Saharan Africa as a continent has been at peace for over a decade, with no substantial cross-border conflicts, and resolution of many civil wars.

I have worked closely with people in many countries across Africa over the last 40 years. While traditional ways of life are still found in almost all rural areas, the speed of growth of many major cities is remarkable and relentless.

Take Kampala in Uganda, which I first visited in 1988. People were dying of AIDS all around us, and a third of sexually active adults were infected with HIV. The country was also recovering from civil war. Kampala is now a vibrant, noisy, thriving, cosmopolitan high-rise city, full of hotels, new offices, and surrounded by new factories. Yet, just 25 miles out of the city, along dirt tracks through the bush, most people live in mud-brick dwellings with thatched roofs, as subsistence farmers, with no running water and unreliable power.

Expect huge investment into Africa

Businesses like Primark, H&M and General Electric are moving into Africa. National economies are being stimulated by rapid rollout of 3G and 4G mobile networks, which has accelerated mobile banking and business. Tens of thousands of Chinese nationals are staying in Africa when Chinese-sponsored contracts end, investing in local businesses. The number of scientific papers published by Africans has trebled in a decade to 55,400.

We are likely to see economic growth of 5–8% a year in many African nations over most of the next 20 years, mainly driven by growth in cities, despite regional challenges and corrupt governments. Manufacturing and service industries will grow fastest within 50 miles of sea ports, as Asia prices itself out of the global market for outsourcing due to inflation.

Nigeria – rapid migration to coastal towns and cities

Nigeria is Africa's largest nation, and largest economy, even though average earnings per person are only a third of those in South Africa. Nigeria will soon have a population of 300 million people, up from 185 million today. It is likely that there will be more than 440 million people living in Nigeria by 2050, which will make it the third largest nation on earth by then.

For the next four decades, most wealth will be in the Christian-dominated cities in the South, because of oil, and because of relative proximity to coastal trade. Most instability is likely to be in the poorest parts of the Muslim-dominated, more rural north, where the terrorist group Boko Haram has its roots. Nigeria could see another prolonged civil conflict, as we saw in the Biafra war from 1967–1970 in which a million died, but this time the result could be partition.

South Africa will struggle to keep pace

South Africa is the second largest economy in Africa, but has seen very slow economic growth over the last decade compared to most other nations in the continent. South Africa's greatest miracle has been peaceful transition from apartheid, widely credited to the calming leadership of Nelson Mandela, and the influence of a generation of prominent black Christian leaders like Archbishop Desmond Tutu.

South Africa's greatest challenge is very high unemployment in many young, black communities, and white dominance of big business leadership, with huge disparities of wealth and opportunity; gated white communities and revolutionary undercurrents.

Sending money home

One consequence of urban migration is hundreds of millions of workers from the poorest nations sending money home. Most remittances in countries like Nigeria or Uganda are from young adults in cities to parents and other relatives in rural areas. Such income will be a significant part of future earnings of rural communities.

Whole industries will grow around the need to move cash across borders. Payments on mobile devices will be far cheaper and more popular than via Western Union or 'human mules', as people are often called who carry cash between relatives.

Global remittances are already worth over $540bn a year and contribute up to half of some nations' GDP. Take, for example, Tajikistan at 47% of GDP, Liberia 31%, Kyrgyzstan 29%, Lesotho 27%, Nepal 22%.

Birth rate decline will add to city migration in Asia

As we have seen, a key driver of migration is people looking for jobs in cities, and an added reason for labour shortages in nations like China and Japan is low birth rate.

Travel around India today and you see children everywhere, on streets, hanging onto buses, crammed into schools – yet China's children are hard to find. The impact of China's one-child policy will be felt for the next 70 years, even if abolished tomorrow. The government has already relaxed some of the rules, and you will soon see more 'double buggies', pushed along the street by proud parents of two young children. Migrants from rural areas are continuing to make up the gap caused by an ageing workforce.

South Korea and Japan need more babies

The same is happening in South Korea. Just 40 years ago, the average couple in South Korea had six children or more. By 2014, that had fallen dramatically to 1.1. This is typical of what is happening in parts of every nation. Global studies show that when income per household reaches around $12,000 a year, numbers of children per couple start to drop dramatically. But we need an average 2.3 children per couple to maintain city population without migration.

If the fertility rate continues to fall in South Korea, without greater immigration, by 2050 South Korea's population will have fallen from 50 million to 40 million, of which 38% will be retirement age.

In Japan, unless something changes, over 1000 rural towns and villages may have no women of child-bearing age by 2050. The government estimates that the population will fall by a third from 127 million over 50 years, and that there will be only 43 million Japanese by 2110 – all because Japanese couples are having on average only 1.4 children.

Japanese society has not welcomed large-scale immigration so less than 2% of the population was born overseas. Expect this to change, following government recommendations that 200,000 new permanent residents should be allowed to enter each year. We can also expect that child-rearing will become more fashionable again, with all kinds of government incentives, promoted as a national duty for Japanese couples.

Population decline has been a national security issue for nations like Russia, which saw a fall of 10 million in a short period, although birth rates are recovering. France is now offering generous tax and benefit subsidies to encourage couples to have children.

Migrations to cities across Europe and Central Asia

From Central Asia to Western Europe, people are on the move. Kazakhstani workers to Russia, Ukrainians to Poland, Poles to the UK, and Britons to America. There are already so many Central Asian workers in Moscow that over 20% of the city's inhabitants are Muslim.

We will see similar migrations from Africa to European cities, with growing pressures on Spain and Italy, who will at times be overwhelmed by highly motivated, younger migrant workers who enter illegally. More than 600,000 Africans are waiting at any time in North Africa, hoping to find a way to cross into Europe. Over 100,000 people a year are entering Italy illegally from North Africa, often at great risk in tiny boats, while migrants from Turkey to Greece have grown 150% in a single year, partly as a result of civil wars in the Middle East.

North Korea is sitting on a migration time bomb. At some point, the pressures on the regime will become overwhelming. In the meantime, expect more military provocations from North Korea. The end of the regime may be peaceful or result in bloody chaos, but expect the Chinese to be deeply involved in any transition.

Wherever they go, new migrants tend to settle in their own cultural communities (almost ghettos). Many will retain their customs and ways of life, alienated from their adoptive nations, adding to local tensions. Birth rates of lower-income immigrant communities will usually be much higher than in wealthy host nations. These imported baby booms will help re-balance ageing populations.

Europe was dying – but expect a baby boom

Over the past decade or two, many economists living outside Europe have been writing off Europe as a region facing rapid terminal decline, destined to become little more than a cultural museum and geriatric park. This is a superficial and misleading view of what is actually happening. However, there are reasons to be pessimistic about the EU, mainly to do with lack of leadership, stifling red tape and social costs, over-dominance by Germany, and problems faced by those who belong to the eurozone.

And it is true that in Germany, on current trends, you need eight great-grandparents to produce a single great-grand-child. That is the simple consequence of couples having an average of just over 1 child. The situation is similar in Italy, Portugal, Spain, Greece and parts of the UK.

However, birth rates in some Western EU nations are likely to rise rapidly, partly as a result of migration, as in the UK. More than 1.7 million a year enter the EU, and a further 1.7 million migrate within the EU – mainly from newly joined EU nations where wages are very low. Most migrants are young, single adults who are likely to settle down and raise families. Another reason why birth rates may rise is that a generation of women delayed motherhood by 10–15 years, and biological clocks are ticking.

10 million more people heading for Britain

For the past decade, more than 500,000 people moved to the UK every year, and just over 300,000 left (many of them British born). Of those arrivals, 40% are from the rest of the EU, but the majority are from all over the world. On current trends, barring the UK leaving the EU, over 10 million people will move to Britain in the next 20 years, and 2 million babies will be born to those 10 million arrivals, offsetting low national birth rates. White children could be a minority in schools in England by 2037. The number of ethnic minority children in primary and secondary schools has soared by over 60% in a decade.

Immigration will continue to be a hot political issue for the next three decades. We will see many attempts (and failures) to control numbers, with growing popularity of extreme right wing groups, and attacks on minorities. However, the UK will remain a very attractive destination. In every nation population size is strongly linked to size of the economy, so the UK economy will also grow.

At the same time, expect serious decline in the numbers of people living in rural areas and smaller towns or cities in countries like Poland, the Czech Republic, Bulgaria, Albania, Slovakia and what was East Germany – as over 15 million younger workers leave for better opportunities during the next decade, many of whom are well educated. Most will only work in other nations for a while, and then return to the largest cities in their home countries.

Germany is likely to develop a more polarised attitude to immigration, with street protests a common occurrence, at the same time as challenges from an ageing labour force deepen, which will threaten economic growth.

Future of real estate linked to cities

In most nations, the future of property markets will be dominated by what happens in the largest cities. In uncertain times, investment in real estate provides stability compared to investment in stock markets. In addition, there is the emotional attraction of property – visible, tangible, with history.

Despite all the real estate booms and busts that we will see in major cities around the world over the next three decades, over \$100 trillion dollars will be added in real terms to the total value of global real estate, from \$180 trillion in 2014, simply because cities are expanding, economies are growing, and numbers of middle-class property owners are rising.

Globalised travellers move near airport hubs

Growth of air travel dictates that all globalised executives will have to be close to a large international city airport, however virtual their teams. This 'hub effect' will also be true of high-speed train links.

Those who are fed up with city life and are part of the middle class can afford the luxury of bucking the trend, going 'back to nature', getting out of cities for a greener life, greater security, lower housing costs. However, the wealthiest will just live in both, with two, three, ten or twenty homes. An increasing number of super-wealthy will have private helicopters and planes that link their offices, homes, hotels and holidays direct, or via big airports.

Future of UK property linked to largest cities

UK property prices will be linked to the future of London,

Manchester, Edinburgh, Glasgow and other major cities. As I predicted many years ago and more recently during the UK real estate crash in 2009, real estate has remained a good long-term investment for many reasons.

◆ Rapidly growing population due to net immigration of over 200,000 a year

◆ Acute shortage of land for new housing in a tiny island, and severe planning controls

◆ Outsourced jobs in other nations returning to the UK as it becomes more competitive due to low wage inflation and exchange rates

◆ Recovery of the banking sector

◆ Strong growth in services and creative industries

◆ UK seen as safer haven for investors than other EU countries or regions where there is conflict

◆ Family breakup means smaller households, more homes

◆ Ageing population, and better care to help stay at home

◆ Equity release by parents to help children buy property

◆ Bank of England policies to keep interest rates low, until certain of recovery, even if the result is a new real estate boom

◆ Low rates of return from government bonds, bank deposits and company shares so real estate more attractive

◆ Many people don't trust pension saving and prefer property

◆ Traditional mind-set/psychology of property ownership as an investment

◆ No capital gains tax on your own home – yet

◆ Tax benefits for personal pension funds that own property.

Future of London

The population of London has grown by more than 1 million over a decade, and will grow by a further million in the next, while the number of houses has hardly increased. London will continue to experience a top-end boost from international buyers who are worried about the future of their own nations, and whether they might need to make a rapid transfer of assets or even of their families. As a result of all this confidence in the market, many other international and national investors will pile in to buy more property.

London will continue to be firmly placed near the top of the world order in popularity as a place to live. Private schools and private health care are world class, and streets are so safe that police don't even carry guns. London is France's sixth biggest city by French population, for example.

Restaurants and wine bars have multiplied, together with cinemas, hotels and nightclubs. London has become one vast work and leisure complex offering the very best of world-class time out for busy executives, round the clock.

London will continue to be a global centre of financial services. Expect a fierce fight from London to remain the main player for foreign exchange. The City will struggle to retain the world's largest collection of foreign banking offices. There will be growing competition from New York and Shanghai, together with Singapore, Hong Kong, Tokyo and Mumbai. London's banks and other financial services will remain dominant employers, even though the total number of workers is unlikely to match that of before the 2008 economic crisis, until 2020.

London will also continue to be a magnet for creative, imaginative people – for free thinkers, digital marketers, computer games companies, film-makers, artists, entrepreneurs, management consultants and advisors. Expect London's tech workforce to grow by at least 5% a year for the next decade, fuelled by new venture capital.

Property in America, Eastern Europe, China and Russia

America's real estate market is likely to have recovered by 2016 across almost the entire country, unless there are local factors such as municipal bankruptcy, as in Detroit. Surplus housing will be rapidly absorbed, loan defaults will work their way through, and the economy is likely to grow well.

Some East European countries suffered over 40% falls in house prices in the recent crisis, and in nations like Ukraine it will be some years before these levels are seen again. In contrast, China's real estate market is likely to wobble from booms to busts across different regions, as the nation rapidly urbanises, in a poorly balanced process driven by migrations, real estate developers, over-ambitious property owners, easy availability of credit, and government policies.

It will take more than 50 years to replace Stalin's world of concrete, identical, low-grade apartment blocks in order to rehouse over 175 million people who still live in them today. His influence will continue to be felt in subtle ways in the minds of the older generation, many of whom will continue to look back with warm affection to the strength of old Soviet Russia.

Future of health

We have seen how the future of every nation is linked to demographics, migrations and cities. But these things are also linked to health: not only how many people are born, but how fit they are and how long they live. And in health, most of humankind will see an astonishing revolution over the next 30–50 years.

The fact is that 65% of all health spending in developed nations is on those over the age of 65, most of whom have several chronic conditions, almost all related to the ageing process. Therefore it could be said that every pharma company and every hospital exists primarily to serve the needs of older people, in those parts of the world.

The greatest health challenges in the next two decades are almost all related to ageing, as many emerging nations also become older.

Shift from sickness to enhancing performance

The whole emphasis of health care is already shifting from treatment to prevention, wellness and improving performance. Many drugs used today to treat illness will be used tomorrow to enhance performance. For the last decade we have seen this trend unfold in sexual health and treatments for memory loss. Drugs like Viagra and Cialis were first prescribed for men with varying degrees of impotence, but both are now more widely used to enhance 'normal' sexual performance, with growing sales on the online black market.

The same has happened with Ritalin and other drugs to enhance brain function, either in hyperactive younger people, or in older people with significant memory loss. In terms of enhancing performance, 20% of all US and UK students are now using such drugs to help pass exams.

In the past, the question might be, 'What do you *expect* at your age?' In the future the question will be, 'What can you do to help me stop *feeling* my age?'

The commonest complaint of older people is lack of energy, tiredness and slowing down. The greatest blockbuster drugs of all time will rejuvenate old bodies and brains by targeting common systems in every cell, increasing the efficiency of mitochondria, for example, which generate electrical power.

Mitochondria have their own genes, they divide and can be swapped between animals and humans. Old mitochondria have been revived in mice and rats, with treatments such as alphalipoic acid in combination with other drugs. The old mice run around faster, and solve mazes more rapidly.

Future of cosmetics, skin care and face lifts

We are seeing a similar trend in cosmetics – performance enhancement in skin. The greatest drivers of sales in cosmetics will be ageing populations and emerging middle classes. The global cosmetics market will be worth around $300bn by 2020, growing by 3–4% a year.

Hundreds of millions of women over the age of 30 will want to look far younger. Some wealthier women will end up paying more than $1000 every year for the latest 'miracle' skin treatments, creams, lotions and other therapies.

The damaged ozone layer still covers 10 million square miles and will continue to fuel tourist concerns about skin cancers. Sunlight will be blamed for an increasing number of disorders, including cataracts and non-Hodgkin's lymphoma (a type of cancer). Skin cosmetics will increasingly emphasise ultraviolet ray protection. Sun screens are now so strong that with their use it is almost impossible to develop a 'normal tan'.

Expect dark brown, tanned skin to become less fashionable in Europe as has been the case in India, with a return to paleness as a sign of sophistication, echoing the fashions of the nineteenth century, when a tan was a sign that you were an outdoor labourer. Increasing numbers of people will view beach holidays in hot countries with suspicion.

We will see reliable research over the next decade that demonstrates clearly that certain formulations really do stop wrinkles, restore the skin colloid that gives the skin its natural thickness, help restore elasticity and make people look up to a decade younger.

Major challenges for the next 40 years

Brain degeneration – Alzheimer's disease is now the commonest cause of death for women in the UK. Over 130 million people globally will be affected by dementia by 2050, up from 44 million in 2015. Expect huge research efforts to find an early marker to detect whether drugs are working, before having to wait 20 years for trials to complete. This research will also teach us more about the physiology of the brain – how we think or remember; where events are stored; how decisions are made; what is conscious thought.

Cancers – most cases are already curable with early diagnosis and the best treatment. Expect many new therapies that teach the immune system to attack cancers, and gene screening to select anticancer drugs based on the precise character of each tumour. Most people with cancer over the next 30 years will be treated by combinations of different therapies. Death from cancer will become very unusual in most developed nations by 2065.

Obesity-related conditions including diabetes – 30% of humanity is overweight, which costs around 2.8% of global GDP (in health care and lost work days), and causes 5% of all deaths. Half of the world will be obese by 2030, as more people become wealthier. One in three babies born in New York in 2015 will develop adult-style diabetes as children because they are so fat. Obesity is costing the US economy over $100bn a year in ill health and lost productivity – with over 300,000 deaths a year, while 20% of all health costs in all developed nations are linked to obesity. Expect new therapies, such as ones based on the hormone thyroxine, which are designed to speed up metabolism without affecting the heart. Expect huge growth in regulations, ranging from chocolate advertising to children, to sugar content in convenience foods, or drinks, and major initiatives to encourage fitness.

Heart disease and strokes – we will see astonishing reductions in deaths worldwide from heart disease and stroke due to screening of adults for blood pressure and cholesterol levels, and because fewer people smoke tobacco. Anti-high blood pressure tablets and statins to lower blood cholesterol will be used by over 350 million older people in 2025. We will see more widespread insertion of small tubes (stents) to unblock cardiac arteries – 127,000 people in America are treated with these each year, whereby a flexible tube is inserted through a tiny hole in the groin, and then guided using a thin wire, through blood vessels right up to the heart. Strokes will also be less common, with better recovery, as clot-busting drugs are used more widely.

Chronic wounds – around 100 million older people around the world will be affected by chronic wounds by 2025, particularly in their lower legs, caused by poor circulation. Expect huge investment in new dressings and therapies to accelerate healing including telomerase, to reactivate old and tired fibroblasts in wound margins. (When cells have divided too many times, the ends of strands of genetic code inside them become shortened so the cells cannot divide any more. Telomerase is an enzyme that lengthens those ends or 'telomeres' back to a more 'youthful' state so they can divide again.)

Bacterial infection and sepsis, including TB – drug-resistant bacteria are a nightmare for surgeons and patients, and make 2 million people ill each year in America, costing $20bn in health care and killing 23,000. If irresponsible prescription practices continue, we could see more than 8 million deaths globally each year by 2045, 150 million deaths over 30 years, wiping out $50 trillion of economic activity. The last major breakthrough in new antibiotics was in the 1960s. Pharma companies do not make big money from antibiotics, because they are taken only for days. Expect new government and industry partnerships. Expect much stricter controls on over-prescribing and bans on use in animal feeds by farmers. The TB pandemic has also been made worse by drug resistance, often linked to HIV infection.

Parasitic infections including malaria – malaria will continue to be one of the world's worst medical problems for the next 20 years, with 100 million cases a year, killing 660,000, especially young children. Expect major breakthroughs in vaccines and treatment for malaria by 2020, with growing numbers of vaccination programmes in every hard-hit nation by 2030.

Infertility – we will see an 'epidemic' of infertile, older aspiring parents. This is because more women wait until age 35 or more to try to conceive, but fertility falls rapidly with age. Sexual diseases are also rising globally and sperm counts have halved.

Care of older people – over 100 million older people in the EU will need care, at home or in an institution, in the next 20 years. Despite popular perception, length of final illness is not much longer than it was 20 years ago, and remains less than two months, even though people are living longer. Most older people die peacefully after a short final illness. Others will need heavy-duty care for a number of years. Expect huge growth in home carers, and growth of e-monitoring of health. Robots will not form any significant part of this solution, even by 2050. Low-cost migrant labour will fill many new, relatively low-skilled, care jobs in the EU over the next 25 years.

Viral pandemics – major health risk

Every year we see new mutant viruses, and as populations grow, mutations develop and spread faster. Mutation is particularly likely when viruses from animals infect humans, or when people are treated with antivirals.

Humankind is very vulnerable to viral attack because we have very few, and relatively feeble, antiviral therapies. There is not a single antiviral today that is as effective as penicillin when first discovered. Antiviral research is 50 years behind antibiotics. Our only really effective weapon is vaccination. Hepatitis C virus is just one threat, carried by 3% of the entire world, including 4 million in America and 215,000 in the UK. Hepatitis B and C kill over a million a year.

AIDS will be a global menace for decades

AIDS has killed over 40 million people with a further 35 million infected, mainly in Africa, and will continue to be a global health threat in 2040. HIV mutated as it jumped from animals to humans decades ago, and is a warning of other mutants to come, against which we will have no immunity, vaccines or treatments.

I have been deeply involved with AIDS work since 1988, when the international AIDS agency ACET started in our family home, as a result of my NHS work with people dying of cancer in London, during which I discovered people with AIDS who were dying in great physical and emotional distress. Today ACET has prevention and care projects in 18 nations, mainly in the poorest parts of the world.

Back in 1987, I said that developing a vaccine against HIV would be very difficult, because the virus keeps changing its outer surface, and escapes every vaccine trick we know. I predicted back then that it would be at least 15 years before a vaccine would be developed, and today there is still no likelihood of an effective, widely available vaccine by 2035.

Treatments have improved, as well as availability, and AIDS is becoming a chronic illness. But there is still no cure, treatments are toxic and are taken for life. We are discovering rare genes that provide partial or complete HIV protection, and which will lead us to gene-linked therapies.

Even if a cure is discovered tomorrow, it will take over 12 years for clinical trials to prove safety, and at least 25 years more to bring HIV under control. TB, for example, became curable in 1944, yet we still have the world's largest pandemic today.

The good news is that prevention works, with falling or stable infection rates in many nations like Uganda where up to 30% of all sexually active men and women were infected at one time. However, complacency will be a constant challenge, in many nations among different parts of the community.

Spanish flu, SARS, bird flu, swine flu

Another mutant virus on the scale of HIV was the Spanish flu epidemic of 1918–19, which spread across the world in months, on foot, horses, donkeys, trains and ships, eventually killing over 30 million people, out of a world population of 2 billion. If a similar highly infectious and lethal pandemic begins tomorrow, it is likely to spread on international flights in days and weeks, not months, with no time for vaccine development or global distribution, and could kill 100 million people within a year. That is why the World Health Organisation keeps warning governments about these threats.

From swine flu to ebola

The genetic code of the Spanish flu virus is almost identical to that of swine flu. Therefore it was worrying when swine flu reappeared in Mexico in 2009. It spread globally in weeks and caused 14,000 deaths, despite mass-mobilisation of health resources, bans on travel, and almost instant lock-down of parts of Mexico.

SARS also appeared without warning in 2003. Over 8,600 people were infected with the virus within a few weeks, despite huge containment efforts, and 860 died. And 1% of carriers were so infectious that even touching a light switch 24 hours after they had done so could have been enough to kill you. SARS was only stopped by aggressive contact tracing and quarantine, in China, Canada and other nations. The outcome would have been very different if a single 'super-spreader' had travelled across Africa in a crowded plane, seeding clusters of infection in remote rural areas.

The 2014–15 ebola outbreak killed and orphaned many thousands, paralysed West African economies, stopped farming, closed markets, and caused widespread hunger and deaths from other treatable diseases, with constant threats of more outbreaks from infected animals in the bush.

How much more evidence do we need? Mutant viruses will be a major future threat, and we will see far greater investment into antiviral therapies, rapid vaccine development and epidemic monitoring as a result.

The ultimate nanotech robot

Around 28 years ago I predicted in *The Truth about* AIDS that doctors would one day use viruses as a therapy. Such an idea sounded very strange back then, but as I write this, I am chairman of a company that is doing just that, to destroy cancer cells.

Viruses are naturally occurring nanotech robots. They are not living, need no food, use no energy – just biological machines. Viruses have legs with sensors to detect what kind of cell they are touching. Once the legs latch onto the cells they are programmed to infect, the body of the virus fuses with the cell membrane, injecting a payload of genetic code.

Within minutes, the genes are read by the cell, and new proteins are being built. Every virus contains instructions to hijack each infected cell and turn it into a virus factory. The cell soon starts to fill with new virus particles until it explodes and dies, and the cycle of infection continues.

Scientists have redesigned different types of human viruses to target, infect and destroy cancer cells without damaging healthy tissue. At the same time, many of these viruses provoke an immune response against the cancer. Viruses can also be used to deliver extra genes, instructing cells to behave in certain ways as part of therapy.

Viruses will be used as weapons of war

These same techniques can be easily used to design viruses as weapons of war, perhaps with receptors that have an affinity to a particular race for example. But while bio-weapons undoubtedly exist in different nations, most will be very poorly targeted, with extremely high risks for those that deploy them.

Some fear that HIV and other dangerous viruses were created in bio-weapons labs, but HIV has been around for many decades and there is no evidence that any new dangerous virus has ever been created and released (yet). However, we do need to take great care to regulate the use of viruses, especially where properties have been altered.

And we also need to recognise that old viruses will *inevitably* be used as 'low-tech' weapons at some point – for example, to deliberately cause a huge outbreak of foot and mouth disease across farms of an enemy nation. Very easy to do – just one person driving a van for a day, dropping bits of infected meat near pigs on a few farms. And how could anyone prove which country was responsible? The cost of a single outbreak in the UK was more than $13bn.

Medical technology will change all our lives

Almost all the greatest medical advances will be from medical technology, pharma or biotech, or a combination. Medical technology alone will transform health care over the next 20 years. Here are just a few examples:

◆ **Endoscopy** – rapid growth of tiny telescopes, keyhole surgery, shorter hospital stays. $75bn a year market by 2022.

◆ **3D imaging** – ability to watch living tissue in astonishing resolutions, 'travel' inside blood vessels, see inside the heart, detect cancer cells during operations.

◆ **Ultra-resolution microscopy** – able to observe things going on inside an individual cell in real time, watch a photon of light excite a retinal cell, a drug molecule attach to a receptor.

◆ **Digitised patient records** – instant availability in the Cloud of all tests, scan images and other medical records. The US Veterans Health Administration has Big Data on 20 million patients, 2 billion text entries, 16 million X-ray images and 1.5 billion prescriptions.

◆ **Computer-aided diagnosis** – let robots treat the sick, using Big Data to predict what will happen. Such tools will transform what doctors need to remember, and how they are trained. Computer-assisted diagnosis will be universal in some countries for some types of conditions by 2025, with doctors forced to use it not by law but by insurance companies.

◆ **Telemonitoring, telemedicine and home diagnostics** – huge growth in virtual medicine and home monitoring devices, where doctors and specialist nurses make decisions in a faraway location. However, we will *not* see many surgeons controlling robots many thousands of miles away, because speed of light is too slow, with delays from surgeon, to robot, to image, to surgeon, as well as risks when things go badly wrong that no one locally can sort out.

◆ **Growth of Do-It-Yourself health care** – web-based diagnostics and mobile apps with a wide range of biosensors, so that many patients know more than their doctors about their own condition.

◆ **Social media and sharing health experience** – scoring carers, rating doctors and hospitals.

◆ **Replacement of reading glasses** by a tiny implant into the cornea, made of hydrogel, to change the curvature of the eye.

◆ **Low cost gene readers** – (see p. 93)

Future of dentistry

Dentistry will also change rapidly over the next three decades, mainly as a result of medical technology. More people will be able to afford cosmetic dentistry, and the governments of emerging nations will provide more access to free dental care.

Treatment will be transformed by huge advances in diagnostics, instant 3D imaging, local 3D manufacturing and printing, plus advances in new tooth-filling materials and 'invisible' braces to correct poorly aligned teeth, with near-perfect results.

Next-generation tooth cleaning will encourage daily repairs of microscopic defects. However the greatest transformation globally will be because of far wider consumption of fluoride, in emerging nations, strengthening teeth of children. And fluoride will go on protecting the teeth of that generation as it gets old, so dentistry will change beyond recognition over the next 50 years, from repair to cosmetic work.

Future of pharma

If you want to know the future of medicines, take a look at the list of drugs that are in clinical trials today, on pharma websites. The global list of potential new therapies is short, unexciting, and stuffed full of 'more of the same' – more anti-blood pressure tablets, and so on. I qualified as a physician over 30 years ago, and the sad truth is that most drugs used today are ones we learned about at medical school, or slight variations of them.

Big Pharma finds real innovation difficult, slow and expensive. The largest five companies have a combined research and development budget of $32bn, while the 50 largest have a combined budget of around $100bn, which is larger than the GDP of the world's poorest 35 nations. Despite all this activity, Big Pharma is likely to generate less than 40% of the world's new drugs over the next 25 years.

Most breakthroughs in the next 25 years will take place in over 20,000 smaller biotech companies, most of which do not yet exist, often partnered with university teams. These companies will typically aim to sell promising drugs to pharma companies at some point before, or during, early clinical trials. Biotech products already account for 21% of the $750bn a year of pharma sales, and are likely to grow by around 7% a year over the next decade, compared to only 4% for small-molecule drugs.

$1.3 billion for a new drug to market

Over the next two decades, the total cost of bringing a new drug to market will rise by at least 4% a year. It already costs over $1.3bn to bring a drug to market in the 15-year process from discovery to early development, through animal studies and full clinical trials.

Of these, 80–90% of new drugs do not make it, and all pharma/biotech will remain a high-risk business. In the past 5 years, more than \$240bn has been spent by pharma on drugs that failed in final clinical trials.

Since patent life is likely in most cases to continue to be restricted to only 25 years, of which 15 are usually lost in development, pharma companies will have to make a good return in less than a decade of sales.

Pharma companies will see lower sales than were typical in the past for many new specialist drugs, especially those with toxic side effects such as cancer chemotherapy, as gene profiling is used more widely to select precisely the right treatment for each person (pharmacogenomics). That means a reduction in 'hope for the best' prescribing.

The price of drugs will fall rapidly over the next 10–15 years, as almost all patents expire on drugs sold today. We are talking about billions of dollars of lost revenue over a decade (and corresponding savings to governments and insurers).

A course of patent-protected drug therapy that costs \$100 today will typically cost less than \$5 as a 'generic' by 2030. Of course, doctors will be offered a range of equally expensive new therapies by then. But most will be incremental changes, tinkering slightly with existing drugs to extend patent life and sales.

To make matters worse for the pharma companies, if a drug shows huge benefits for a disease like malaria in the poorest nations, the company will be under huge pressure to give it away 'at cost' for ethical reasons.

Some large pharma companies could lose up to 35% of revenues almost overnight if forced to withdraw one or more well-accepted 'blockbuster' drugs because of unexpected health risks.

Orphan diseases will get special treatment

Yet in spite of the above, our world needs a profitable pharma industry able to take risks to develop next-generation therapies. That is why we can also expect more concessions by regulators, seeking to balance patient safety with the need to accelerate new drug development, particularly for people who are otherwise certain to die soon.

Governments will expand lists of so-called orphan diseases, where numbers of sufferers are too few to attract much pharma interest. Orphan diseases will attract special subsidies, tax incentives, fast-track approval, better pricing and longer patents.

Expect new models for drug development where knowledge and patents are owned by the public, with work funded by the taxpayer, while production and distribution are carried out by pharma companies – as seen in AIDS research. Expect big changes also in medical publishing. More public bodies that fund research will insist that published results are freely available to all. Expect new patterns of collaboration: co-opetition, crowd-sourcing, open innovation, crowd-funding. Super-wealthy patrons will also fund many biotech innovations, as social enterprises.

Many new pharma blockbusters

While many pharma leaders have claimed that the days of new blockbuster drugs are over, the truth is that from time to time we will see gigantic sales and profits from key breakthroughs. Just imagine the sales from a new drug proven to delay the onset of Alzheimer's by 3 years. Other examples will include breakthroughs in rheumatoid arthritis, asthma and diabetes, and drugs that make people 'feel' much younger. As I say, many of these new therapies will probably have started out as a concept in a biotech company or a university lab.

Future of biotech – altering the basis of life itself

We are without doubt living in the age of the gene. This will take us way beyond biotech discoveries to sell on to pharma companies. It is hard to comprehend the gigantic steps that humankind is now taking to redesign the very basis of life itself.

Every form of life on earth is programmed in the same biotech language of DNA and RNA. We share almost all our genes with amoeba, insects, earthworms, rats, rabbits, and horses. We can cut and paste sections of genetic code very easily, without needing to know in advance what the results might be. Human genes have been added to mice, cows, sheep, rabbits, rats and fish, to name just a few.

Large numbers of designer animals have been born. Several million mutants are made in European laboratories every year, each of which is a unique mix of two, three or more different species, for example, transgenic sheep programmed to produce human hormones or other complex molecules in their milk. Scientists have also created a goat with genes from a spider, so that spider web proteins are excreted into the milk. These proteins can be extracted to create a kind of textile fibre which is highly elastic and almost as strong as Kevlar.

Expect humanised cows to produce low-fat milk. Another goal will be cows that produce human breast milk. Biotech farming raises new animal welfare issues – for example, in the case of cows that are programmed, or driven by hormone injections, to produce many times their natural daily yield of milk.

Ability to read your genetic code (genome)

By 2025, doctors will be able to read an individual's genetic code in less than 2 hours for less than $3500, enabling us to predict our medical future with far greater accuracy – using Big Data, Cloud Computing, combining tens of thousands of genomes, medical records, lifestyle data.

It took $3bn and 15 years of work to decode a single genome. Expect costs to fall towards $500 by 2035, using nanopore sequencing and other techniques. Expect gene readers on devices as small as today's USB sticks by 2040, taking 30 minutes to decode each strip of genetic code.

Big Data has already identified genes associated with speech, memory, murder, addiction, excessive risk-taking, shyness, obesity, faithfulness and happiness, among other things. And once a gene is located and a test devised, the test can be used to select early dividing embryos before implantation after IVF, raising a host of new ethical issues. It is one thing to decide not to implant embryos that carry genes which guarantee a very serious, lifelong illness, but quite another to select embryos for some enhanced characteristic.

Researchers have already found that a high proportion of murderers on death row in the US share a common gene or genes, raising profound questions about responsibility or therapy. Having the 'wrong genes' has been cited in mitigation against sentence of execution in America over 50 times since 1994. Men with XYY chromosomes are more likely to commit murder, while the gene affecting production of monoamine-oxidase-A in the brain is called the Warrior Gene, because it is linked to very aggressive behaviour.

Ability to alter your own genes

Once you find a rogue gene in your own genome, which is almost certain to make you very sick one day, why not try to correct the defect? This is the basis of gene therapy, and as we have seen, a relatively simple method is to use human viruses.

Humans will experiment with different ways to enhance the genes they have naturally. Some athletes are already pushing their bodies even harder with injected gene fragments, which have short-term effects and are very hard to detect. Bio-doping will be a major problem in the Olympics, and is already beginning to raise questions about the validity of every new sporting record.

Who owns a species?

The world will soon have to face more big questions about ownership of gene-mutated animals. Is it right for a company to own an entire species? Is it right to create a species which by its genes is guaranteed to suffer? Both questions were raised by the creation of the first type of oncomouse, designed to develop fatal cancer 90 days after birth. The oncomouse was created in America for the testing of cancer treatments and is commercially owned, protected by patent.

Patents on human genes

Is it right for companies to own human genes? A man in the US developed cancer and gave cells for research. The genes were used to develop a diagnostic test and the process was patented. He was furious. 'I own my own genes,' he said. He challenged the company and fought them all the way to the Supreme Court, but lost his case. As a result, humans do not have the right to own their own genes in America.

We urgently need gene technology to feed the world and prevent disease – but we do need to ask what kind of world we are creating, now that we have the ability to alter the very basis of life itself.

New ways to make babies

We are going to look deeply at ageing and how to stop your own biological clock. But first I want to take a look at how reproductive science is going to change every aspect of giving birth.

Every year puberty comes earlier in both boys and girls. By the age of seven, 27% of African-American girls and 7% of white girls in America have obvious pre-puberty body changes, for example, breast enlargement. Female cells produce oestrogen so the larger a girl is, the more oestrogen in her bloodstream. And there are also naturally occurring oestrogens in some foods, plus contamination of water supplies with oestrogen from contraceptives.

Children having babies

Expect to see much younger children as 'parents', with 9-year-old boys impregnating 9-year-old girls.

Doctors are having to rewrite medical textbooks. What is normal, and who needs treatment? Children are having to cope with adult hormones before they are emotionally ready. Doctors will therefore take steps to delay puberty in significant numbers of very young children in developed nations by 2030, at the request of worried parents.

A sterile generation?

Environmental oestrogens may also be the reason why sperm counts have halved in many nations over 50 years. On current trends, 50 million men will be unable to father children because of this by 2050. If this decline continues at the same rate, sperm counts will be seriously low in most men globally within 80 years. However, this will hardly affect overall birth rates in the current century. At the same time, cases of testicular and prostate cancer are increasing.

As we have seen, most women in developed nations are waiting longer to have children, and the mean age of mothers at first birth is now 30 in many EU nations. That means many women have been ovulating for over 20 years before they first try to become pregnant. Yet by then, fertility is already in decline, and complications more common.

Epidemics of infertility

Expect epidemics of infertility caused by a combination of older women trying to conceive and rapid spread of chlamydia. Over 48 million couples are unable to conceive from many different causes, despite all efforts, while 44 million abortions take place every year. In many nations, abortion rates will continue to fall over the next two decades, as contraceptive use improves, and as attitudes harden against abortion as an alternative to protection.

Numbers of babies or young children available for adoption in developed nations will also continue to fall. Despite there being 18 million young children in the world with no parents, many of whom struggle on the streets to survive, international adoptions will also decline, banned already in many of the poorest nations.

We will continue to see unease, particularly in many emerging nations, over abortion. Imagine a busy hospital in Delhi or Moscow with two women sitting next to each other, both with problems in early pregnancy. One wants to see the gynaecologist about 'terminating the pregnancy' while the other wants to see the paediatrician for advice on 'saving my baby'. If a gynaecologist talks about 'terminating a baby', or an obstetrician about 'saving a pregnancy', both will likely be condemned as uncaring – or even unethical in their attitudes.

Era of the precious child

We live in an era where anything that might threaten the health or emotional happiness of a baby or younger child is severely frowned upon. We see this in concerns about safety of children in cars, exposure of children to undesirable influences at school or online, and in even greater outrage over paedophilia than in the past. This new era worships the image of the little child, as a symbol of innocence and perfection in an increasingly tarnished, polluted and self-centred world.

Child 'cocooning'

'For the sake of the children' will be used as a motto to justify more or less anything, from marital fidelity to getting married in the first place or getting divorced, cleaning up the environment, or banning cigarette advertising.

Parents will become even more obsessed with well-being of their child, creating cocoons in which (they hope) each is totally protected from risk. So, for example, fewer children will ride bikes on their own in the park or walk on their own to school. As a reaction, we will also see a new generation of parents who believe children need to be allowed to grow up in the 'real world', less tied to adults for every waking moment.

Retired mothers giving birth for the first time

Expect a growing but controversial fashion for women in their late fifties or early sixties to have babies, using donated eggs or their own, held for years in freezers before use. Or even women in their seventies by 2050, with longer life expectancy. The next two decades will see extraordinary advances in child-making technologies, each of which will push the boundaries of social acceptability. However, expect to see a reaction against 'playing God', and a growing desire for 'naturalness' in conception as well as in home births.

Human cloning will continue to fascinate

Animal cloning has been possible for a long time, first conducted in frogs in the 1950s. Mammal cloning is relatively recent. The technique is now well developed using fresh or frozen cells.

1. Remove the nucleus from an egg.
2. Inject the nucleus from any adult cell into the egg
3. Give a small spark of electricity to simulate fertilisation
4. Incubate the cell in a warm watery bath full of nutrients

All the genes in the nucleus are activated by the cytoplasm of the egg, and the cell begins to divide to form a new embryo. If such early embryos are implanted in a womb, they grow into an identical twin of the adult donor. If they are harvested instead, they can be used as sources of stem cells to treat the person who donated the adult cell.

Many claims for human clones but when will we see them?

Many laboratories have carried out human cloning experiments, and some claim that their embryos failed to implant or miscarried. No cloned babies have yet been shown to the world as babies, but it can only be a matter of time.

Even if such cloning is successful, 'parents' and doctors are likely to feel rather sensitive about the new person they have brought into the world, and may want to protect such an unusual child from being stigmatised in any way. So there may well be a significant time lag between a clone being born, and the world learning the truth about what has taken place.

Big market for human clones

There is certainly a considerable market for cloning. Over the years I have had a large number of requests to my website from people asking me if they can be cloned, even though I am strongly against it.* One woman told me that she wanted to clone her dad who was

---

* http://www.globalchange.com – cloning section. The reason for all these cloning requests is that my web pages about human cloning controversies are some of the most popular online resources on that issue.

dying, offering her own womb as a surrogate: 'I intend to see that he goes on in this world.' She wants to give birth to her own father. If she has frozen cells, she may succeed one day.

Another woman suffering from infertility wanted to use her own cells to make a baby rather than use donated sperm and eggs. A student wrote that 'it would be so neat' to be cloned. However, verified claims of birth of the first clones will cause a backlash in those who already feel science is drifting out of control.

Cloning will be very popular among some wealthy people: the ultimate in pedigree children. Supermodels could make money selling cells from their bodies to cloning merchants, who offer childless couples the child of their dreams by creating a clone and then implanting it in a surrogate. In future humanised apes could also be used as surrogates. Scientists are already able to sustain a mammal foetus in late development inside a completely artificial womb. However, human surrogate mothers are easy enough to find and hire online, despite ethical questions and laws in some nations.

Cloning will mean that infertile couples can have a twin of the father or mother as their newborn baby, or that parents can 'recreate' a dead child, or that a clone can be created to assist in tissue donation for the existing child or adult. These will be the justifications used. However, there are enormous safety and psychological risks for the child. Malformations and miscarriages are very common in cloned animals. For these reasons, cloning is unlikely to be used widely as a technique to create designer babies for at least the next 35 years.

Even if the cloned child is healthy, what will be the emotional impact of growing up knowing that you are your mother's or father's twin? What about the pressures from a parent to 'relive' their own genetic potential – for example to see how musical he or she might have been if given music lessons? Of course, parents often create these pressures anyway, but they could be even greater were the parent trying to prove something about their own genes, by hot-housing their cloned twin as a child.

Designer babies – made to order

Scientists can already design young children to order, using some of the same technology used routinely in IVF. The easiest way is to take a cell from a number of early embryos (morula) before you freeze them, ready for later implantation. Then analyse the genes of each one and use genetic Big Data to match for the most desirable features.

Cloning raises interesting long-term possibilities: women no longer need men to fertilise their eggs, and can produce an entirely female society. Or we could create an entirely male society, once animals have been humanised sufficiently to carry humans in their wombs.

And for those whose genes are already fixed, plastic surgery will continue to offer remarkable remoulding of faces, ears, necks, breasts, buttocks and thighs and will become increasingly common as a death-defying generation attempts to stop the ageing process.

Cloning the dead – or the extinct

Animals have been cloned using frozen cells, so any human can in theory be recovered from the grave as a baby, so long as cells are suitably frozen before death, or shortly after. Viable living cells can usually be found in someone for up to a week after death, so cell removal can be delayed for some time. Another way to clone the dead will be from cell cultures, fed each day in a warm place, which can usually be maintained for many decades. This means that a child dying of cancer could be 'recovered', allowing parents to give birth to an identical twin.

As I predicted some years ago, we are now quite close to recovering extinct animals – by using genes in frozen tissue, for example from mammoths buried in tundra – or to partially recovering them by adding a few clusters of recovered genes to an existing animal such as a horse 'to see what happens'.

Altering the human race

Of course the easiest way to alter the human race is the oldest method of all: mass sterilisation or genocide. Some 60,000 forced sterilisations of women with 'unwanted mental and physical characteristics' were carried out in Sweden from 1935 to 1976, with similar practices in Denmark, Norway, Finland and Switzerland. Meanwhile 20% of the entire world's population are already banned by law from having children if the state decides that their genes are not worth reproducing – in China.

Ultimate miniature factories

Genes are the ultimate in miniaturisation. A conventional laboratory to make insulin would occupy a vast area and cost several billion to construct, needing huge numbers of staff. Yet that entire production unit can be compressed into not just the size of a house, not just one room, not merely a single flask or test-tube, but into the cytoplasm of a single living cell.

Once a single bacterium receives the human gene for insulin, it carries on dividing forever, eating food and making insulin. Insulin production becomes as simple and elegant a process as brewing beer.

Every complex chemical you can think of will be made by gene technology in brewing vats containing bacteria or animal cells. Medicines, vaccines, precursors of new plastics, new fuels – whatever. More complex substances can be made in genetically engineered insects or in the milk of mammals such as cows and sheep.

Growing whole organs

Whole organs may also be grown inside young animals of suitable size, or in humanoid organisms (strange clusters of human tissues, providing blood supply, and so on). Organs are already being built layer by layer, using bubblejet printer cartridges full of nutrient jelly and different types of human cells.

Expect many ethical questions about gene technology to be dominated by the 'yuk' factor, which will determine not whether something is right (which can be too confusing to think about) but merely whether it is acceptable to the majority of people.

Bio-computers

Biotech will be used in new generations of intelligent machines, and chips or digital sensors will be routinely connected to a variety of living tissues. As we have seen, many successful experiments have already been carried out to grow brain cells onto the surface of chips and chips have been fused with brains of paralysed adult humans so they can control machines by thought.

How close is a monkey to a human?

It will not be long before humonkeys are with us. Perhaps such embryos already exist. The technology is proven. Hybrids are very easy to create. Take geep, for example, a combination of goat and sheep made by rolling together two balls of cells from two different embryos shortly after fertilisation.

But how many human genes does an animal have to have to gain human rights? We differ genetically from monkeys by less than 2%, and from amoeba by around 14%. So if you are adding 1% of human gene material to a fertilised monkey egg you had better brace yourself for the results – a mere 0.3% of human gene material could be more than enough to give the monkey speech.

Can monkeys go to heaven?

Theologians, philosophers and lawyers need to think what their reaction will be when such a hybrid is displayed to the world, as it most surely will be. Is it a monster to be destroyed? Does it have human rights? Can it be eaten? Is it morally responsible before a court of law? Can it be tried for murder? Is it allowed to marry and procreate with 'normal humans' or to mate with other animals? Is it in need of salvation? Does it have a soul?

Many biotech inventions are already blurring the distinction between animals and humans. It could all produce a crisis of faith for many, brought up on the traditional teaching that humans have been created 'in God's image'. So what is that image? Are monkeys 98% of the image of God? Is all life a manifestation of the image of God to some degree or another?

In my experience, biotech specialists almost always hate

controversy, and are sensitive to the delicate nature of their work. Many have an understandable fear of uninformed public reaction and shun the limelight, particularly if their work involves the use of laboratory animals or aborted human foetuses. They may choose to keep quiet about some of the experiments they do in private.

New ways to stay young (forever?)

So then, we have looked at future health challenges and how they will be overcome by med tech, pharma and biotech. We have also looked at changes in how people will reproduce, and the huge ethical questions raised by being able to redesign life.

Now we need to turn to the ageing process itself. How long will people live? How will health care revolutions interfere with the ageing process itself?

How long will we be able to stay alive?

The life of every reader of this book has increased by an average of 15 minutes in the last hour – in line with what has happened in many cities and nations of the world over the last two decades, in people with reasonable education and a certain amount of wealth. To many, this is very surprising, but not to those who study international statistics for life expectancy.

Take London, for example, where the average life expectancy of the entire city population increased by a year between 2004–6 and 2008–10 – both for those at birth, and for those aged 65. You see the same in Japan and Germany. In many emerging nations, life expectancy is improving even faster. But what about the next 50–100 years?

Governments, corporations, life insurers and pension funds are required to make accurate forecasts for life expectancy. Most official forecasts are hopelessly incorrect.

Here is the truth about life expectancy, and why there has been collusion by governments and corporations to underplay the situation. Every time you add a year to the expected life of an individual, you add over 3% to their pension deficit. So adding 5 years to projections can wipe out the entire reserves of many large corporations, or make government liabilities soar.

Slowing down or reversing the ageing process

Scientists have already produced mice that live to the human equivalent of 160 years and earthworms that live to the equivalent of 500 years. The gene activated in long-living worms is the same one often found in people who live until at least 100. Scientists at Harvard Medical School reversed the ageing process in mice by increasing levels of NAD protein. This protein restores communication between DNA in the nucleus of a cell and the DNA in the mitochondria.

As a result, the body tissue of a 6-year-old mouse was converted back to the age of a 2-year-old. It would be the equivalent of some of the tissues in a 60-year-old man or woman becoming as young as those in a 20-year-old.

Some animals do not age at all

We have identified types of rockfish and some whales that show no signs of normal ageing. Rougheye rockfish live to 200, while other rockfish live only to the age of 20, even though they are identical in every other way. Naked mole-rats can live in captivity for over 28 years, 9 times longer than similar-sized mice. They show little sign of ageing and never develop cancer. The same for whales, where individual life expectancy can vary from 20 to over 200 years in the case of bowheads, depending on their genes. Aldabra giant tortoises live for up to 255 years, and ocean quahog clams can live for over 400 years.

We are also learning from animals that regenerate, such as lobsters, naked mole-rats and planarian worms, and learning from animals that regrow limbs, such as lizards.

Common mechanisms of ageing in every cell

Almost every group of cells, in every organism, in every corner of our planet, is ageing in similar ways. Insects, worms, frogs, fish, mice, tigers, elephants, monkeys and humans – it makes very little difference. You will find a mix of:

◆ cell loss or atrophy without replacement
◆ nuclear mutations (and epimutations) that cause cancer
◆ mitochondrial mutations
◆ cell senescence – useless cells that resist death
◆ telomere shortening – as we have seen, ends of genes shorten with each cell division until they prevent cells dividing
◆ junk inside cells that stops cells working properly
◆ junk outside cells such as atheroma blocking up the arteries of the heart
◆ random cross-linking of proteins outside cells, e.g., reducing elasticity in skin.

Each of these common mechanisms will become a target, in the search for 'negligible senescence'. Touch one mechanism, such as mitochondrial mutations, and you may improve the function of 37 trillion cells in a single human being.

Alteon 711 is an interesting compound that produces a permanent reduction in blood pressure levels in old mice and rats, as well as restoring elasticity of the skin. Sadly, clinical trials found only a small effect on arteries and no effect on human skin, but we can expect many more such trials, targeting a fundamental part of the ageing process.

Gene mapping is showing us precisely which genes are the ones to slow down ageing, in the list of long-lived animals above. All genes have the same function. They tell cells to build proteins of a particular shape. So once we have found the right genes, pharma companies will try to make the proteins to sell as therapy, while biotech companies will try to activate the same genes inside your body instead.

Using stem cells to grow new organs

Another way to keep people young is to repair old organs by injecting them with fresh stem cells. Such treatments have already begun and will be routine for many conditions by 2025 in developed nations. As I predicted in *The Genetic Revolution*, despite many claims, there is no justification for taking stem cells from embryos or foetuses. We can get adult cells to revert to more primitive types, to repair just about any tissue we want. Even better, when we use a person's own cells to repair their own bodies, we don't see rejection by their immune system, unless they already have an autoimmune disease.

Bone marrow is a favourite source of stem cells, as techniques for bone marrow extraction are so well developed, for treatment of leukaemia.

We have seen repairs of retinal damage to restore sight, and improvement of heart function. Some think that stem cells build new tissue in organs like the heart, but more likely is that they release cytokines or special chemical messengers, which aid repair by other cells. So we will also see research into the production of cytokines to be injected into damaged organs.

Repair of brain or spinal cord

Cells from the olfactory bulb, high up inside the nose, will be used widely to repair the brain and spinal cord. The bulb is the organ that we use to smell, and is packed with mature brain tissue and brain stem cells. We have already seen successful repair of broken spinal cords in animals, and partial spine repairs in humans, with people regaining some sensation and movement.

All nerves naturally regrow at around 2mm a day, but in the brain or spinal cord this growth is stopped by scar tissue and debris. Given the speed of recent progress with stem cells in animals and now in humans, it is very likely that at some point in the next three decades someone with a newly cut spinal cord may recover complete sensation and movement. That is, so long as the injury is treated early enough, and the spinal cord either side of the wound is completely undamaged. We are already seeing some early success in repairing severe spinal cord damage.

Head transplants – to get a new body

Such a breakthrough in spinal cord repair will open up the longer term possibility of head transplants, to enable someone to survive who would otherwise die very soon, using the body of someone who has died from severe brain injuries. Head transplants have already been successfully carried out in rats, dogs and monkeys.

The procedure was well developed over two decades ago. Under anaesthetic, the 'old' head is cut off, and the new one stitched on, with careful connections of major arteries and veins as well as the windpipe and gullet. During the process, the transplanted head needs to be cooled to protect the brain from damage during the short interruption in blood supply. In these animal studies, there was no attempt to reconnect the spinal cord or other nerves, nor was there any attempt to prevent the transplanted head from being rejected by the immune system, so the transplanted heads rapidly deteriorated after a few days. However, the experiments continued for long enough for animals to wake up, and in one case a laboratory worker was bitten by a monkey after the operation was completed, which the researchers took as added proof that the mental processes of these reconstructed animals were intact.

Head transplants in animals or humans may seem a rather grotesque, weird and unethical idea, but if someone is already completely paralysed from the neck down, and is dying from something like combined total liver and heart failure, there is no practical reason why their head could not be transplanted today onto the healthy body of someone who is totally brain dead.

And of course, once spinal repair techniques are perfected (and they will be), head transplants could allow an older person to jettison a worn out body and enjoy becoming a young adult again (from the neck down).

The astonishing truth about future life expectancy

Leaving aside such an exotic and controversial possibility, and only taking into account medical advances in the general ageing process that we considered earlier, we can see how human ageing could look rather different in the longer term.

More than 320,000 people are 100 years old or more, around the world. By 2050, that figure could be more than a million in Japan alone, with a further 4 million in America and 280,000 in the UK.

But these modest figures assume very little innovation in health care.

Let me take you through a thinking process that I have discussed with hundreds of actuaries, whose job it is to predict life expectancy – for banks, insurers, pension funds and government.

My grandmother is a guide to your future

Let us start with my own grandmother. She was born in 1905, retired officially in 1970 at 65, but continued to enjoy working part-time as a physician until she was 82, playing bridge most afternoons and also playing golf twice a week. She died a decade later.

Even if we were to say that each generation can only expect an additional *5 years* of life, that would mean the same grandmother today would retire at 75, then work part-time as a physician until her 92nd birthday, with over a decade of full retirement ahead, before she died at the grand age of 102. Indeed, one of my cousins has just died at the age of 103, with all her mental faculties intact.

The real future of a 40-year-old today

Now let us look at a more recent generation. Let us suppose that a woman called Jane was 40 years old in 2015, and is now reading this book. If she was from Western Europe, Japan or North America, government figures would give her an average life expectancy forecast of 82, or 42 more years, which takes her to 2057. However, the fact that she is reading this book gives her an extra 5, because it means she is in an upper socio-economic group: well-educated, middle class. So on average she would still be alive in the year 2062, at the age of 87.

But life expectancy forecasts keep on changing. As we have seen, to keep pace with endless small corrections made over the last 20 years, we need to add an extra 2.5 years in every decade. So on that basis alone, without even considering any major advances, it is perfectly logical to add a further decade over the next 45 years. That would give an average life of 97 years for our example – which takes Jane to 2072.

However, that is of course far from the full story. We have

already seen the huge number of medical advances that are already upon us. If you look at the rapidly growing pace of medical research and innovation in medical technology, it is reasonable to assume that knowledge and capability in health care will continue to double every 24 months.

That means we will know 10 times as much as today in a decade, 100 times as much by the end of the following decade, 1000 times as much by the end of the third decade and so on. Therefore, we are bound to see several major advances in health care between now and 2050, and these must surely add at least 5 more years to Jane's life during that period, which takes her to an average life expectancy of 103, and the year 2077.

The most spectacular medical advances that Jane will witness between now and 2077 will of course be in the final two decades, from 2057 to 2077, because of this relentless acceleration of health-related science. During that 20-year period there will almost certainly be more medical advances than in the whole of human history before that point, many times over.

It is hard to fully comprehend the scale of health advances over the next 62 years. To help us, look back 62 years into the past for a moment, and consider what life was like in 1953. Just think how much health care has improved since then. Nevertheless, the accelerating speed of innovation means that we are likely to see many times greater advances in the 20 years from 2057 to 2077, than we saw in all of 1953 to 2015.

So it is perfectly reasonable to add a further 5 years to Jane's average life expectancy to allow for what new medical advances are likely to offer her during 2057 to 2077. That would mean a 'true' life expectancy for Jane of at least 107 years, which would take her to 2083. And because this is only an average, it means some of her generation will still be alive at the age of 120 in the year 2096, while a few may see the dawn of the 22nd century.

Social meltdown or a welcome transition?

We can see now why most actuarial experts believe that commonly quoted figures for life expectancy are completely misleading, and a dangerous basis on which to project the future of societies, burden of future health care, and so on. This will be one of the world's greatest social adjustments, and will affect every aspect of every nation, the solvency of every pension fund, and the balance sheet of every large corporation.

It will also affect your own average life expectancy of course, assuming that today you are in reasonable health. Most people are out of step with their own biological clocks. They are expecting their own lives to wind down much earlier than is likely. And they have also underestimated the costs of funding their retirement.

Some forecasters have made dire warnings about social meltdown, with countries crippled by tens of millions of ancient people, who have no money left, but need constant care. While there is an element of truth in this depressing picture, it is also true that, as in the example above, most older people will enjoy very extended working lives, biologically much younger than those at the same age a decade or two ago, and will also enjoy extended retirement.

Health messages will start to backfire

In spite of the above, we can expect a boomerang effect from all this progress on health care when it comes to health messages, a kind of double-think. On the one hand an obsession with ageing and with staying healthy forever, and on the other an increasing apathy about personal health. These will coexist and can already be seen in the same people at different times. Personal health has always been a fairly irrational issue and will continue to be so.

So, for example, we will find 80-year-olds who decide to enjoy all kinds of risky activities for the first time in their lives – who have no wish whatsoever to live to a very old age in a very frail state, in dire circumstances, and are more than happy to 'go out with a bang'. Expect more headlines like that of the woman who celebrated her 100th birthday in the UK by going skydiving. More eating, drinking and smoking – 'Who cares. Life is for living. When life is short, eat dessert now.'

Expect many people in their eighties and nineties to enter with great energy and passion into new relationships, particularly after major bereavements, which in the past might have led to permanent loneliness and isolation.

First Life and Second Life

By 2040, childhood, youth and young adulthood will be defined as up to 30 years old, because of delays in settling down to have children, and longer education or training.

First Life will be defined as 30 to 65 years – what people used to consider their normal working lives. **Second Life** will be defined as 65 to 100 years – an identical length of adulthood. A period of many surprises, new skills, new jobs, new purposes and patterns of life. Old age will be those over 100.

Growing costs of health care – and rationing

So in the light of all this, how on earth will government health budgets cope? Well for a start, it is clear that every nation that provides free medical care will be faced by almost unlimited demand, which they will deal with in the same way as in the past, by rationing – mainly by making sick people wait, and making some wait a very long time.

Doctors have been rationing scarce resources for over 100 years. Expect debate about these choices to become more strident, linked to social media, especially from 2015 to 2022, in nations that are trying to repay national debt. Health will be in competition with education, infrastructure, defence and other government departments.

Every health specialty will also be in competition: cancer competes with asthma, hip replacements with stroke rehabilitation. Within specialties there will be competition, for example, more money for the breast cancer budget or for the prostate cancer budget?

Future of Obamacare

Nearly every developed nation except America provides free health care to all, 'as part of living in a civilised society'. In many nations, universal access to health care has become as widely accepted as universal access to education, but this will be questioned. We can expect gradual introduction of a wide range of small health charges, to stave off bankruptcy of health services and as a further rationing tool, to choke off demand.

America spends more per head on health than any other nation by a wide margin. But until recently, 17% of non-retired adults in America had no health insurance at all, and faced huge worries if sick. Despite popular perceptions, most health care spending in America is also now funded by taxes. By 2020 it is likely that the numbers without any health insurance will halve to around 30 million, partly as a result of new regulations and state initiatives commonly referred to as Obamacare. But one thing is clear: health care will need to be more cost-efficient in America, with stricter controls on insurance claims and authorised treatments, and clampdown on massive fraud. At present there are many incentives for over-treatment, and over-billing is hard to prevent.

Future of NHS in the UK

As the UK's largest employer, the NHS in the UK is facing a deficit of up to $35bn by 2020, with insolvent hospitals, and risks of meltdown. We can expect rapid shifts towards community care, fewer hospital beds, shorter stays, more community-based clinics, and more privatisation in a bid to cut costs. Private health insurance and treatment will grow, as people become more fed up with waiting lists, and more worried about quality of NHS care.

Expect a crisis in general practice as many family doctors retire over the next decade, with acute shortages of new doctors willing to work under greater pressures, for less money. The same is happening to hospital nursing, where chronic understaffing and stress will lead to more resignations. As a result, more doctors and nurses will be employed from other nations, some with poor English and cultural understanding.

Better outcome measures

Surgeons will be measured by numbers they treat successfully, complication rates, length of hospital stay and numbers they kill. Expect a rethink. These crude measures are encouraging bad practice – for example, premature hospital discharge, which may be 'safe' but is stressful, painful and unpleasant. Surgeons may also refuse to operate on those who could be a 'bad risk', because of obesity or other conditions.

Medical tourism and medical migration

One way to reduce health costs for individuals, insurers or government is to move patients abroad for treatment, and we will see a lot more of this.

'Medical tourism' is already a $40bn industry, growing 15% a year, with over 11 million people annually travelling to another country for private treatment (a million Americans alone). If privately funded, this is often combined with a convalescent holiday in a nice hotel. The savings can be huge: private health care in Brazil is only 25% of the cost in America, India 73%, Mexico 50%, Thailand 65%, Turkey 60%. Within the EU itself there are also major cost differences – for example, dental treatment in Hungary is far cheaper than in Paris.

Governments are already signing contracts with private providers in other nations. Thousands of elderly people have moved to Eastern Europe and Asia for long-term care and rehabilitation. According to the German government, over 400,000 older people cannot afford a German retirement home – a cost that is growing by 5% a year, and 7000 are in retirement homes in Hungary alone.

We are also seeing the migration of health professionals. Vietnamese doctors and nurses, trained at huge cost by their own nation, are working in Thailand. Filipino nurses are attracted to work in the UK. This is a very worrying and unsustainable situation for 'donor' countries that can ill-afford the escalating costs of losing the majority of those they train to wealthy nations. Expect some kind of training tax in future, or binding contracts with those trained at government expense.

★

So, then, we have seen how a billion people moving to cities will transform our world, and how demographics is the key to the future of every nation and market, how life expectancy is radically changing, and how ageing itself could be halted one day. Now we need to look at the most powerful force in the world: the power of tribes and how we all relate together.

Chapter 3

TRIBAL

TRIBALISM IS THE MOST POWERFUL FORCE in the world today, more powerful than the entire military might of America, China, Russia and the EU combined. Tribalism is the basis of all relationships, brands, families, communities and nations, but is also responsible for the darkest moments in human history.

Most people belong to many tribes

Neighbourhoods are tribes, members of sports clubs are tribes, football supporters are tribes. If there were no tribes, human beings would create them in a day. We need tribes to exist, to make sense of our world.

If you want to understand the forces on someone's life, whether client or friend, their motivation, the basis of their values and decisions, you must first understand that person's tribes.

Tribes will create new languages

We see tribalism in our love of national languages. Gaelic in Scotland was more or less a dead language 30 years ago. Now it is spoken in shops, heard on radio, taught in schools, and road signs are in both Gaelic and English. With French radio there is a strict limit on the amount of English language music that can be transmitted on air. The medieval French tongue *langue d'oc* is also experiencing a revival.

Language preserves ancient literature, poetry and songs –and vice versa. Language communicates who we are – even the accent in which we speak our mother tongue reveals our tribe. That is why it was so provocative when the new president of the Ukraine announced in early 2014 that it would be illegal in future for children to be educated in Russian in Russian-speaking parts of the country.

New tribes will also create new languages of their own, whether street slang or 'texting' speak, or as players of global online games.

Why people are hungry to join new tribes

As many as 2 billion people around the world have lost their birth tribes, or tribal ties have weakened. The most common reason is that they have moved to towns, cities, or indeed other nations, where old social ties are less strong. Another common reason is that their parents have split up, which might bring pain in their family tribe.

Tribalism is a basic human instinct that every culture celebrates, whether in birthdays, or marriages, or festivals. We all need to belong. And into that gap have come new tribe-makers. Brand directors, marketing managers, football coaches, social media gurus, club owners, church leaders, mosque preachers, music celebrities, mother and toddler groups, head teachers of schools, university professors or even friendly neighbours. Each creates new groups of followers or supporters.

Tribalism has driven 50 million from their homes

There are 50 million refugees in the world today, most of whom are victims of tribalism. Every day, over 30,000 more people are forced to leave their homes and 33 million are sheltering with friends, family or in camps within their own nations. A million more seek asylum each year, and a further 10 million are stateless – with no passport and no means of getting one. The poorest parts of the world house 86% of refugees; 6 million are internally displaced inside Syria; 4.5 million more in Colombia; 1.4 million in Sudan and 1.3 million in Iraq,

I have met many refugees and their children in over-crowded, muddy camps, living in temporary huts of earth and corrugated iron. It is a huge decision to leave everything and flee. For every refugee, there are many others who also live in great fear, but choose to remain. I estimate that over 350 million people today are either refugees or thinking about becoming so, have been refugees in the last decade, or have relatives who are refugees at the moment – 4.8% of all humanity.

Tribalism and the EU

Tribalism will dominate and threaten the future of the European Union, as a Tribe of Tribes. There is no common language or shared culture, and national interests are fiercely defended. The EU has muddled along, avoiding many tough decisions, but struggles to respond rapidly in a crisis, so will continue to be vulnerable to global shocks.

The European Union is likely to remain a cluster of inter-tribal compromises, dominated by Germany, and held back for at least the next 5–10 years by economic malaise in many of its poorest members. The EU is very good at passing new laws for trivial matters, and very bad at tackling fundamental issues. But hundreds of new laws make life more difficult and expensive for factories and retailers, and enforcement varies from country to country.

More strains in Europe from monetary union

I predicted before the 2008 crisis that tribal and economic strains in Europe were likely to become immense. It is hard to see how the eurozone will survive in its current form without even greater pain and unrest. Countries with very different economic problems and business cycles remain locked together by common exchange and interest rates. Expect further steps to closely integrate Euro economies, with more loss of national powers.

Greece has been overwhelmed by government debts, greater than 170% of the size of its economy while its economy shrank by 25% during 2008–2014. If there is no agreement to write off much of the debt, Greece is likely to default, and could well end up leaving the euro. Balance sheets of European banks are better prepared than they were, but such an exit could well be destabilising for the eurozone as a whole. Markets will speculate about which nation might be the next to exit.

The wider EU project is in deep political trouble, as I also predicted, with 30% of European MPs belonging to protest parties like UKIP (28% of vote), France's National Front (25%), Denmark's People's Party (27%) and far-left Syriza in Greece (36%). Meanwhile, most people in Europe distrust EU politicians, few can name their Euro MPs or the president of the European Commission, and voter turnout is low.

America will continue to be a dominant EU partner

America still invests 3 times more in the EU than in the whole of Asia. And EU investment in America is 8 times that in India and China combined – while a third of all global trade is between the EU and America. The future of the EU will be overly dependent on the American economy for the next two decades, even though the only hope of strong economic growth will come from trade with emerging markets.

Farming subsidies still account for 40% of the entire EU budget. But as we have seen, the future depends on rapid investment in innovation, next-generation manufacturing, precision engineering, aeronautics, biotech, medtech, nanotech, Big Data, Internet of Things, mobile financial services, e-commerce, new venture capital, enterprise zones, joint ventures on emerging markets, and so on. So where is the *equivalent-sized* EU budget for such things?

The European project may yet be saved by some of the 500 million people from emerging nations who would like to live and work in the EU, legally or illegally. Many are highly educated, entrepreneurial, and bring investment with them, while others do unpopular jobs for low wages.

Corruption and control in the European Union

The EU will continue to be a corrupt, monolithic, non-accountable and wasteful institution. For the past 19 years, auditors have refused to sign off the accounts as accurate. In 2013, for example, they reported that €6 billion had been spent 'in error' – up 23% on the year before.

So how on earth do so many 'errors' and fraudulent decisions get made? I was asked to give a lecture on 'Ethics in Leadership' to some of the most senior leaders in the European Commission. At very short notice, I managed to get hold of an e-voting system, with a handset for each member of the audience, which allowed them to make secret responses to my embarrassing questions. Their answers were very disturbing but hardly surprising. The lecture was recorded and an edited version is on YouTube.*

Many participants admitted that they had recently been put under pressure to do something that they thought was morally wrong. In many cases this was something so serious, that in their own country it would have been likely to be on the front pages of the newspapers, should it have been revealed. What is more, most felt they had no choice but to obey. The person asking them was usually their own boss, and they had no one to turn to.

Trapped by fear

One leader came up to me afterwards, in obvious fear, to reveal a severe moral challenge he faced, in which he felt trapped. Looking over his shoulder repeatedly, he told me in a hushed voice how he felt corrupted, and did not know what to do. He feared what would happen to him or his family, if it became known that he had revealed what was happening. I was able to give him some practical steps to take.

It was clear in discussions with participants that the EU Commission pay, perks and other privileges are so generous, and employment prospects so poor if someone leaves the commission, that few can contemplate leaving. And, as I always say, when an executive is afraid to walk out over a matter of principle, he is already in danger of losing his soul. I am certain, therefore, that corruption will continue to be a feature of day-to-day life in the European Commission and in every agency that is subsidiary to it.

* http://www.globalchange.com/leadership-ethics-and-dealing-with-corruption-eu-commission-lecture.htm

Despite all this, size and inertia will almost certainly enable the eurozone to muddle along for some considerable time, perhaps even for a generation or two, even if there are changes in the list of Euro or EU members.

Tribalism will reshape the United Kingdom

The vast majority of the UK lives in England, a nation within a nation that will struggle with identity, except during international sporting events. England has no national language (English is global), no well-recognised tribal dress, and has often been defined in the past by being British – which has irritated many who are Scottish, Welsh or Northern Irish.

Discussions on public spending are not going to get any easier and whoever is in government will face pressure to cut costs or raise revenues, or both. And the less attractive government debt becomes to the markets, the more borrowing costs will rise.

Choices on tax or spending will therefore be very limited. This is what we can expect:

◆ further cuts in government spending
◆ strict control of public pay awards
◆ increase in taxes for middle and high earners
◆ allowing inflation to drift well above 2% targets at times, diminishing the value to lenders of low-interest government bonds
◆ low corporation tax and other measures to encourage investment into the UK, and headquartering of multinationals
◆ continued growth in UK strengths such as fashion, film, music, design, pharma, architecture, consulting
◆ recovery of banking and financial services – with new revenue streams, related particularly to emerging markets
◆ expansion of UK automated manufacturing, e.g., car industry
◆ attracting a new generation of wealthy and highly talented settlers, who see the UK as a refuge

- encouraging sovereign wealth funds to invest in new infrastructure
- growth in exports to many emerging nations, benefiting from historic trade, cultural and language ties and relatively low UK wage inflation.

UK fantasy finally fades of being a global power

The UK has long had one of the highest figures for military spending in the world as a percent of GDP, but this level of spending will be almost impossible to maintain over the next decade.

The UK will continue to nurse a fading fantasy of being a global power, the second police force of the world after America – but this already looks absurd in the light of dwindling armed forces. In the 1940s, Britain still ruled over 25% of the world's land area from London. It is hard for this independent-minded, island nation to cope with the thought of being ruled by the EU from Brussels.

There is a real risk that a referendum on EU membership will result in a 'no' vote, even if there is a wide range of concessions from the rest of the EU on things like migration.

Likely breakup of the UK

Expect a further vote on Scottish independence in the next decade, especially if the UK as a whole decides to leave the European Union. A second vote could well result in the breakup of the UK, despite arguments that oil revenues will be too low to sustain Scottish ambitions. And if not, we can expect a third vote, some years on. Tribalism is a very strong force, and the global trend is firmly set towards autonomy and self-government.

Royal reforms and an English flag flying

Tribalism will save the monarchy, albeit on a smaller scale, because otherwise there would be so little left of British or English culture. The fundamental problem with the monarchy is that royalty is based on genetic discrimination and family lines. This genetic elitism will seem increasingly bizarre and morally suspect to a people who have fought for equality of opportunity, fairness, and lack of discrimination.

Expect to see a rebirth of the English tribe: a fresh energy in a new generation who want to be as English as the Scots are Scottish, or the French are French. National state funerals, the last night of the BBC Prom concerts, international football matches and other events will help focus this new sense of tribal identity.

Future of Germany as the central tribe of Europe

Germany will continue to be the dominant economy and voice in the EU, particularly as the French economy continues to falter. Germany has the largest population of any nation in the EU, as well as a strong economy built on high-tech engineering. Such dominance in the EU was an inevitable consequence of the re-unification of East and West, after the collapse of communism, but may cause increasing resentment in future. Germany's economic growth is likely to be held back to some extent by a rapidly growing number of older people, and by a shortage of low-cost, skilled labour, unless migrants enlarge its workforce significantly.

Germany's geographical position at the heart of Europe will ensure it has a vital role in brokering tensions between Russia and the rest of NATO. Germany will be a very important partner in economic development for such neighbours as Poland. It will take at least 20 more years for all the economic differences to melt away between former East and West Germany, and for historic reasons for Germany as a nation to feel fully comfortable in exercising a strong leadership role.

France – tribal protests and radical change

France has been a dominant influence in the EU, straddling nations in north and south, as one of the world's largest and most socially minded economies. However, France is in the midst of a profound economic and social crisis that will take at least a decade to resolve. The economy has been moribund, while public spending is 58% of

GDP – more than any other European nation. Debt is 95% of GDP. So how will change come about?

A central part of French history is revolution by the masses against a powerful elite. In 220 years, France saw 11 radical and sudden regime changes. And today, the tradition of protest continues. For example, over 1.5 million people took to the streets in 2006 in a series of 'Liberty' marches against a new law that would have made it easier to fire workers under 26 years old who had less than 2 years of service. In 2010, more than 3 million people took to the streets in a series of protests over many weeks, against a proposed increase in retirement age from 60 to 62 for many public workers.

The scale of such protests has made France volatile, hard to govern and hard to reform. Voters are likely to go on favouring governments that promise higher social spending than in Germany and the UK, even if that means borrowing more money, breaking EU rules, and imposing punitive taxes on wealth creation or business in general.

So what of the future of France? Voters will continue to look for a leader who will save the nation, in the spirit of Napoleon I or General de Gaulle. They will also tend to look more fondly than the UK on the EU, as France was the nation that gave birth to it, and continues to see itself as a twin-power to Germany within it. However, the National Front won 25% of their EU votes in 2014, on an anti-EU ticket, and anti-EU protests could grow rapidly. In some ways, France is likely to remain fiercely tribal. For example, in its hostility towards the use of English in speeches by government officials to international audiences.

A radical transformation is likely to be seen eventually, but until it comes, expect further stagnation.

Future of Russia's 160 tribes

Western Europe's future stability and well-being will depend on many factors, but among the most important will be peaceful co-existence with Russia.

Russia will remain strongly nationalistic, as a mega-tribe of 160 different ethnic tribes, 140 million citizens spread across 11.5 time zones. Russia is a nation that has been forged by hardship and comradeship in adversity. Siberia makes up more than three-quarters of Russia's landmass, with average temperatures below freezing, while 50% is forest and 11% is tundra, a bleak and treeless, marshy plain.

Russia's future economy will depend on energy prices and exchange rates, both of which collapsed in 2014: Russia is the world's largest producer of oil, second only to America in gas production. Oil and gas account for 70% of export revenues and government spending is hugely dependent on them.

Russian desire for strong leadership and nation

The Russian tradition is of strong, autocratic leadership, and powerful figureheads like President Putin will continue to enjoy popular support, so long as these figures deliver increased living standards, improved security and better public services, or at least so long as living standards do not drop too much as a result of the leadership's actions. President Putin is likely to continue his strong grip on media and political movements, by popular consent.

Just 110 of Russia's many oligarchs control 35% of Russia's wealth, some of it gained rapidly by dubious means, at a time of chaos following the fall of communism. Government agencies have a long-term strategy to place great pressure on oligarchs who are 'living off Russian money' in other nations, as well as in Russia.

If you talk with members of the generation who grew up under the Soviet regime, you will continue to find warm nostalgia, tinged with slight sadness, when they look back to life as it was under Brezhnev. They will continue to point to full employment, regular pensions, stability, public order and respect for Russian traditions. But Russians born after 1980 have no such adult memories, and are already 35 years old today.

Daily life in big Russian cities can be expected to be similar to that of many European nations, with vigorous consumerism, capitalist culture, and middle-class wealth. However, we may also see what many Russians would describe as loss of 'soul' or 'dushá' in smaller cities like Samara or Tolyatti, with very high divorce rates, addiction, depression, and lack of purpose or moral strength.

Russian foreign policy and military renewal

Russian leaders are likely to promote a free-trade area with border nations such as Georgia and Ukraine (but not China), to rival the EU. They will seek to influence former CIS nations with a combination of diplomacy, economic measures, media messages, military pressure and less obvious actions.

President Putin will continue to fret about what he sees as persistent American efforts to undermine Russia, whether economic, diplomatic, military or covert. He will also worry about similar activities by some European nations. The stronger the EU becomes and the more united NATO is, the more threatened Russia will feel.

Russia lost over 20 million lives in the Second World War, which is 60 times the toll of UK military deaths, and 90 times the toll in France. It is very hard for non-Russians to fully grasp the emotional force of that disaster on the national psyche, and on Russian pride. It explains the 'Never Again' and 'Don't mess with Russia' mantras that are set to influence foreign policy for several decades. The nation is also deeply scarred by the loss of the Soviet empire, as Britain was with regard to its own empire in the 1950s–1980s, and is fiercely proud of its heritage, culture and military strength.

Deep unease and anxiety over NATO and the EU

Therefore, Russia is likely to remain bitterly opposed to any further extensions of EU or NATO influence or control, close to its borders, and will be easily provoked by fear and mistrust to vigorous actions of many kinds to prevent this. Such steps would be likely to damage Russia's economic growth, and we will see Russian rhetoric that may feel like a throwback to the Cold War. However, such rhetoric will be popular at home, unless people are hit by major, prolonged declines in living standards that they come to blame on the government rather than on sanctions or other actions by foreign powers.

Russia is likely to want to spend more on defence than any

other nation except China and America over the next two decades, and to seek strategic alliances with China, to reduce political and trade risks to the West.

Russia is already an unbeatable power in the wider European region in terms of tanks and rockets, artillery and troop numbers, but also in locally stored tactical nuclear weapons. NATO has little local strength in comparison, without resorting to the threat of first nuclear strike, which is almost unthinkable.

Challenges for Russia

Despite former superpower status, Russia's economy was only the size of Italy at the start of 2014, and shrunk to the size of Spain with the collapse of oil prices and EU sanctions. A sustained regional conflict would rapidly destroy a significant part of Russia's wealth.

Internal security will remain a key issue: the interior ministry bill exceeds by far state spending on health. Other challenges include capital flight by Russians moving wealth to 'safe havens' – $170bn in 2014 alone; low life expectancy in men (64 years – 50th in world), partly related to alcohol; corruption – ranked 127th in the world by Transparency International; lack of strength in manufacturing; Islamic separatists; threat of a 'coloured revolution' inflamed by social media; and a crumbling legacy from tens of thousands of Soviet-era tower blocks.

Despite these things, expect a more vibrant, self-confident, militant and wealthy Russia within 15 years, but still bound tightly to global markets, and constrained by them.

Tribalism will undermine Ukraine

Since Tsarist times, Ukraine has been called the 'bread-basket of Russia'. It was the wealthiest part of the Soviet Union, with coal mines, heavy industry and large-scale grain production. It declined rapidly after the breakup of the Soviet bloc, due to bankruptcy, under corrupt and incompetent governments, to the point where it refused to pay Gazprom for heavily subsidised Russian gas, on which the entire nation's survival depends.

The Crimea will remain under Russia's control following its seizure from Ukraine in 2014. The Crimea contains Russia's most important naval base and was a highly valued part of the Russian nation, until ceded by treaty to Ukraine in 1957 in exchange for cheaper gas, at a time when such an 'administrative' step had limited significance in the context of the wider Soviet empire.

Ukraine is likely to split permanently along tribal 'fault lines'. People in the east of the country are mainly Russian speakers who feel strongly Russian in culture. Their region is dominated by coal mining, which used to generate most of the nation's wealth.

As in many other civil wars, the situation has been complicated by volunteer fighters and mercenaries from many nations (particularly Russia), and by maverick local leaders who are difficult for either side to control.

The nation will only be held together if a huge amount of autonomy is granted to eastern areas, in a peace process supported by Russia. Whether this will be within a federal structure of some kind or with the east effectively absorbed into Russia remains to be seen.

We could well see a 'frozen conflict' for many years, similar to those still in place today in South Ossetia, Transnistria, Nagorno-Karabakh and Abkhazia, following their own breakaway votes from post-Soviet republics in 1991–1993.

Impact of tribalism on future conflicts

Across the world there have been hundreds of civil wars since the Second World War, of which twenty are ongoing and most of which have been simmering for two decades or more. But there have been very few traditional wars.

We have probably seen around 30 million conflict-related deaths since 1945, compared with 100 million between 1914 and 1945. So our world as a whole has been relatively peaceful, and continues to be, despite news headlines.

Most current conflicts are in poor nations in Africa, the Middle East and places like Ukraine – which together produce less than 7% of global output. Therefore the impact on profits of global corporations has been very small over the last two decades. Only 2% of American, British and Japanese foreign investment is in such places, for example. Yet the risks of conflict remain and indeed may be growing.

American supremacy will continue to create tension

More than $1.8 trillion is spent every year on weapons and other defence costs, or 2.5% of global GDP, down from 4% in the last days of the Cold War, equivalent to $250 per person on earth. Combined sales of the largest 100 arms companies is around $320bn a year.

However, 40% of all global military spending is by one nation alone: America, which burns up more in this way than the next 15 highest-spending nations combined. This is a truly spectacular imbalance of military fire-power, and will be unsustainable in the longer term, as we will see. Next is China with 9.5% of global military spending, followed by Russia at 5.2%, UK 3.5% and Japan 3.4%.

America needs to spend just 3% of GDP on arms to achieve such dominance – compared to Russia, which today spends 4% of a much smaller economy, China 2%, India 2%, UK 2%, France 2%, Israel 6%, Saudi Arabia 9% and Oman 12%.

This relentless build-up of ultra-powerful weaponry will continue to feed tension, resentment and fear over the next two decades. America's army, navy and air force will be dominant globally for the next 15–20 years, despite rapidly increasing military budgets in Russia and China.

However, the perceived 'moral strength' of America and its reputation as the world's 'police force' is likely to continue to weaken rapidly around the world, following adventures in Afghanistan and Iraq, news reports on abuse or torture of prisoners, held sometimes for years without trial, and because of routine killings using drones of foreign citizens in other nations.

China and Russia will enter a new arms race

So how long will it take China to catch up with the global military power of America? The answer depends on whether you measure this in size of armies or smartness of missiles and other tech. Even if China were to raise military spending from 2% to 5% of GDP, and even if China's GDP were to grow 4% faster each year than America's, it would probably take over two decades for overall capability to catch up with US military might, unless America slashed spending.

Russia will not be able to create such global strength in 40 years, but within 5 years could easily mass a million troops in Eastern Europe, up from half a million today, backed by huge numbers of lower-tech weapons, and smart tactical nuclear delivery systems. So, then, both China and Russia will be able to engage in significant military excursions in their own regions, if they choose, even if far-flung conflicts of any size will be difficult to sustain should they act alone. Only America will have the global power to try to stop them, which, on the whole, it will be very reluctant to try to do.

New nuclear threats and the Space Race

Expect to see major nuclear scares over the next 30 years as various countries or groups claim to have got hold of nuclear weapons or material, or to have developed their own, and threaten to use them.

We will see an accelerating nuclear arms race in a growing number of emerging nations, with rapid upgrades of small tactical nuclear weapons by Russia and America.

America will really struggle to develop an effective anti-ballistic missile defence, following many failed attempts to shoot down intercontinental rockets in tests, despite spending almost $100bn in 12 years. Russia and China will also try to crack this problem. The trouble is that intercontinental missiles travel at 10km per second, and can release large numbers of decoys in flight. And 'ordinary' looking satellites could also be launched, containing hidden nuclear devices that could be detonated while flying over a country like America or Russia.

No nuclear warhead has been used in anger since 1945. As I say, expect someone to use this threat somewhere and for massive international confusion about how to respond. Do other countries threaten to go to war against a nuclear weapon-using nation, if a warhead is used by such a country in self-defence, after repeated warnings to an aggressor? How would such a war be waged? Where do you target your first or second strike(s)? How many warheads do you retaliate with, of what size, and how rapidly do you press the fire button? How do you counterstrike against an invisible terrorist group that has no national support base? What happens if a group threatens again, and explodes a second warhead?

Countries in such a crisis may have only hours or at most a couple of days to work out how to respond.

National arms industries

As I predicted, there has been significant consolidation in the arms industry, and there will be more to come. Defence research is only cost-effective when there are large economies of scale. That means selling to other nations whose policies and behaviour may make many uneasy, despite the argument that if one country doesn't sell to them, then another will just step in.

Rethink about high-tech weapons

High-tech weaponry will not be enough to win future wars. Most wars will be much more ordinary: guerrilla wars fought wall by wall and house by house, ethnic conflicts or terrorist attacks; mucky wars where tank commanders park their vehicles inside a large children's hospital, where civilians are caught up in bombing attacks; traditional military hardware, fired in shopping precincts, around public libraries, by ancient stone bridges and in fields of corn.

Landmines and other messy weapons

New weapons replace old, which move down the arms chain, into the hands of the poorest (and often most unstable) nations where they are frequently used for internal repression. Then arms fall into the hands of criminals.

Weapons are also lost or unaccounted for, like the machine gun I stumbled across in woodland near London one day. Landmines are a global menace, designed to be hidden and 'lost' from the moment they are scattered. Tens of thousands of square miles will remain uninhabitable because of the indiscriminate use of anti-personnel devices, which will remain dangerous for at least three more decades.

Over 110 million mines have been laid and lost, affecting at least 70 countries, and 2 million more are planted each year. Each mine costs $700 to detect and recover, in work that kills many experts every year. A million ordinary people have been injured or killed in 25 years, mainly children (who often pick them up as toys), women and old people.

A further 100 million landmines are neatly boxed in military stores across the world, waiting to be used. Landmines will continue to be scattered widely, not only to protect bases and kill armed men, but also to stop farming, travel and trade.

Power of the few will break the mighty

Gigantic military strength is almost useless in delivering many types of strategic objectives – as America has repeatedly discovered.

For 50 years, America has struggled to 'win' a single 'foreign' war, and even more to 'win' a lasting peace, whether in Vietnam, Iraq or Afghanistan. This will reduce America's willingness to embark on yet another major war in the next 10–15 years, barring a NATO-triggered response to a major Russian offensive against Europe, or more major terror attacks.

As Stalin once said: 'A single death is a tragedy, but a million deaths are just a statistic'. Surveys show that Americans paid more attention to the beheadings of two US journalists in the Middle East than to any other news report over the previous 5 years. As a direct result, 75% of Americans said they supported air strikes against Islamic State in Iraq, with 66% supporting air strikes against rebels in Syria. This was a complete reversal – 12 months earlier, only 20% supported missile attacks on the Syrian government after chemical weapons were used.

Such huge emotional reactions to tiny numbers of American deaths are proof of how vulnerable the nation is to being provoked and goaded into large-scale military reactions. This makes further beheadings of hostages or similar atrocities inevitable. Enemies of the US will ask: 'What will it take to tempt America into another asymmetric conflict that will wear it down further? Another ten journalists beheaded, or would it take twenty, or a larger attack on US soil?' The answer of course is that it will depend on many different factors, but probably far fewer deaths than many might suppose.

Fewer unilateral decisions to embark on major wars

As we have seen, by 2030, global military power will be more equally distributed, with the relative decline of American military dominance, and this will also result in an eventual restructuring of the old UN security council.

Individual nations will be less able or likely to embark on major military action some distance from their borders, without acting jointly with several other nations. This also means that major multinational wars (or a Third World War) will become less likely, but expect many minor conflicts over resources/borders/sea-bed rights and other similar issues.

Worrying results from war games

Every large nation in the world is playing war games on a regular basis, the Pentagon more than most, exploring outcomes of imaginary conflicts in faraway places.

However, many such war games reveal the same pattern as in the Middle East. Small, highly motivated groups on the ground, with tiny budgets, easily provoking large, foreign military powers into long-term fighting at enormous cost. War games also show rather worrying outcomes from any scenarios that begin with a sudden, major Russian assault.

The greatest weakness of American military strategy is that the public is not usually prepared for more than a handful of American forces to be killed abroad. Servicemen are rarely motivated enough by the 'cause' to engage in widespread suicide missions. Therefore, future military strategies will be based mainly on technical power, firing long-distance weapons, at eye-watering cost, using very few human beings on the ground.

So a young drone operator sits in an American city watching live video, firing smart missiles into targets in a nation he has never visited, on the other side of the world. He thinks the enemy are *terrorists* that could threaten America.

On the other side, perhaps, is a young man with a gun who will soon sacrifice his own life as a local hero, for his own people, and for the 'rightness' of his cause. He thinks that he is a *freedom fighter*.

The trouble is that the history of warfare shows that those who fight with greatest passion for the 'rightness' of their cause tend to win in the long term. So which of the above has the strongest passion?

Terrorist or freedom fighter? This battle over perception will be central to many future conflicts, as during the Second World War with the French Resistance, and with the Nicaraguan Contra movement that was covertly funded by America in the 1980s, along with the Afghan mujahideen.

More double and treble agents – with strange results

America's intelligence agency budget has more than doubled in real terms since 2001, to $75bn a year, while Russia's intelligence spending has also soared. Expect huge growth in double agents, treble agents, quadruple agents – people or networks working for more than one intelligence service, infiltrating activists and militia groups, playing one off against the other with disinformation and subterfuge (such as sending a fake report to a drone operator, hoping that women and children will be killed 'by mistake').

Expect many strange events and news headlines. At times the numbers of spies planted inside some smaller terrorist cells may form a very significant proportion of the number of genuine members, as has already happened from time to time in Northern Ireland. Expect many moral dilemmas, and legal action in future – spies will often have to prove they are *not* spies by carrying out attacks or atrocities themselves. And one day the shocking truth will be revealed… with ethical and legal questions.

This strange world is being shaped further by the massive expansion of cyber-monitoring and surveillance, which in future will be added to by many tens of thousands of tiny low-cost drones, to watch us from the skies. (See Chapter 1 for more on cyber-crime and state monitoring).

Hybrid wars – blurring of war and peace

We will see combinations of traditional military; threats and economic bullying; humanitarian aid; paramilitary groups; informal militia (volunteers and mercenaries); concealed, rebadged or disguised armed forces with official deniability; criminal gangs; terrorist acts; drone assassinations; insurgency and cyber-destruction – all accompanied by social media, fear campaigns, subtle propaganda, bending the truth.

The gap between war and peace is already blurred. And future conflicts will be very confusing, hard to interpret – with conflicting reports, and uncertainty about who the 'enemy' is, or if there really is a conflict at all.

Covert activities will include commercial espionage; buying members of parliament as consultants; buying up key companies; blackmailing influential bankers, business leaders, media owners or government leaders; and funding dissident groups. Blackmail will be a particular risk for high-profile business leaders who take senior jobs in some emerging nations, where they will be targeted, compromised and corrupted, with the aim of controlling them when they return home. This will mainly be about enhancing national interests and economic growth in a hyper-competitive world.

Challenges from failed states

Time and again, the might of the most powerful nations will be tempered by the difficulties of ensuring stable regime change. Whether in Zimbabwe, North Korea, Sudan or Syria, it will become even clearer that mending so-called 'broken states' by sending in foreign armies in traditional fighting machines is a near-impossible task.

One of the greatest challenges will be how to find ways to bring stability and security by other mechanisms, which may include friendly support from neighbouring countries, IMF development loans, NGO activity, use of UN peacekeepers, and so on.

The net result of all these trends will be a radical reshaping of military spending by all major military powers over the next two decades. It will always be true that 'real' wars will require 'boots on the ground'. Tens of thousands of troops, artillery, tanks and other hardware will always be persuasive when massed close to borders. But we can also expect developed nations to invest in more drones, smart missiles, rapid response troop vehicles and helicopters, and better intelligence, for longer-distance operations.

Tribal leadership will also change corporations

Whatever country, army or corporation we look at, tribal leadership will be the most powerful type of leadership in our future world. Every great politician understands how to appeal to an entire tribe, as does every great CEO.

Team leadership is always limited by team size, usually to less than twelve. But tribal leadership can take a hundred thousand people in the same direction, as members with a common vision, inspired by the same dream, marching in step together as a powerful force for change.

Tribal leadership is about relationships rather than structures, aspirations rather than goals. We see tribal leadership in popular movements around the world. Anything that strengthens your tribe will strengthen tribal leadership. Expect huge investment by corporations in tribe-building. Team days, offsites, staff conferences, celebrations and client events.

Every company is a tribe of tribes

Every organisation is a tribe and there can be many tribes inside corporations: front and back office, HQ and regions, sales and credit control, research and marketing. Tribalism in a company makes us proud to belong. Tribalism can weld teams together in a healthy and competitive way. Corporate tribalism raises key issues: can we impose a dominant national culture on a global business – for example, as a *Swiss* bank? What about cultural adaptation?

Tribalism will be one of the most powerful tools managers use to increase productivity, competitiveness and loyalty. Every great manager needs to understand how to create and maintain a happy tribe.

The more inspiring a leader is, the larger that person's tribe will be. It's a law of the universe. The fastest way to change an organisation will be to address the tribal culture. Tribalism is the reason why most mergers fail to create value: take care to honour and celebrate each tribe, and your business is more likely to grow.

Tribes of friends produce three times more manufacturing output than acquaintances and 50% better decision-making, with greater trust, honesty, open communication and respect.

Family business is all about the tribe

A significant proportion of new wealth in many emerging nations will be created by small companies with fewer than twenty employees, of which most will be family owned. They will continue, despite legal challenges, to favour employing relatives, friends, and friends of friends. Expect new government initiatives to help provide venture capital and loans for smaller businesses, as a way to create jobs.

Brands and tribes

Every brand creates a tribe and the more powerful your tribe, the more powerful your brand will be. Apple is the world's most valuable corporate tribe – worth around $117bn, followed by Google at $107bn, IBM at $76bn and Coca-Cola at $80bn, then GE, McDonald's, Samsung, Amazon and Toyota. Each superbrand will spend billions over the next 20 years to promote their tribal identity.

Consumers in many nations are already exposed to 30,000 brands. Tribal gatherings are an advertiser's dream. Create a tribe and money follows. Many more global brands will hide inside local 'tribal' packaging, becoming more 'glocal', especially where the brand is too closely linked to one nation, culture or religion.

All great marketing will appeal to tribes

Traditional marketing is dead. Customers have moved on and left marketers behind. I have met leaders from all the largest advertising agencies who between them control global campaigns for most multinationals. They are facing an anxious future.

Their big TV campaigns, press releases, mailshots, events, billboards, cold calling of customers or Twitter feeds – all of these marketing plans still work to some extent, but belong to the last century. Even worse, some techniques just alienate customers – like cold calling, or emails, or unwanted ads.

Most young people in developed nations are moving from old-style live TV to time-warp TV, where they skip the ads. Students in the UK spend an average of 9 hours a day on mobile email, texting and social media sites – and less time watching TV. The average student spends 90 minutes on texting alone, and 60% say they might be addicted to their mobiles. So we need new ways to reach them.

But the cleverest campaigns will all be about creating *new* tribes. So, for example, a Christmas ad featuring a huggable penguin goes viral on YouTube, and becomes an instant hit, with a run on anything that looks like the character, so creating a new tribe.

Selling to youth tribes

Falling birth rates will mean smaller youth tribes in many nations. And here is another issue: radical or quirky, eccentric youth fashions will be harder to create or sustain.

Young people today in most developed countries are far more likely to wear the same kind of clothes as their parents, listen to similar music, frequent similar bars and clubs, have similar hairstyles, and hold similar political or religious views. The main exception to this will be in children of migrants who adopt the culture of their new nation and reject that of their parents.

The M generation, whose entire adult lives have been lived in the third millennium, is on the whole unused to protesting, and is politically relaxed. This may well change in some communities, but there is little sign of it right now.

Surveys of 13–19-year-olds in the UK show them to be the most driven generation for 100 years – excelling in their careers is one of their most important goals. Many teenagers are starting up their own businesses at school, often using digital skills, or are taking part-time jobs. They are also keen to give time as volunteers.

This ambition to succeed is also driving youth tribes from middle-class backgrounds in India, China and many other developed nations. They also want to get educated and get a good job. They also want life outside of work, dream of long-term relationships, and hope to have children one day.

Selling to older tribes

As we have seen, 1 billion people will be over the age of 65 by 2025. This tribe accounts for 50% of US income and 75% of all financial assets, and the UK is much the same. Expect a wide range of products tailored to the 'grey market', such as cruise ships, golf breaks and health spas. This is a generation that thinks young, with a mental age of 60, physical age of 70 and actual age of 80.

Redesign for older customers

Expect a rethink about packaging, restaurant menus, instructions and marketing materials, which are usually printed too small for older people to read without glasses. Most people over 50 who stay in hotels will tell you similar stories about accidentally using conditioner instead of shower gel because the text was too small on the bottle. Who wears reading glasses in the bathroom? I realised the other day that I had no idea of the make of my electric razor because the logo is so small.

Some role models in advertising will age 30 years. Grey power will be more visible on the high street, in clothes shops, sports shops, car showrooms, garden centres, travel agents, theatres, cinemas and restaurants.

Personal pension plans and investment funds will be growth

areas, and face-to-face banking will be especially aimed at those who are retired. Equity release from homes will be a common way to boost pensions.

Delayed inheritance for middle-aged workers

More than $10 trillion dollars will pass from one generation to another in the next decade in the US alone. These days, people may be in their sixties or seventies before both parents have died. By 2050, they may be working at the age of 75, and caring for an older parent at the same time.

Expect an army of fit and active 75-year-olds to become volunteers for hundreds of charities. These organisations will provide a sense of family, purpose and belonging.

People with no pension

At the other end of the social scale, we will see an elderly underclass – people who work part-time until they drop in their late seventies or eighties (or in their nineties by 2040), unable to survive on miserable state pensions, out of touch with their children.

A huge problem will be growing numbers of people in 20 years' time who failed to invest adequately in a pension fund. A separate crisis will be experienced by those whose pensions have been hit by low yields or inflation, or because their pension company went bust as life expectancy jumped. Others will run out of cash, after raiding their capital or making very foolish investment decisions, following deregulation of pensions in nations like the UK.

Impact of later retirement

As I predicted, compulsory retirement is already illegal in countries like the UK – seen as a form of ageism. Many older people will cash in a partial pension at any stage from 55 to 75 and will top up with part-time work, or low-paid, full-time jobs for worthy causes.

State pension age for all workers will be set at 70 years by 2025 in many developed nations, for those who are younger than 40 in that year.

However, those with adequate personal pensions will retire,

or semi-retire, whenever they like. A key recruitment strategy in ageing nations will be tempting people in their seventies out of retirement. It may be hard to imagine the need to do this today, in nations where up to 40% of young people are still out of work because of economic crisis, but hard times will pass, wages and exchange rates will adjust, and the experience of older workers will be needed.

Shift from marketing to information and revelation

I don't like the word 'marketing' because in future it will imply overselling, hype, spin, presenting a distorted version of the truth. Brands that oversell will be quickly exposed. The best products in future will 'sell' themselves. The more you have to 'market' a product, the more people will assume that the product is not worth having.

As we have seen in Chapter 1, the most powerful messages in future will be information and revelation in a personal 'conversation'. At the same time, expect many attempts by retail marketing, advertising and brand agencies to use ever more exotic ways to develop concepts and messaging in a fight to gain customer attention – including neuromarketing, which studies how our brains react to brands, slogans, shapes, textures, smells, ideas, memories, hopes and dreams.

Reaching tribes through social media

Most people are quicker to believe the opinion of a stranger on a social media site than a marketing executive, chairman or CEO. And the more colourful and negative the social media review, the more customers are likely to read it, especially in China, where 66% of consumers rely on social media reports before buying.

Hotels or restaurants that consistently have 5* reviews will be less likely to get bookings than ones which score 4* or 4.5*. Customers want to hear authentic, varied and balanced opinions of real people and mistrust information that looks as though it is automatically generated.

Every one of your future marketing messages, slogans and

campaigns is likely to be scored by the online community. It is already happening. So your company ad on Google or Facebook or any other website may appear with a star rating, based on customer experiences.

This is great news for all smaller companies with excellent products or services but tiny marketing budgets. Quality and customer enthusiasm is what will really count in future.

Threat to Google from tribes

Google faces a huge challenge because search results are being damaged by marketing techniques, to distort listings, and to give added prominence to certain web pages.

Google's answer was to try to turn the entire web into an author network, with each author and web page ranked by the rest of the community for influence, respect and authority in their field. That meant mapping 5 billion people onto the whole web in social terms: who reads which pages, who knows whom, who writes what?

Facebook has 1.4 billion users a month, more than the population of China, and an annual income of $2.8bn. With 1 trillion page views, Facebook had the power to enable Google to do what they wanted in a single step. That is why Google was so disappointed not to be able to buy Facebook, and why it was also obvious that Facebook would itself move into search activities. So Google tried to create a rival with the launch of G+, which has 300 million users – not enough.

Millions of fake identities on social networks

In the meantime, marketing companies have hit back, creating tens of millions of fake people on social networks with fake friends, fake life events, fake activities, fake posts and fake product preferences. Their hope is to influence search results.

There are probably over 1000 social media companies in China alone that exist solely to fool the algorithms of Taobao, one of China's biggest e-commerce platforms. Each online store displays recent sales figures – and larger figures attract more customers.

Pretend customers linger on web pages to make pages appear 'hot' on many different websites. We will see many more such attempts to corrupt search results with fraudulent data.

Search results that you see in future will be altered by your previous activity. Imagine someone who is very sceptical about climate change science. Such an individual may think he is searching the whole web for updates on the science, but in future he will only be shown results that confirm his own views. This matters a lot, particularly if people do not realise that the search engine is censoring results in this way.

Does Facebook have a long-term future?

Facebook has made few radical improvements and will soon look tired unless fresh direction is found. Facebook use is already falling rapidly in the UK, a nation that led much of the world in online sales and networking.

New sites will spring up almost overnight, aimed at younger users, but only one or two will become global players. Old social sites will be under huge pressure to allow people to move all their digital timelines, content and networks.

Another major risk to sites such as Facebook is that significant numbers of people will decide to 'get a life' by rejecting a hyper-frenetic virtual existence. Is it really sustainable to expect users to spend up to 8 hours a day on social messaging – exchanging relatively unimportant and superficial gossip-type items, one fragment or photo at a time?

The average smartphone user feels compelled to pull a phone from a pocket over 230 times every 24 hours. Head-mounted devices will only increase the number of times we check a display.

Most people would say that social media strengthens friendships, but what about real intimacy and personal attention? Expect a premium for the real, the authentic, breathing the same air, being '100% present', enjoying the total moment. Expect growing numbers of people to turn off their devices as a matter of principle for at least an hour a day.

Tribal fashion, clothing and textiles

The fashion industry has always been about tribes: what kind of person do you want to be? With whom are you identifying by the way you dress?

Expect more tribal-influencers like 18-year-old Bethany Mota who rapidly gained more fashion followers each month than *Vogue*, *Elle*, *I* and *Cosmopolitan* put together with her YouTube video clips about what clothes, makeup and accessories she had tried out. Expect hundreds of highly influential 16- or 17-year-olds, each with several million social network followers who read their blogs or tweets or watch their videos, to follow suit.

Future of the fashion industry

The fashion and textiles industries are worth over $1.8 trillion, growing 5% a year, employing 75 million people. At present 50% of global growth in apparel sales is in China, which will probably overtake the US as the largest market by 2018. But prices globally have been falling in real terms for two decades, and will continue to do so, with competition and scale economies.

In the US, the industry employs 4 million people, in 280,000 outlets for clothes and shoes. I met an American cotton manufacturer recently who makes 1,400 pairs of socks *every minute*. Just think about the challenges of selling individual pairs to 84,000 different customers around the world every hour, ordering, supplying, marketing.

Fashion is worth over $40bn a year to the UK economy, employing over 800,000 people – more than telcos, car manufacturing and publishing combined.

How catwalks and fashion launches will change

Fashion parades will continue to push towards every extreme, with models parading semi-nude, completely veiled, clean, muddy, soaked, icy, body-painted – anything to get attention. But none of this will create popular third millennial fashion.

Expect a backlash against the traditional catwalks in New

York, London, Paris and Milan. Four weeks of shows, thousands of events, tens of thousands of outfits. Some fashion leaders will explore ways to completely reinvent how they launch their collections, for a web-mobile world, where attention spans are only seconds.

Traditional styles will endure at work

Executive workplace clothing for men is likely to remain unchanged for the next 30 years, as a globally accepted but visually boring uniform. It is striking how little men's suits, shirts and ties have evolved since the year 1901.

Identikit suits for men will remain the 'safe' norm, usually with shirt and tie, as will similarly sober dress styles for women, adapted heavily for life in countries like Saudi Arabia, Brazil, Malaysia or India.

Exotic and eccentric styles will continue to be frowned on, seen as conveying an image of eccentric and risky decision-making. Exceptions will of course be in fashion, design and other creative industries such as software, App development and many startups. And on 'dress-down' days in some corporations.

Expect leisure fashion cycles for women to be as short as 12 weeks for some design houses by 2025, requiring shorter supply chains, faster design to production, in an ever more frenetic attempt to increase sales. Some of this retail hyperactivity will implode with big losses, to be replaced by slower seasonal stock changes.

New fabrics and textures

Expect revolutions in fabric properties, especially in new ranges of synthetic fibres. These will create exciting opportunities for designers: clothes that change colour, new textures, textiles with nanotech treatments that self-clean or air-clean. Expect to see wide use of intelligent clothes with displays and sensors that change with temperature in colour or texture, or made of material which itself changes colour with temperature, or with accessories 'wired' with functionality, such as belts, hats, glasses, watches, gloves or trainers – for example providing readouts of distance runs.

Future of cotton and polyester

Cotton is a really important industry for many emerging markets, and supports over 300 million jobs. We grow 25 million tons of cotton every year on 2.5% of the world's arable land, mainly on smallholdings of around 2 hectares, and the global cotton trade is worth $12bn a year. The largest exporters are America and Africa, and the largest hoarder is China, with stocks equal to more than 6 months of global output.

The cotton industry will continue to grow, much in line with global population, but will decline as a proportion of all fibre types. This will be the case even in tropical nations where cotton has a key advantage over polyester in absorbing moisture. Cotton is being displaced by polyester at a rate of around 7% a year in the US.

Expect huge improvements in water use, pollution reduction, productivity per acre, pesticide reduction, and promotion of independently certified, ethical, sustainable cotton. In contrast, synthetic fibres are simple, chemical products, made from oil. Expect a public relations battle over whether polyester or cotton is the most sustainable and responsible fabric to wear.

Future of sport – tribes at play

Just like fashion, sport will continue to be dominated by tribalism: support for individuals, local teams or national champions, celebration of extraordinary physical skill, cheered on by tribal admirers. And then there is the huge social status from 'owning a tribe' such as a football team.

In some ways the world of sport will change only slowly. For example, we can expect very few significant alterations in rules for most sports, and few new global sports. Sport will continue to be a focus for entire nations, with huge media pull for important live events, some drawing audiences of more than 1 billion. Revenues from broadcasting and related advertising will continue to dominate the sporting calendar, while most leading sports celebrities will earn far more from corporate sponsorship deals than from winning competitions.

However, we will see more news stories about how results have been fixed, by gangs linked to betting syndicates in countries far away from the event itself. Multiple scandals will threaten to bring entire sports into disrepute – with football in the frontline after years of problems in cricket. Just about every kind of major sporting event will be implicated. Some ruling bodies may turn out to be implicated or corrupt themselves.

Expect huge bets on, for example, whether there will be three free kicks before half-time, or whether a particular player will be injured or will score a goal, and similar things in cycling, Formula 1, and so on. And as we have seen, there will be many questions in future about the credibility of athletics world records in the light of biotech doping.

Future of family and relationships

So, then, we have seen the importance of tribalism for the future of the EU, for nations, companies, brands, marketing, fashion and sport. But the family is *the* primary unit of tribalism. How will family tribes change in future?

Despite nonsense predictions by many social scientists over the last two decades, family life has continued relatively unchanged in most parts of the world. Couples develop relationships, usually get married, want to have children, and often live in extended family situations, especially in emerging markets or immigrant communities.

Family breakdown

Developed nations – and a growing number of emerging economies – are experiencing a cluster of trends that can influence each other. Rise in family breakdown; more absent fathers; emotional upset and behavioural problems in children; poor school performance; and risks of adding to an unemployable and disaffected underclass. Teachers, social workers, probation officers and judges in family courts see these trends every day.

In the UK, most couples over the last 10 years have decided to have children without getting married. This is despite most studies showing that happiest couples, and ones most likely to stay together, are those that are married, particularly if they have had few other relationships before their wedding day.

The popularity of marriage will vary with income. Wealthy, middle-class couples in some nations are far more like to marry before they have children. Many of the poorest and least educated are rejecting marriage altogether.

Absent dads

The UK has one of the highest percentages of absent dads in the world: fathers who have little or no contact with their children, following breakup of the relationship. That means absent male role models, less money to support the children, and higher costs for housing. Family breakup is often a fast-track to poverty.

Family breakup is also strongly associated with higher risks of mental illness in children (and later on in adulthood) of addiction, risk-taking, teenage pregnancy, suicide and relationship breakup as adults. So we are likely to see a generational impact, beyond 2050, from events in families over the last decade alone.

The impact on such children is often made worse by the fact that in many cases both parents are struggling to survive financially, both working full time, possibly with more than one job each. So parenting is often outsourced to childminders, friends or relatives.

The pendulum always swings somewhere new

Over the next three decades, we are likely to see a partial swing away from previous patterns of 'sexual liberation'. In some countries we are already seeing a significant *rise* in the age of first sexual experiences.

For example, in America, the number of 15–19-year-olds who have had sex before 15 fell from 19% to 11% in women, and from 21% to 14% in men, in just 12 years from 1995 to 2008. In nations like Uganda, these trends have been driven by fear of AIDS – most Ugandans have attended at least twenty AIDS funerals in the past decade or so, usually of relatives. But more globally, we are seeing a rethink about what sex is really about in many communities.

Rise of responsible and conservative teenagers

A new generation is emerging that is the most socially conservative for a decade in countries like the UK. Not only has there been a sharp drop in teenage pregnancies to the lowest rate in 40 years, but more young people are rejecting alcohol, drugs and sex at an early age.

One in six admitted to taking drugs in 2014, half the level of 2003. Only 9% are drinking alcohol each week compared to 25% a decade before. The numbers who have ever tried alcohol also dropped from 61 to 39% over the same time period. Smoking also fell from 41% to 24% – with numbers of regular smokers down to only 3% compared to 9%. These are huge changes, born out by repeated studies, and also by the experience of retailers/suppliers on the high street.

This generation is likely to question what kind of life they want for their *own* children. Some will want to give their own children more parental time than they had themselves when they were young, even if that means working fewer hours, and having a lower standard of living. Such future parents will also be less likely to place their own young children in full-time professional childcare.

Older people as anchors and free childminders

Many grandparents will find themselves helping out with grandchildren, and will become much-loved role models in many areas of life; many happy long-term relationships will be formed, and of course grandparents will save the family money that would otherwise be spent on childcare. As we have seen, for economic and family reasons, more households will have three generations living under the same roof. Some grandparents will provide welcome stability at times of family strain, but others will place impossible stress on the marriages of their children.

We are also likely to see more informal fostering or adoption in wealthier nations of retired people as substitute grandparents, or aunties or uncles, by parents with children at home, where generations of blood relatives are separated by distance or family tensions.

A growing number of children share the same mother but have different fathers, with these father-figures coming and going over the years. Such children will often experience complex rivalries with step-brothers or sisters, and complex relationships with grandparents.

Web censorship and child protection

Many parents of young children that I talk to are very anxious indeed about how to protect their children online. They have sleepless nights worrying about what access to allow, what is fair, and if their children will be teased or bullied if parents don't allow various things. And they know that whatever the family rules are, their children may be getting unrestricted access anyway, to every kind of very disturbing 'adult' material, through friends at school.

Parents are horrified to learn from repeated surveys that most 8–10-year-old boys and girls have watched very explicit sex videos. And that most 14-year-olds feel it is part of normal life to be bullied into sending photos of their genitalia to classmates (sexting).

In the UK, 20% of all 11–13-year-old girls are already secretly padding their bras before they go to school, because they feel embarrassed to be flat-chested at such an old age. Just another small aspect of the wider issue of teenage angst, self-doubt and social pressure that are the result of a hypersexual culture.

Parents of teenagers are anxious in every nation

I have seen this same parental anxiety in every part of the world, through the work of the AIDS charity ACET that I started years ago. Our educators have seen over 5 million high school students, teaching classes in high schools on relationships and sexual health, in twenty nations, ranging from Russia to Kazakhstan, Thailand, India, Uganda and Ireland. We usually find it is the parents who are most keen for our lessons to take place.

Governments of nations like China, Russia, Malaysia and Thailand – which tend to have a more autocratic approach to what they think is good for people to watch or read about – have already taken the lead in global efforts to clean up the web. Remember that 85% of the world's people will be living in these parts of the world by 2025.

These regions are on the whole far more traditional than Europe or America when it comes such matters, and watch with growing incomprehension what they regard as the 'moral decay' of many developed nations.

Expect more government-imposed filters and other initiatives, aiming to regulate access to 'corrupting' websites, to be active in over 50 nations by 2025, covering over 60% of the world's population, up from 35% today. Even though 400 million people already use private networks to get round such censorship, these networks will become illegal or require a special licence in many countries.

Outrage over abuse of women and children

Another sign of change in developed nations like the UK and America is the massive outcry recently over celebrities who abused their status in the 1970s and 1980s to sexually abuse teenagers and younger adults.

In the 1970s and 1980s many British women accepted that it was normal (but nasty) if a work colleague pinched their bottom in a lift, or tried to put a hand up a skirt in the office. Today, such acts may mean a prison sentence if repeated – even if they took place decades ago, and even if the woman didn't complain about it at the time, or at any point during the following 35 to 40 years.

So while many societies have become hyper-sexualised, as seen in advertising, music videos, fashion, magazines and TV, it is also true that many societies in developed nations are becoming more sensitive about sexual abuse of women and children in particular.

Marketing executives, designers and film-makers will all need to tread carefully as they seek to navigate these changes, sensing what is no longer appropriate and will now risk offence. For example, one of the most iconic adverts of the 1990s was a poster campaign for Wonderbra with the slogan: 'Hello Boys!'. The posters were so eye-catching that they were blamed for some car accidents by male drivers. Whether such a campaign would be so widely acceptable today is open to question.

Growing number of commercial sex workers

Prostitution will continue to be a growth industry in many nations where up to 10% of men have paid for sex. In the UK alone, one in 20 students (100,000 across the country) are paying their way through university with jobs as prostitutes, escorts, lap dancers or filmed performers. One in five students have considered the option. Globally, at least 40 million women are commercial sex workers, while a further 40–60 million are in less formal arrangements, providing men with sexual companionship in exchange for food just to survive. Around 12 million women and 2 million children are 'slaves' – trafficked, tricked, trapped – in one of the fastest-growing criminal activities in the world. Expect many new regulations and deregulations as governments struggle to respond to demand for prostitution.

Rethink on age of consent

In Spain the legal age of consent is 13, compared to 21 in Bahrain, 18 in Turkey and India, 17 in Ireland, 16 in UK, 14 in China and 12 in Angola. In some nations, all sex outside marriage is illegal, as in Kuwait where the minimum age for marriage is 15 for girls and 17 for boys.

Expect a major debate on the issue in nations where ages of consent are higher for same-sex relationships, as in Finland, Greece, Austria and Malta. Expect harmonisation downwards in some European countries. We will also see a relaxation of laws in some of the 79 nations in the world where homosexual acts are illegal.

However, any future debates about ages of consent in general will be dominated by one argument: if we do lower the legal age further, it will mean more adults escape justice, because they will not have broken any law by grooming and seducing (even) younger girls or boys.

The romantic dream will remain strong

The romantic ideal is very powerful, has not changed in over 200 years and will endure for the next 200. One reason is the powerful genetic instinct of human beings to form intense bonding relationships.

Almost all young people hope one day to find an amazing person who fulfils them in every way, with whom every day is treasured. If the romantic ideal remains unchanged and powerful, and if breakup is more often the reality, then it tells us that our future world will be full of disappointed people. And also full of people whose self-esteem has taken a knock as a result of an unhappy or broken relationship.

All this will guarantee that in many nations the market continues to grow for relationship advice, marriage counsellors, agony columns, confidence-building activities, dating agencies, romantic city breaks, Valentine's day gifts, bedroom fashion wear, sexual therapists, and a very wide range of other products and services to help couples keep their romance alive.

And marriage or re-marriage is likely to become more popular again in some nations where decline has been greatest, even if the event takes place only when a baby is expected or shortly afterwards.

Sex industry adds to worries about performance

Recent research cited by *Forbes* magazine and the BBC showed that 4% of websites and 13% of web searches are pornography related, based on global search teams and an analysis of the world's million most popular sites. These figures are lower than often quoted in older studies – more women are online these days and e-commerce means that the web is used for more things.

Even the most popular video porn sites have only a tiny fraction of the traffic of sites like YouTube. The busiest of such sites globally is used by 2.5% of all online users, with around 32 million visitors a month. Revenues from selling porn have fallen sharply over the past decade, because of wide availability of free online content.

Research suggests that 2% of men are addicted to online porn, and a further 30% experience various degrees of dependency, which can damage their relationships. Dependency on online porn is one of the commonest complaints cited by women in American divorce papers.

Professional help for sexual performance

There can be little doubt that widespread consumption of porn has changed expectations in some men (and women) about their own relationships and capabilities, often in completely unrealistic, and possibly damaging, ways.

One thing is certain: many more men are seeking professional advice because they are anxious about their own sexual performance. At the same time, more women are also seeking ways to achieve greater satisfaction, or to give pleasure to their partners.

Most men over 50 have some degree of mild erectile dysfunction from time to time, a potential market of up to 300 million men by 2025. And 5% of 40-year-old men and 20% of 65-year-old men have serious long-term problems with impotence.

Sales of drugs like Viagra and Cialis are already worth more than $4.3bn a year. Expect a wider range of such drugs in future, with faster action, longer effects, at lower cost – some of which are likely to be available from pharmacists without prescription in some nations by 2030.

Busy professionals are becoming too tired for sex

Busy young professionals may be in relationships, but their love-life may often be non-existent, which can increase the temptation to look elsewhere. One of the common causes of lack of intimacy in younger people is chronic tiredness and stress. Couples are often affected by long working hours, young children, broken nights or night shifts, financial worries and crowded housing with lack of privacy.

A growing number of male and female executives will be faced with a choice between aggressive pursuit of an exciting career or a fulfilling long-term relationship, with well-balanced children and (hopefully) a happy love-life.

Arranged marriages will decline

Over a billion people live in communities where marriage partners are chosen by family, and where marriage is still regarded as a noble and exclusive institution, with dire consequences for unfaithfulness, or for pre-marital sex, especially in the case of women.

Expect more frequent culture clashes in traditional families now living in a developed nation, where children are rejecting arranged marriages, or where there are few suitable matches for parents to select from in the host nation in which they have settled.

More virtual relationships and e-marriages

It is already the case that 20% of all new romantic relationships start online in some nations, with someone that the person would never have otherwise met. Video links such as Facetime or Skype will become increasingly important to hundreds of millions of couples, and wider families. However, it will continue to be very rare for an enduring romantic relationship to remain primarily or completely virtual.

Gay marriage and diverse expressions of family

Expect gay marriage to become very widely accepted as a normal expression of long-term commitment between two men or two women, across almost all the EU, most of North America and a growing number of other nations. It is easy for residents of such nations to think that the rest of the world is just backward, and will soon fall into line with modern thinking, yet laws for gay marriage will continue to be viewed with deep hostility in many of the 72 nations where *all* homosexual activity is still criminal, let alone marriage.

We are likely to see increasing polarisation over this issue between developed and emerging economies, with greatest opposition to gay marriage in strongly Islamic or Christian nations like Malaysia or Nigeria. Nations like Russia and Belarus will also tend to be fairly traditional in outlook for the next decade or two.

The word 'family' is already being redefined in many developed nations by those who believe that alternative models are equally good for individuals and society as a whole. Families with two dads or two mums – using surrogates or sperm donors to create their children. Families with children from one, two, three or four different relationships, or children made by combining genes from three parents.

However, more studies are likely to confirm the findings of a large body of research suggesting that, on average, the lowest-risk environment for the emotional well-being of a child is in a happy home in which it is cared for by its own biological mother and father.

Extended families will cluster together

Despite many predictions about the atomisation of society, most people in developed nations like France, Spain or the UK are still living within an hour or two's drive of parents, and not far from where they were born.

What is more, more young adults are at home until around age 30, or spend long periods during their twenties with one or both parents. A major reason is economics, with rising house prices, more time in education, and higher unemployment. The same has been happening with grandparents, who are more likely to be living under the same roof as one of their children than they were a decade ago, often helping with grandchildren. This is particularly the case if their own child is a single parent.

Products for the 'precious child'

I have already described the 'era of the precious child' (see p. 97).

Part of this growing obsession with children is due to families having fewer of them. The entire hopes and dreams of two parents are often focused on the development of a single child.

We will see rapid growth of products, services, techniques and educational tools to 'hot-house' child development. Ways to encourage your child's genius to shine. How to create a musical prodigy by the age of five. How to help your child to be trilingual by the age of three.

Entire industries will spring up to service the hopes and worries of pregnant mothers. Ways to encourage child development before birth. Hyper-nutrition to boost brain development in the womb. Exposing the unborn child to ambient music or other stimulation. How to give your child a perfect birthing experience.

Some of these things may matter more than most people

realise. For example, we know that the genes your child inherits are permanently affected by your own nutritional status when conceiving, and by environmental factors in the lives of your own parents, and grandparents. So what happens when your unborn child is still in the womb could possibly affect the well-being of your great-grandchildren in subtle ways. Such insights will just add to the pressures felt by mothers-to-be.

Changes in drug and alcohol use

We have already seen how a younger generation in many nations is spending less on alcohol or drugs than a decade ago. People are usually introduced to these things by others in the same tribal group, and consumption is often a social activity.

Alcohol will be a growing problem

Alcohol dependency is one of the world's most complex challenges. Globally, alcohol kills 3.3 million people every year, and 3 times as many teenagers than all illegal drugs. It is responsible for 7.6% of all male deaths and 4% of all female deaths. Half the world's population does not drink alcohol at all, but those that do consume on average 17 litres of pure alcohol each year. European figures are higher than the global average.

In America, 6% of the population, or 16 million people, drink more than their bodies can cope with long term, and 10% of all health problems are related in some way to alcohol consumption. Around 40% of all crimes across America are committed while under the influence of alcohol. In the UK, 9 million people are 'problem drinkers'. The cost of alcohol misuse to the UK economy is over £21bn a year.

We can expect a wide range of measures in many nations, including education about health risks, stricter controls on sales to young people, and higher taxes on alcohol (the single most effective measure in reducing consumption). Expect more investment in specialist centres and support teams to help people break a serious drinking habit, and more research into medications that take away the craving to drink, or interfere with pleasure pathways inside the brain.

Tobacco sales switch to the poorest nations

Tobacco will continue to be a huge global industry, as companies switch marketing from developed to emerging economies. Smoking kills 419,000 Americans a year and costs $100bn in health care as well as productivity losses. However, the proportion of people who smoke in the US has fallen from 43% to 18% – after 50 years of health campaigns, social pressures, taxes, restrictions on marketing, and a ban on smoking in public.

The government of China is also likely to become increasingly hostile to smoking over the next three decades. China lights up 1.6 trillion cigarettes a year (25% of the population smoke, more than 300 million adults), making it the world's largest producer and consumer.

Most Chinese smokers are male and smoking kills over 400,000 men a year, a figure expected to rise to 2 million by 2025. On the other hand, the Chinese tobacco industry is one of the largest sources of state revenues, with total sales of more than $100bn.

Tobacco smoking is the usual door-opener to cannabis smoking. Therefore it is no surprise that cannabis use is falling in countries where smoking is out of fashion. Research clearly shows that cannabis use is not addictive, and less dangerous to life than tobacco or heavy alcohol use. However, cannabis alters important brain pathways, and heavy use often affects personal motivation, aspiration and achievement, especially in children and young people, and even more so if stronger types of cannabis are taken. Risks of psychosis are 5 times greater in people who smoke 'skunk' cannabis every day. In the UK, a six-year study suggested that one in four people with hallucinations, delusions, paranoid ideas or schizophrenia were mentally ill because of smoking extra-strong varieties of cannabis.

How the drugs economy will evolve

The global trade in illegal drugs is worth around $400bn a year – now included in official GDP figures of EU nations. That includes 450 tons of heroin, mainly from Afghanistan, which (after seizures by police) supplies 17 million addicts. A further 17 million people are addicted to cocaine or crack, of whom 40% live in America and 25% in Europe.

The global drugs economy will continue to be highly profitable, funding wider criminality and terrorism. Trade in illegal drugs will continue to destabilise several nations.

Failure of drugs control

America has spent over $1 trillion since the 1970s on targeting drug cartels in Latin America. In 2006, Mexico declared a 'war' against drug gangs. In the space of 8 years, 100,000 Mexicans died and 27,000 disappeared. A similar 20-year crackdown in Colombia cost 15,000 lives. Yet there is no evidence that these efforts cut consumption in America. The number of heroin addicts doubled to 680,000 in 6 years, and the price of heroin halved in real terms between the 1980s and 2014.

Uruguay and Bolivia have now liberalised laws relating to illegal drugs, and other Latin American nations are likely to review their own laws over the next two decades.

In the US 55% of voters now support the legalisation of marijuana. The logic is that as prohibition failed for alcohol in the 1930s, drug policies are also set to fail, and merely encourage criminality. Decriminalisation in some American states will be watched closely. Expect small steps in the same direction in many other developed nations, while death penalties remain in some emerging economies for drug trafficking. At the same time, the Netherlands is now moving to tighten up drug laws, having had the most liberal attitudes in Europe to drug use for a generation.

Falling drug use in many tribes

The numbers of people taking heroin, cocaine, crack and cannabis have fallen over the last decade in many other nations, despite wide availability of cheap heroin from Afghanistan. In the UK, for example, cannabis use fell from 11% of the population to 7% in the 10 years to 2011, while LSD use has also become less popular. Heroin and crack use fell from 332,000 to 298,000 in the 6 years to

2011. As we have seen, alcohol consumption has also fallen significantly – especially binge drinking in young people.

Expect huge growth in consumption of 'designer drugs', however, created by chemists, of which ecstasy is one of the best known. Each experimenter can make several types of new drug a year, none previously seen in government laboratories nor classified under 'old' drugs laws. Most of those who take these designer drugs do so on an occasional basis, but there are many unknown risks. Governments will struggle to respond to this trend.

Future of crime – tribal patterns

Crime rates have fallen in almost every developed country, in a consistent way, over the past 40 years. In many parts of the UK, for example, rates of reported crime have halved for various types of criminal activity. In the past, crime tended to rise or fall as unemployment rose and fell, but the link appears to be broken now. So what has happened and what will criminality look like in future?

Why recorded crime is falling in many nations

Societies in general are becoming more caring and sensitive. This is based on a wide range of historical trends going back hundreds of years, well described by Steven Pinker in *The Better Angels of our Nature*. Here are some examples:

- ◆ Attitudes to women have become more respectful as part of the feminisation of culture; human rights are widely supported; fathers are expected to be involved in caring for their children; most urban dwellers are very squeamish when watching the slaughter of a chicken; cruelty against animals makes many people very angry.

- ◆ Cruel and degrading punishments such as beheadings, burning people to death, public torture and slow deaths for political enemies are almost unknown today in developed nations.

- ◆ Falling rates of drug addiction means less crime. A single heroin or crack addict may need hundreds of dollars a day to buy drugs, and may commit several crimes a day to survive. In some communities, a small group of addicts can be responsible for most thefts.

◆ Better security. Car theft used to be very common, but is now almost impossible. Cash machines are better protected. Burglar alarms are more reliable, and more likely to be connected to police stations. Locks on windows and doors are more likely to be robust.

◆ Crime is moving online. E-commerce and online banking have created more than 1 billion people to target with scams, frauds and other activities. Every business has become a target for online theft. The risks of being caught are low, and prosecutions are very difficult across borders. These crimes are often not reported properly in official statistics.

Expect further progression towards less violent and aggressive societies over the next two hundred years – punctuated by shocking lapses into atrocities and anarchy, mostly in wars, civil conflicts or terror attacks.

Expect better ways to close down online scams at the speed of light. Expect recent falls in traditional types of crime to stabilise. Expect more wealth to be stolen online than in all other kinds of small-scale criminal activity, by 2020.

Despite falls in crime in many nations, we will see a rapid growth of private security services for people with wealth, because of the unsustainable and growing gap between rich and poor. Private security in America already represents three times the amount spent on the police. Countries like Russia and South Africa have ten times as many private security guards as public police officers.

★

So, then, we have seen how tribalism is the most powerful positive and negative force on earth: the basis of teams, brands, customer groups, nations, and families. The balance to the tribal Face of the Future is the Universal one, which includes globalisation, manufacturing, retail, travel and banking. The two faces pull in opposite directions. So what will be the drivers of a more Universal future?

Chapter 4

UNIVERSAL

THE FOURTH FACE OF THE FUTURE, universalism, is the exact opposite of tribalism. Universalism means English and McDonald's everywhere. Tribalism and universalism feed each other, each the reaction to its opposite.

Globalisation is an unstoppable force: the result of the free movement of capital, technology, goods, services and information across national boundaries. Globalisation will continue to increase competition and lower profit margins in many countries.

Future of regional trading blocs

Expect more of the world to be aligned within regional trading blocs, allowing tariff-free movement of goods and services. The number of regional trade agreements increased from 100 to over 250 in the last decade alone. Expect strengthening of NAFTA, ASEAN, a Russian-based bloc, and a Southern African trade area, in addition to the EU. And expect growing frustration as many countries realise that they are losing control of their own economies, as a result.

With the expansion of regional trading blocs, interest rate or tax differences between nations become less sustainable, and capital flows unstoppable. Governments will be forced to harmonise laws, taxes and benefits. Countries out of line with what the global investment community thinks is reasonable will rapidly lose foreign direct investment (FDI).

Costs will converge and power will be centralised

In a globalised world, market forces mean that commodity prices tend to converge in different parts of the world, and this will also be the case with prices for labour, despite resistance in developed nations like America and calls for trade barriers. So China's wages will rise, and Europe's will fall, relatively. Expect organised labour movements to campaign increasingly against free trade and in favour of trade blocs.

Global investors, such as pension funds and sovereign wealth funds, will become increasingly involved in big corporate decisions, effectively hiring and firing the most senior executives and exercising a veto on strategy. Trading by institutions is already 90% of the volume and value of transactions on Wall Street. Institutions already own the vast majority of US stock.

Future of mega-corporations

Our world needs more economies of scale to achieve greater efficiencies. Expect to see many more mergers – and also de-mergers as corporations make mistakes, or refocus on key areas.

Scale will reduce choice. It may seem surprising, but even a market of 10 billion people will be too small to support more than two main airline manufacturers – Boeing and Airbus. The same will be true of mobile phone operating systems and their communities of App developers; our world may be able to support three, but not four. Android and iPhone will endure beyond 2025, but Windows for mobile may struggle. Expect similar consolidation in telcos, defence, banking, car manufacturing, pharma, the film industry, energy companies, and so on.

Illegal cartels and semi-monopolies will grow in numbers and strength – typically raising prices by around 20%. Past examples include: airlines fixing the costs of $20bn in air freight – which led to fines and compensation of more than $4bn; car part manufacturers fixing a huge range of component prices; rail and subway contract price fixing in Brazil; Libor interest rate fixing in Europe and America; and the huge semi-monopolies of Apple, Google and Amazon.

Global citizens

We will see a new breed of hyper-mobile globalised individuals with no national loyalty or identity and no commitment to any geographical area, yet with friends in every city. These industrialised techno-gypsies consider themselves global citizens. They will be hard to tax and hard to count in census surveys, as well as hard to police.

We see them already: for example, the senior executive who spends more than half the year away from home, equally divided between two other continents, and who decides to take a flat in another city, which she visits frequently. Where is her home?

Future of global manufacturing

All manufacturers will find extra cost savings, and so the prices of most goods will fall in real terms over the next three decades. They will achieve this with greater automation, larger factories, better design, thinner and stronger materials such as carbon fibre and composites, more recycling, improved energy efficiency, shorter supply chains, lower stock levels, and by moving factories from nation to nation, to regions where labour costs are lower or to where demand is growing fastest.

Future of trade, logistics and supply chains

Moving a container 150km by lorry from Birmingham to Southampton costs the same as moving the same container 10,000km by sea from Southampton to Beijing. It is cheaper to transport melons from Istanbul to Naples than to drive melons from a village up in the Italian mountains, to the same market.

This overwhelmingly huge difference in freight costs will be one of the single greatest drivers of future global trade, despite increases in energy prices. It is the primary reason why global trade has grown at twice the rate of global production over the last 30 years.

Look out for trade growth in Latin America and Africa – both of which have huge manufacturing potential close to the sea. Areas with major container ports will on average grow up to 40% faster over the next three decades than cities, regions or nations that are landlocked.

Take Uganda and Kenya, for example. Uganda has no port and all exports travel on huge trucks along hundreds of kilometres of dusty single carriageway road. Follow the same trade route in the other direction and it takes you down into the heart of rural Africa: Burundi, Malawi and beyond.

Expect over $22 trillion a year of global trade by 2030, up from $13 trillion in 2015. The use of shipping containers has grown twice as fast as international trade, as companies seized the opportunity to be more efficient. But the container revolution is now complete, and so the growth difference will ease.

Regional trade will grow – and global trade will slow

'Outsourcing' jobs to low-cost nations is a controversial and sensitive subject, as I have discovered on my website and YouTube channel. Just mentioning the word can cause a massive hostile reaction on social media, mainly from people living in America who are scared by the rise of China, and think their jobs are threatened.

However, these people are behind the times. Ten years ago, many global manufacturers were stampeding to move their factories to China and other parts of Asia to save costs, while banks were shifting call centres and IT support teams to countries like India. Several years ago I predicted that outsourcing would start to go into reverse, which is exactly what has happened.

The simple model of outsourcing factory jobs from America or Europe to Asia is nearly over. Asia is becoming more expensive. Long supply chains are easily disrupted by sudden events. Cultural gaps, tariff barriers and varying exchange rates can often be troublesome. Local demand in Asia is also growing.

So we will see more clusters of regional suppliers, delivering components to make products that will often be sold within the same area. That is why 'south to south' trade will grow significantly (e.g. India to Brazil, China to Malaysia, or South Africa to Tokyo).

Such trade doubled from 12 to 24% of global trade from 2000 to 2011, and will increase to more than 40% by 2030. Half of all trade in Asia is already within the region itself.

A significant amount of offshoring is already being replaced by nearshoring or reshoring of manufacturing – 'jobs moving back home'. Jobs are also moving around Asia. So Intel has built a new $1bn chip factory in Vietnam, just a few miles from the border with China where labour is twice as expensive. Samsung has switched almost all manufacturing of electronic goods out of South Korea to many other lower-cost locations within Asia.

How to save money on logistics

At least 30% of all trucks on the road in the EU are empty, transporting nothing but air over 150 million kilometres a year. Tens of thousands of journeys a year are wasted carrying identical end products, components or raw materials in opposite directions from different producers, factories, warehouses – literally passing each other on motorways. Expect new websites to sort this out, and to become money-spinners.

We will also see great efforts to speed up shipping. Automated cranes can already unload a giant container ship and reload it in 24 hours, re-sorting containers on the dockside as the Post Office sorts letters and parcels.

Every day counts. An average delay of a week on the shipping time to a particular country can mean a loss of up to 25% of trade, depending on how time critical those deliveries are. It is often 20% more expensive to trade with a low-income country than a middle-income country, because of lack of infrastructure, red tape, slow customs, form-filling and maybe pressures for bribes to keep goods moving.

Paperwork and customs delays still account for over 10% of all shipping costs in many countries. We will see huge efforts by the World Trade Organisation and governments to solve this with secure electronic bills of lading and other freight records, together with wider use of electronic tags on every item.

Many emerging economies will also invest in combined rail,

road and port facilities. Mexico has spent over $220bn on such a super-hub in the past eight years.

3D printing – overhyped yet revolutionary

Custom manufacturing will grow – whether personalised clothing or high-speed development of prototypes using 3D printing. However, 3D printing has been much over-hyped. Around 10–20% of all homes in developed countries will own a 3D printer by 2040, but this will have very little impact on sales of pre-manufactured products.

3D printers are limited in the kind of materials they can print with, and in the size of what they can make. Next-generation printers will use raw materials that can be 'fired' in a microwave or domestic oven. Resolution depends on nozzle size, and the better the resolution, the longer printing takes. Home-based 3D printers will be too small to make larger products without assembling them from many different pieces.

Having said this, 3D printing is already a very important technology to prototype new engineering parts for an auto company, or for dentists to create false teeth. For example, with a 3D printer, Airbus can make a new bracket for an aircraft door using 90% less titanium.

Robots taking over the world?

Despite all the talk of robots taking over most menial jobs and putting tens of millions out of work, the growth of robots in factories has been slow – up from 92,000 to a mere 170,000 a year from 2000 to 2012. Compare this to growth of smartphones, for instance, and the pace is snail-like. Sales of such robots are likely to increase by around 7% a year – mostly in the auto industry, which owns most robots in America. Robots will become cheaper and more intelligent, but smaller models will still cost over $20,000 each in 2020.

Expect rapid growth in military robots – with tens of thousands of drones owned by the Pentagon alone, raising the prospect of swarms of small, flying robots being thrown into the air above a major battle zone, at a cost of less than $1000 each. However, they are not true automatons (yet), as each has a human pilot back at a military base.

Domestic robots are already here, of course – cleaning floors, for example – but other uses will be hard for consumers to justify, apart from control devices in things like heaters or fridges as part of smart homes. The biggest personal use of robotics will be in cars – self-parking is already well accepted as a feature of new vehicles, and self-drive will be common too.

Robots as personal servants or friends?

The greatest nonsense of all has been the notion that within a couple of decades, in most homes, you will find a walking, talking cyborg-type robot that smiles, tells jokes, does a range of household tasks, or helps with personal care, and becomes a close friend. The truth is that it will be many decades before such machines become cheaper, better and more acceptable to people than real human beings.

However, we will see major advances in devices that think 'intuitively', able to infer meaning from things. Google is investing a huge amount in 'Semantic Search', for example, which goes beyond the keywords you enter to try to understand what you are really thinking about.

We are still a very long way from being able to have a sophisticated conversation with a robot, on a wide range of themes, where you cannot tell if a human is replying or if it really is just a machine. Expect many more experiments, with far more realistic conversations by 2025.

Future of Asia as a global growth engine

When historians look back in 500 years' time they will record this period as the 'Century of Asia', built on manufacturing and cheap labour.

India and China will dominate our globalised world, with a third of world population, and relentless economic growth, driven by low-cost labour and emerging middle-class consumers. More than 85% of all the world's new graduates in science, technology, engineering and maths (STEM) over the next two decades will be from Chinese or Indian universities. Expect to see the same pattern in software development, medical research, business studies and accountancy.

Asia now represents over 40% of the world's GDP on purchasing power parity (PPP) terms. It is the world's factory with complex regional supply chains, smelting 76% of the world's steel and emitting 44% of global pollution. However, apart from giants like Toyota and Samsung, the region still has few truly global players. Expect this to change, especially in areas such as Chinese e-commerce, or Big Data companies in India, or biotech in South Korea.

Expect joint action by China and India on a growing number of issues by 2025, acting together as a powerful force in global politics. India's growth will be held back by poor infrastructure, while China will be burdened by its ageing population. Both countries will start experiencing severe shortages of highly trained managers, engineers, scientists and other groups, reflecting in a salary inflation of more than 20% a year for the fortunate few. Both nations will also continue to be affected by corruption.

Future of China – shifting from factory exports

China is a wealthy 'nation of nations' with a huge middle class, gigantic manufacturing capacity, its own dotcom boom, the world's largest high-speed rail network, and one of the best educated work-forces in the world. But China is evolving rapidly and for many globalised corporations manufacturing in China is becoming a rather old-fashioned idea, because of rising costs.

China is now the world's largest economy according to the World Bank, on the measure of purchasing power parity (PPP), which looks at what the local currency will actually buy, after adjusting for international exchange rates. But even on an absolute dollar basis, China will be the world's largest economy by 2024, propelled by a threefold rise in annual consumer spending from

$3.5 trillion in 2014 to $10.5 trillion by 2024. This will all be part of a transition from an export-led, manufacturing economy to a more balanced economy serving Chinese consumers.

As a direct consequence, global trade in the renminbi (RMB) will rise. It has already overtaken the euro as the world's second most important currency for trade after the dollar.

Expect consumer spending in China to continue to grow by at least 7% on average each year for the next 15 years, with occasional dips in the adjustment process. By 2025, China's consumer market will be three times larger than Japan's.

President Xi Jinping is becoming the most powerful leader that China has seen since Chairman Mao, with popular agendas such as stamping out corruption, breaking up state monopolies, faster economic reforms, greater equality and developing China as a powerful nation. We can expect him to run China efficiently, to a grand master plan with visionary investments for China's future.

China's leadership will do all it can to maintain economic growth above 5–6% a year for the next two decades, to reduce risk of civil unrest. It is likely to succeed. The memory of revolution is recent, strong and unsettling. Every adult in China aged 65 today has vivid memories of life as a young adult under the Red Guards and the Cultural Revolution led by Chairman Mao.

The workforce in China

As we have seen, at least 300 million of the poorest Chinese people will migrate to cities over the next 25 years, seeking a better life, and providing extra labour to compensate for the ageing workforce. A further 600 million middle-class people will be expecting better choices, personal freedoms, and will be increasingly strong in their private opinions about how their region should be governed, about pollution and corruption, size of their families or future well-being of their children. Expect China to further develop its own form of democracy, allowing regional voting for candidates with different policies, even if technically as part of a one-party state, within the limits of national policy.

China will continue to age as a society because of the one-child policy. Shortage of younger workers has been partly hidden by migration from rural areas. An additional challenge for China is that many families over the last 30 years have chosen to have a boy as a single child – either by selective abortion or in some cases infanticide. There is now a significant gender imbalance – 50 million women may be 'missing'. More Chinese men will look for a lifelong match with someone born outside China, using dating agencies and other means.

China will relax further its one-child policy, worried about meeting the needs of an ageing population, and about the lack of younger workers. The population of working age is shrinking by several million a year.

Regionalisation within China

There is more than one China: culture, tastes and fashions vary hugely from one part of the country to another, together with what is permitted locally. Over 400 million people do not speak Mandarin. Expect large companies to decentralise their decision-making within China rather than concentrate leadership in a city like Shanghai or Beijing. Expect more localised product development, branding and marketing.

Freedom of speech, religion and fertility in China

As we have seen, Chinese is already the dominant language of the web, and many of the world's greatest online companies over the next two decades will be born in China. Expect the government to continue to walk a narrow line between embracing the freedoms of the virtual world and wanting to control it.

Senior government leaders recognise that many profound changes are inevitable soon if the nation is to transition peacefully. They recognise that major unrest could be triggered not only by lack of jobs and lower economic growth but also by anger over corruption, inflation, inequality, pollution, over-zealous censorship and lack of religious freedom. The government also fears wider contagion from regional unrest in places like Xinjiang, among Muslim Uighars, and also in Tibet.

Stamping out official Chinese corruption

Expect rapidly growing numbers of arrests for corruption. Many suppliers of premium retail such as watches, perfumes and hotels have been hit by an absolute ban on expensive business gifts and extravagant lifestyles by public officials.

The fifty wealthiest members of China's National People's Congress are said to own more than $94bn. Expect many more probes into how and where leadership wealth was made. Over 250,000 officials have been prosecuted, removed from office or punished in other ways in less than three years.

Renewable energy will improve China's environment

We are already seeing investment on a vast scale into renewable energy, especially wind power, to reduce air pollution in major cities (and seize the global market in renewables). Expect far-reaching measures to reduce water pollution and food contamination. China now requires 15,000 enterprises to publicly report their air pollution levels, water use and heavy metal discharges in real time – until recently such matters were government secrets.

From export-led growth to domestic-market dominance

China's image as the factory of the world will change, as costs of manufacturing in China continue to rise. China will lose jobs to nations like Vietnam, Cambodia and Myanmar – even to Europe, Mexico and the US. China's future economy will be driven more by domestic demand from its own growing middle class, and by investment in new technologies such as high-speed rail, wind energy and biotech. Growth of retail spending in China is likely to exceed GDP growth by 3–5% on average over the next decade, as middle-class consumers save less, and draw down their assets.

China buying up the world

A growing part of China's sovereign wealth is being diversified into new investments in other nations: property, farmland, mines, factories, utilities and other infrastructure. Back home, expect booms and busts in Chinese real estate, with risks of a severe banking crisis due to poorly controlled lending and accumulated bad debts, particularly in the state sector.

We will continue to see bold, visionary moves by the Chinese government, resulting in giant industrial enterprises and breathtaking infrastructure projects. China will continue to spend between 6–8% of GDP on infrastructure for the next decade.

Territorial disputes and armed conflicts

Expect China to expand regional influence, largely through economic means, with a range of strategies. China is unlikely to be territorially ambitious, except in the case of sparsely populated islands, which would enable it to extract new energy or mineral resources. China will have challenges managing all the territory it already controls, including Tibet.

As with Russia, events from the Second World War are likely to continue to overshadow foreign policy, in particular the relationship with Japan. This particularly relates to alleged atrocities which are downplayed by many Japanese leaders.

Expect ongoing complaints by many global businesses and smaller investors that business is difficult in China. Expect some multinationals to pull out altogether, blaming a wide range of barriers to business including corruption, red tape, hostility by government to companies that take profits out of China, careless attitude to intellectual property, ruthless self-interest, lack of transparency in business dealings, etc. Revlon, L'Oréal (Garnier brand) and Yahoo were among the first to abandon China.

Chinese companies to watch

Alibaba – world's largest e-commerce platform, specialising in business to business sales.

Lenovo – bought IBM's computer business, now world's largest PC maker, bought Motorola's smartphone business and IBM's server business. Third-largest smartphone maker after Apple and Samsung.

Huawei – second-largest telco equipment company in world, banned from US and Australia public sector contracts over fears that its equipment could be used to spy on behalf of the Chinese government.

Xiaomi – China's Apple – smartphone and tablets; threat to Samsung.

Tencent Holdings – 650 million users of messenger App, fifth-largest internet company in the world in 2014 after Google, Amazon, eBay and Facebook. Highly innovative.

Baidu – main search engine in China, with 66% of market, fits in with government rules.

ZTE – one of world's 10 largest smartphone companies, also telco network equipment. Expect huge success for their ultra-low cost smartphones.

China's economy will be three times the size of India's in 2025, as it is today, but we can expect that India will close that gap in the longer term.

Future of India – growth of global services

India is a highly globalised nation of nations, the largest democracy on earth, and the third largest economy in the world in terms of PPP. India has a key advantage in international trade and service delivery because English is a national language, alongside Urdu and many other languages, unlike in China where English is hardly spoken.

Expect India's economy to grow 5–7% on average over the next decade. However, just as China is becoming too expensive a location for many multinationals in terms of outsourcing manufacturing, India is becoming increasingly expensive for outsourcing of services. Salaries are rising 3–5 times faster for senior managers in some sectors than in Europe or America. And as in China, India's long-term future will depend on growth of its own internal markets.

A single State, Andhra Pradesh, has over 200 million citizens, of which 75 million speak Telugu. Karnataka state has 52 million people, including Bangalore. The minister for health oversees no less than 114 medical and pharmaceutical colleges, while the minister for education has 15 universities, 131 engineering colleges and 600 industrial training institutions.

Young and highly ambitious, well-educated workforce

Half the population of 1.2 billion people are under 26, and this single fact will drive economic growth more than any other over the next 30 years. More than 66% of the national wealth is generated by India's 646,000 towns and cities, and this will increase rapidly with the arrival from rural areas of a further 300 million people over the next 25 years. Population growth is also the reason why income per head has remained much lower than China, despite national economic growth – more wealth but more mouths to feed.

India's central government will continue to exercise far less national power than in China, and this will mean fewer large-scale national programmes for energy, infrastructure, industrial parks, and so on.

However, India is a nation of industrious, well-educated and highly ambitious entrepreneurs, and is exceptionally well connected globally with hundreds of millions of people in its diaspora, often in highly influential roles across the world.

Despite outward signs of busy chaos, India will remain one of the best places in the world to make things happen fast. This is a country that is able to deliver from an empty concrete shell with no facilities a complete working call centre with trained staff and 24-hour video links to Europe, less than 12 weeks after signing a contract.

Religious caste and corruption in India

India will continue to be a highly tribal and religious society, with many internal tensions, particularly between the majority Hindu, Muslim, and to a lesser extent Christian, communities. Expect outbreaks of ethnic violence, triggered by accusations of favouritism by authorities to one group or another, particularly in periods leading up to elections. The caste barriers of India are becoming less severe, especially in cosmopolitan cities, but the whole caste system will look even stranger in future, in a global system that increasingly adopts human rights legislation.

Corruption will continue to hold India back, despite popular anger and calls for reform. It is institutional, and at every level – some estimate that politicians and government officials may be pocketing bribes of more than $3bn a year.

India's global status

Expect India's profile to grow rapidly. Indian influence and culture will also grow thanks to more than 200 million Indian managers and executives working around the world. India's voice is still missing at the table of the five permanent members of the UN Security Council, at G7 leadership summits, and so on. This is likely to change by 2030 as part of a restructuring of the UN and other bodies.

Future of America

While China has been a natural base for global manufacturing, and India for many global services, America is the dominant 'home' location, with 128 of the world's largest 500 multinationals, accounting for 70% of all global trade. China is rapidly catching up, with 95 already.

America remains in many ways the most globalised nation on earth, despite all the calls from activists for more trade barriers, and will continue to be a premier destination for well-educated, highly skilled migrants. America's future will be redefined globally by the emergence of nations such China, India, Brazil, Indonesia, Malaysia and the recovery of Russia.

At the same time, America will continue in some ways to be one of the most isolationist nations, partly a consequence of geography, with such huge distances to Europe, Asia or Africa. America's multinationals will continue to dominate global trade and services and America will also continue to be the only global superpower for the next 20–30 years, despite relative decline in GDP. America will continue to be self-confident and nationalistic, rallying around the American flag and other symbols of the American way.

America will take more than a generation to adjust to a more modest world status, as further global superpowers emerge. It will still be the case in 2025 that most US citizens have never owned a passport. This will mean that a new generation will lack experience of how people think and feel in other nations, which will result in lost opportunities, and will reinforce isolation.

Oil and health revolutions across America

The US is likely to become a larger oil producer than Saudi Arabia by 2020. Shale gas could add 3.3 million jobs and around $500bn a year to the US economy by 2020, depending on global oil prices.

America will continue a transition to health care mainly funded by the state (already the case today), despite much hostility to the concept of free care. As we have seen, the US spends 30% more per person on health than any other developed nation – around $750bn, of which up to 10% is lost because of fraud.

America will continue to be a gun-loving and violent society, compared with Europe. America has the world's third-highest murder rate per million people – beaten only by Honduras and Venezuela. Guns are used to kill around 10,000 people a year, and almost twice that number commit suicide using a firearm. Ordinary citizens own over 300 million non-military pistols, rifles, shotguns and machine guns – more than the size of the entire adult population.

Influence of race and religion on future US life

America will also continue to be deeply challenged at times by issues of racial equality and prejudice, and by the fact that 45 million voters now speak Spanish as their first language.

Over 11 million people in the country are illegal residents, and have been there for an average of 13 years. America spends $2bn a year keeping illegals in detention, more than on the prison service, and the nation spends more on immigration control than on all Federal law enforcement. Expect steps to be taken (eventually) to formally recognise most of the remainder as members of American society.

Despite a rapid decline in church attendance, America will remain deeply influenced by religion. Six out of ten Americans believe that God heals people in response to prayer. Four out of ten believe that God created humans just 10,000 years ago, and six out of ten oppose (almost) all abortion. Churches in America will tend to become much larger or much smaller, with a decline of medium-sized congregations.

Globalisation of retail and e-commerce

National and regional retailers are being hit by a wide range of global customer trends, each of which could destroy them in their present form. Indeed, every single trend in this book will affect retail to one degree or another.

Mega-chains will dominate retail growth

In many EU nations, over 70% of all retail spending is in just four or five retail chains, and across the EU as a whole, 50% of all food sales take place in just ten chains. In Germany, 37% of all food retail is now in budget stores like Lidl or Aldi. Expect to see a similar unstoppable trend in every other nation, driven mainly by global or regional retailers, unless governments pass laws to halt these semi-monopolies.

As a result of all this consolidation, national food and drink markets will be dominated by small numbers of central buyers, setting national prices for milk, or bottled water, or other basics. This will be a very tough period for local farmers.

National price wars will become regional price wars. Big regional chains will push some national food industries against the wall, because they are able to import huge volumes of lower cost (and possibly lower quality) alternatives from other nations.

Sales by chains in the EU have grown rapidly – by up to 25% over the last 14 years, but floor space has often grown at twice that rate, so productivity has fallen. And the value of total EU food sales has also fallen over the last decade or so. One reason is of course that more people are eating out more often. That could mean a sandwich in a coffee shop, or a restaurant meal. The fact is that living standards will continue, on average, to rise across Europe, so buying food to cook at home will become less important to customers.

Too many new stores

Across every type of retail we have seen more shopping centres and other new outlets built, but for every square metre of new retail space, another metre needs to close and will close. Therefore, we can expect pressure on rents for commercial retail space, and see the demise of huge numbers of smaller stores, as well as some hypermarket outlets. And that is without taking into account the growth of online sales.

Many large out-of-town grocery stores will close across Western Europe over the next decade, as middle-class shoppers shift away from large weekly purchases, to buying food several times a week from local stores, open 24 hours a day and owned by large chains.

Buying food 'just-in-time'

Around four out of ten adults in the UK have no idea by 4pm what they are going to eat later that evening. Impulse, grazing, and exploring are part of the daily leisure routine, even though this is an expensive way to feed oneself. But then the average supermarket shopper throws away up to 30% or more of the fresh food they buy.

Each community is different, and the most successful chains will use Big Data to predict different product combinations to stock in each local store for maximum sales. Over 60% of their trade will usually come from people who live less than 700 metres away.

Price, quality or brand?

Retailers will have to be clear about how they aim to grow. Competing on price alone will mean a savage fight to the bottom on profitability. Only the largest and most efficient retailers will survive such a contest, and many will experience huge profit losses in the battle.

Apart from scale, the only other reliable way for retailers to compete on price will be to stay very *small*, with tiny overheads, trading from local market stalls, on street corners, or using virtual equivalents such as eBay.

Future of supermarkets and food retail

Hypermarkets, supermarkets, convenience stores, corner shops, niche outlets – all are faced with similar challenges when it comes to selling food.

There are 7 key things that each can try to offer customers but it will be almost impossible to score highly on all of them, and still make a profit. To some extent, these same 7 factors affect every other type of retailing – whether fridges or carpets.

PRICE – SPEED – CHOICE – QUALITY –
EXPERIENCE – INSPIRATION – TRUST

So a convenience store may focus on speed and experience, while the hypermarket offers lower prices and better choice, and the premium niche store goes for quality, experience and inspiration. The middle market in groceries is going to be squeezed further by discounters as well as premium outlets.

But they all need to focus also on trust. Without trust a food store has nothing to sell, which is why reputation is vital in this industry.

Touch – smell – feel

One of the most important reasons that people shop physically rather than online is because they want to inspect what they buy, explore what is available. But the other day I wandered into a supermarket and found most of their fruit and vegetables in tightly sealed plastic packaging. Expect more stores to direct fumes from their in-house bakery into the store entrance, or offer tasting sessions with regional cheesemakers or wine experts.

Improve the customer journey through the store

Many superstore layouts are specifically designed to confuse customers a little, so they take longer journeys, which are constantly interrupted by end-of-aisle special offers.

I went shopping recently in a store I used to visit quite a lot. The entire layout had changed. Nothing was where I expected. I had to keep asking where basic things were like bread, milk and eggs. At every corner, a stack of unrelated products were shouting for attention – wine boxes with the milk and dairy section, chocolates and batteries in the fruit section. What a mess. Designed to encourage impulse spending of course but guaranteed to frustrate and slow down a considerable number of people. As we saw in Chapter 1, customers are becoming very, very impatient and every second counts.

Piles of stuff in the aisles on special offer may seem like a good idea to the team trying to shift that product line, but then you see customers bashing trolleys into each other because the aisles are partly blocked. These kinds of errors may have worked in the past and supermarkets may think they are being rewarded with additional sales, but in future they will find they are more likely to annoy and alienate customers.

Smart offers at great prices

Every large store should be using Big Data to create clusters of special offers, vouchers, discounts, sent to customers at home or on email or in SMS, based on things it 'knows' they will like.

Expect more retail chains across Europe and other nations to print price comparisons on every receipt, showing every customer how much their total bill would have been at 3 or 4 other main competitors. If customers have saved money, wonderful. If they have spent more than they would have done elsewhere, the store will print a voucher equal to the amount they are 'owed', to spend against their next shopping bill.

Specialist food retail outlets – many opportunities

We will see the return of the small specialist food store (at least in higher-income areas), satisfying customers who are looking for expert advice and inspiration from retailers who really know about their products – e.g. cheese shop, butcher's, deli.

Many niche stores of all kinds will be very successful (not just in food retail), offering specialist ranges of products to highly selective consumer groups for a premium price. The best specialist stores will do well, typically run by a single owner-buyer-retailer who hopes to have similar tastes, interests and style sense to its customers.

Street markets

Street markets will continue to be popular: providing buzz, energy, 'street atmosphere', local variety, niche experts, and constant variety. Expect larger chains to experiment further with trying to create market-stall atmospheres in parts of their larger retail areas, and large shopping malls to look to create street markets within their walls. All in response to the greatest challenge of all to traditional retail grocery stores – boredom. Same products, same look and feel, same experience. Customers want consistency, but they also need to explore and be excited.

Global e-commerce more than $5 trillion by 2025

Online sales are an even greater threat to traditional retailing than large chains or budget warehouses. Global online sales will roar ahead to more than $5 trillion by 2025, from $1.6 trillion today, with most transactions taking place on mobile devices.

Over 30% of all UK shopping apart from groceries is already online, growing at 10% a year, mostly via mobiles, and more than twice the level of sales per person as in America. E-commerce is also growing at 30% a year in Asia. It all adds up to the biggest change in retailing for a generation, and will mean huge pressure on all physical stores in mature markets like the EU. And as physical retail declines, so we will see lower tax revenues from business rates.

Forget about shopping online or offline. In future, online and offline will completely fuse into one activity. Online shoppers will be almost entirely mobile: just as likely to be placing an order on a train, sitting in the park, watching a film, or in a boring meeting at work.

Already one of the most common places for people in certain nations to do some of their online shopping is inside a traditional store – maybe comparing prices, researching, looking at customer reviews, perhaps ordering from the store's own website.

Expect new waves of disintermediation – where whole tiers of business get wiped out by technologies that allow people to go direct. An example is estate agents or travel agents, many of whom are being swept aside by websites that allow buyers and sellers to connect at the speed of light. The best will survive, but only because of their specialist knowledge and excellent websites.

Global premium retail

With over 500 million new middle-class consumers over the next 20 years, and rapidly growing numbers of super-wealthy, expect a boom in premium retail sales – whether of luxury handbags, fashion accessories, perfumes, gadgets, jewellery, lingerie, watches, fast cars or yachts. The global market will be particularly strong for aspirational brands like Rolls Royce, Maserati, SunSeeker yachts, and so on.

The majority of middle-class consumers in most emerging markets will continue to chase premier European or American consumer brands for the next decade. While we can expect several new global superbrands to emerge from India, China and Latin America over the next decade, most will struggle to engage top-end consumers in developed nations before 2025.

Some consumers will react against endless premium malls and airport retail areas, with identical collections of boring outlets for global brands, and favour niche brands instead.

Threat from your own online store

Cannibalism is a word we will hear more of. Here is a typical story from a mid-size retailer:

◆ Competitors with no physical stores are undercutting our prices on their websites.

◆ Our own website prices are the same as in our stores.

◆ We can afford to cut prices online and still be profitable, but risk killing sales in our stores, or enraging our partners who also stock our products in their own stores.

◆ As a result, we are shrinking in market share every year.

Most stores will be strongly tempted to stick with the same prices online as offline, risking future growth. Some retailers will experiment with setting up a completely new online channel to run cut-price sales separately from their own brand. Others will face the risks head-on and invest heavily in online discounting.

Overall, the result is that the volume of retail space will fall rapidly in the towns and cities of developed nations. Outlets that remain will need to offer something extra, appealing to the emotions of customers in order to make physical shopping feel worthwhile.

Google and other large players like Amazon and eBay will sweep up huge sales with instant displays of 'unbeatable' offers, matched to web pages recently looked at by customers. Many shoppers will never get past the first display line of a Google search. The same is already happening to the travel industry.

Future of Amazon, Alibaba and similar retailers

Amazon is the world's ninth largest retailer after companies like Wal-Mart, Carrefour and Tesco, with $74bn of sales a year, or $150bn if you include sales from other companies using it to sell their own goods. Amazon's assets are a global superbrand, with a simple website, and highly efficient warehousing and distribution, shifting a billion items a year.

Amazon's greatest *hidden* asset is its ability to provide any small business with its own e-commerce pages, created in minutes, with instant payments, cheap warehousing and fast delivery. Amazon already lists over 230 million items for sale in America alone – 30 times that of Walmart.

Two million businesses already sell on Amazon. This is likely to double by 2020. Most will sell exclusively through Amazon, especially where those businesses are able to shave a little off competitor prices. Amazon's revenues will also be boosted by pay-as-you-go cloud storage – already $9bn a year of sales.

Websites like eBay will create a new generation of young entrepreneurs, whose entire careers since junior school have involved buying and selling bits and pieces online – whether used toys, bikes and cars, or old china, camping equipment or spare solar panels.

Expect a boom also in micro-facturing – tens of thousands of home-based entrepreneurs who are making, marketing and shipping their own products, some using the most expensive 3D printers to fulfil orders.

Why home delivery is unfit for the future

In the UK, over 1.3 billion online products are delivered each year to homes – time-consuming because so many are not in when the delivery van arrives. We will see a boom in click-and-collect retailing across every developed nation, following extraordinary growth in Germany and elsewhere. Order online and decide where to collect: local garage or coffee shop. Every metro station in London will be a click-and-collect depot by 2017 – the process has already started. New delivery hubs will develop, shared by many online retailers and other delivery companies.

Many retailers will start to offer same-day delivery, for a premium price. A customer will place an order, which will be routed to the nearest store. Staff immediately order a taxi and get the package ready. The taxi uses a locator App to guide them to the customer, whether at home or work or in the local gym. For longer distances and higher-value products in rural areas, commercial drones will make the delivery.

Retail in emerging economies

From Uganda to Congo, India to Vietnam, we will continue to see an almost identical retail experience. Despite all the retail trends listed above, almost all shops for the next decade will continue to be the roughly the size of a single shipping container – never much wider or deeper or higher. One outlet next to another for mile after mile.

Such shops, typically with brick walls and tin roofs, are often the living rooms of the families who own them, and are their bedrooms at night. Lit by a single light bulb, such stores have an almost identical range of products as ten or twenty other similar shops within a few hundred metres. We see clusters of clothes shops, clusters of metal working shops, clusters of furniture shops. In fact, the most important rule in retail location has always been co-opetition. And this will be as true in the slums of a megacity as on the streets of Paris or New York. Jewellers will continue to cluster, fish sellers will cluster. Retail clustering will dominate physical retail globally for the next 100 years, as it always has done.

Malls will take off in all emerging markets

At the same time, expect growth in top-down mass-retailing in emerging markets, despite e-commerce. Big companies will invade a completely new area where there has never been a single store a fraction of the size before. The first mall in a new area will usually be relatively informal, not air-conditioned, housing smaller shops. And then premium malls will follow, identical in many ways to malls in Europe, Singapore, Beijing and North America, and at international airports.

Expect radical changes in retail in emerging economies, therefore, particularly in India, with hundreds of millions of middle-class consumers, tens of millions of small retailers, and very little retail space at the moment that is not a container-sized box.

Boom in informal retailers

Alongside container-sized outlets, shopping malls and open markets, expect hundreds of millions of informal retailers to provide a significant proportion of total sales for many local products such as water, soap, rice and flour – selling at traffic lights, on the pavement and from bicycles or small stalls. The key for every maker of lower-cost products in megacities will be these networks of informal agents.

Manufacturers will divide more products up into tiny packages or bottles, to use for a single day or week, for those on very low incomes (bottom of the pyramid). Hundreds of millions of informal retailers on the street will be children in 2025 – street selling will often be their only means of survival. This will cause moral outrage in tourists from wealthy nations located many thousands of miles away, who think that all child labour should be banned.

Retail in Latin America heads online

Latin America is also experiencing an online revolution with more than $100bn of sales, including $6.2bn in Mexico, growing 40% a year. In Mexico 58% of adults have online access compared to 46% in Brazil, 67% in Argentina, 59% in Chile and 34% in Peru.

Most consumers in the region are very uncomfortable about buying online, because they do not trust the payment system, but that will change fast. Most online sales are still on websites owned by traditional retailers but the big threat from pure online retailers will really begin to be felt by 2019. Sales per online user each year will grow fast – already averaging $600 across Latin America: $900 in Mexico, $750 in Brazil and $450 in Argentina.

How will Latin Americans *pay* online? Few people have credit cards or bank cash cards, so newer types of payment will take off. PayPal, for example, is already used for most online sales in Mexico. A hundred million people in Latin America are likely to move straight into a PayPal or mobile payment world, having never had a bank account or plastic card before.

Most web sales will soon be on mobiles in Latin America

Mexico saw 6 million new mobile users in 2014, and smartphone sales averaging 49% a year. In addition, 60% of 25–34-year-olds own a smartphone. In Brazil, most online sales are influenced by what people read on their mobile devices.

The number of middle-class consumers in Latin America has grown by 50 million in just 10 years, and their needs will be met by larger retailers. In Brazil 56% of the population is now middle class, totalling 113 million people. We are seeing the same pattern in Chile, where you will find Latin America's largest shopping mall – Costanera. In Peru multinational retailer Cencosud opened fourteen huge new retail stores in a single year.

Future of financial services, banks and insurance

Globalisation depends on free movement of money for goods and services, and financial services will therefore follow many of the retail trends we have seen above.

Finance, trade and digital technology all go together. Many predicted the death of banking as we knew it, following the 2008–2013 crisis, but our world needs strong banks just as it needs hospitals and schools. Banks are fundamental to every civilised society.

When a financial institution's reputation dives, the end soon follows. At the height of the crisis in early 2009, a friend of mine who owns a global business ordered a van to drive around the country containing around $2m in cash 'just in case'.

Trust is the most important thing a bank has to sell

Without trust you have no bank. You could say that trust is the only thing a bank really has to sell. The rest is tinkering with products and services. The fundamental issue for many banks I work with is how to rebuild trust after scandal upon scandal, with billions of dollars spent in fines and lawsuits. This will require a revolution in culture and day-to-day behaviour – we will look more closely at this in Chapter 6.

Banks and their shareholders have been punished, mocked, blamed by societies. Owners of banks have lost huge amounts of money. But the main owners of bank shares are of course pension funds, so all of us have been affected. We can expect more global regulations to force banks to hold more capital, with lower limits on the levels of risk-taking. But if regulation is too severe and returns on investment fall too low, no one will invest in banks, banks will be poorly led, bad to work for, with old technology, vulnerable to hacking, and providing last-century levels of service.

Rise of third millennial banking

Common sense will prevail in banking. Investment banking is being separated from retail and corporate banking. We will see further regulations. But we can also expect to see some regulations relaxed by 2025. New types of banking services will also evolve, with ingenious work-arounds, enabling better investment returns with better managed risks.

Many predicted the decline and fall of the City of London as one of the world's dominant financial centres. As I said at the time, this was overstated. The City will continue to be one of the world's most important communities of the smartest and most experienced financial experts, from over 100 nations. The City will also continue to be one of the greatest generators of GDP in the UK. However, even 5 years after the onset of the financial crisis, the sector was employing 20% fewer people than before.

Future of retail banking

Retail banking will become far more mobile, automated and highly competitive. Banks make profits by collecting and hoarding cash, and lending at interest. But when cash itself ceases to exist, what then? In an electronic society there is nothing physical to collect or give out. Old-style banking becomes a meaningless concept, used to describe a defunct industry that now trades not cash but electronic impulses. In future you will buy any financial product, via any channel, from just about any source you could imagine.

As we will see later, banks will become telcos, and telcos will become banks, along with a string of new non-banking competitors who have all applied for banking licences in Europe and elsewhere.

Instant mortgage switching

Most senior bankers I talk to recognise it is only a matter of time before a mortgage will be switched from one lender to another by an authorised broker, with a single mouse click. Once the legality is established, expect such loans to be moved up to several times a month by broker robots constantly looking for better deals on identical terms. It will spell the death of traditional lender-borrower relationships.

Revolution in peer-group lending

Expect rapid growth of peer-to-peer lending, social lending or crowd-funding websites. Already $5bn is lent on such platforms each year and this will probably rise to more than $25bn by 2020, $60bn by 2025, with average savings of at least 1% on interest rates from banks. Peer-to-peer lending is just a small fragment of the rapidly growing 'shadow banking' industry, and regulators are slowly catching up. Crowdfunding platform Kickstarter alone is raising over $3m a day for entrepreneurs. In the past, such lending has been by individuals to individuals, but hedge funds and other financial agencies are piling in to provide lending capital.

Boom in micro-loans and savings associations

One of the most radical and exciting innovations in banking is micro-loans. I have seen at first hand across different parts of India and Uganda the extraordinary impact of micro-loans on the poorest of the poor. There are now over 10,000 micro-finance institutions worldwide, growing 15–20% a year, and serving 200 million people, 25 million of whom are in India, with a total of over $50bn in loans / savings. Consider that in India alone over 500 million people have no access to banking. Globally the figure is over 2.5 billion.

A while ago I met fourteen women living in a slum area who formed a savings group in Delhi. The agreement was that each person saved money each week, recorded in their own book. After they had saved for a number of months, they were able to take a loan for up to four times the amount they saved, with 12 months to repay ten instalments. Such a scheme means you are borrowing off other members of your own community, and each person in your group is guaranteeing all fourteen loans. Typically, over 97% of all loans plus interest are repaid on time. These loans are used to start small businesses.

Micro-loan schemes are usually profitable, popular with many governments and are a gateway into traditional banking as well as micro-insurance products. Millions of savers have now been through two or three loan cycles and are proving creditworthy to traditional banks. That is why many investors are entering the market.

Future of corporate banking

High-end corporate banking will remain people based, including treasury management, global money flows, advice on mergers and acquisitions, multi-currency, and multinational deals. Low-end corporate banking will go the same way as retail, moving to mobile, with a wide range of web-based portfolio management tools.

Future of private banking

Private banking used to be mainly wealth management for older, typically female, customers (because women live longer), with whom private bankers often had a long-term advisory relationship. New private banking clients will typically be younger, hyper-connected global citizens, micro-managing their affairs and with highly complex and rapidly changing business needs, demanding responses day and night at the speed of light.

A growing area for private banking will be philanthropic advice. Private bankers help make wealth for their clients faster than most can spend it, which creates a problem, since most clients are worried about spoiling their children or grandchildren, and cannot invent enough new ways to use the money themselves.

Great wealth is usually toxic to the well-being of children and family harmony. There is no evidence that people who have great wealth are happier as a result. Indeed, most research points in the other direction, and this is confirmed by my own experience of working with ultra-wealthy families. Great wealth brings its own pressures: family anxieties about maintaining the wealth, worries about personal security, tensions with non-wealthy relatives, fears about children being spoilt by wealth, or even abducted. Great wealth can distort *every* friendship – are they only interested in me because of what I own?

Expect to hear more about social enterprise and impact investing – where the purpose is not just to make money but to do something that has a positive impact on society or the environment, even if the returns are lower than with other forms of investment.

We are likely to see at least $10bn set aside by some of the world's wealthiest, over the next decade, to tackle a range of important issues, following the lead set by Bill Gates, Warren Buffett and others. We will look more fully at the growth of philanthropy in Chapter 6.

Why cash has such a long future

Despite predictions by bankers and 'digital gurus' about a cashless society, cash has never been so popular in many parts of the world. Many people love cash: for its anonymity, convenience and speed – and because it is invisible to the tax man. Cash use will continue to grow in the EU until around 2025, despite huge handling costs for retailers and banks.

Between 10% and 20% of all earnings across the EU are untaxed, depending on the country. Such informal cash transactions are now reflected in official estimates of the size of each nation's economy, along with revenues from illegal drugs and prostitution. (The latter is worth at least £4.5bn a year to the UK economy alone.)

EU nations with the largest 'shadow economies' include Belgium, Spain, Italy and Greece. The higher the tax burden on employers and workers, the more widespread tax avoidance tends to be. India's untaxed earnings percentage is at least 20%, if you include 85% of all workers who pay no tax. China's is probably around 10%.

Expect rapid growth of virtual cash: untraceable, anonymous units of value such as Bitcoin, traded across the internet. Virtual cash will be hated by governments, because it underpins the dark web, and is used to trade drugs, buy arms, pay ransoms, hire assassins or fund terrorists. China has already banned Bitcoin and we can expect other nations to follow – while the rest will seek to regulate or tax its use (which will be difficult).

Future of e-payments

We will see more than 200 billion web payments a year by 2025, up from around 50 billion today. A third of all such payments today are on smartphones, but this proportion will rise to at least 70% by 2025. As we have seen, most e-commerce transactions in the UK are already on mobile devices.

Most retail payments on mobile devices take place not in Europe or America but in Africa. And for several years, most m-payments in Africa were in Kenya, where over a third of GDP is already traded each year using the M-Pesa alone. Around 25% of the entire population of Africa already has a mobile money account of some kind – compared to only 2% in Latin America. Africa has redefined retail payments, and Asia will be next. Take Singtel, for example, which has around 430 million registered SIM cards in its customer base, including partners. Of that, maybe 200 million are unbanked, with no access to financial services. I expect that up to half of these will carry out their first m-banking transactions over the next 5 years.

Free telco-banking

As we saw in Chapter 1, the cost of providing free phones, tablets, bandwidth, video calls and so on is falling rapidly towards zero. The cost of biometric ID is also falling, and it will soon be impossible to buy a smartphone without finger print recognition.

At the same time, revenues that can easily be captured by mobile payments are increasing fast, as mobile payment systems become more widely used. When you combine the two trends, it becomes clear that there will soon come a point where companies will offer free smartphones, video calls, voice calls, mobile computers, broadband, perhaps even throwing in free TV and movies – on condition that customers only use a specially set up smartphone for payments. Indeed, it is already starting to happen.

But that spells the end of telco contracts. It also means the end of traditional retail banking. The most important and urgent question for the board of every large retail bank and telco is this: When telco and banking fuse into one, who on earth will own the customer relationship?

The answer is not the bank. At least, not without partnership, or without huge gaps in understanding what the customer is actually doing.

As we have seen, one of the most important things to know about any mobile customer is where they are right now. But banks are blind to location. They may have credit card and current account statements, but this only tells them about yesterday. They desperately lack the live intelligence that only telcos own. What is more, the same telcos also see every web page, every search term, which Apps are downloaded, who the person calls and when. So we can see that hybrid companies, telcobanks, may be able to gain a huge advantage in owning the customer, combining the insights from telcos with a wide range of next-generation financial products and services.

Fight to own the new global standard

As we have seen, scale is everything in a global world, so there will be very few winners in telcobanking. The telco company Qualcomm has dominated mobile phone technologies for 2G, 3G and 4G for many years. So much so that up to 70% of its costs are legal, defending patents. In a similar way, there will only be room for maybe two or three mobile payment systems.

Expect a huge fight among consortia of banks, telcos and IT companies, seeking to impose their systems as global standards. The prize will be billions of dollars in royalty payments, from every financial institution, retailer and telco, for the following two decades.

We will see many new alliances between telcos and financial services, like Vodafone's with Visa and Nectar, in the race to create these new global platforms. We will also see campaigns by companies like Apple and Google to promote their own payment systems as the new global standard.

A key complication, however, is that if a telco seeks to become a bank, it immediately becomes subject to all kinds of limitations on the amount of capital it uses, its reserves policy, and so on, in places like Europe and America. This may mean that most innovation in telcobanking is pioneered in emerging nations.

Why most banks are far too small

You could say that banks are primarily IT companies, trading electronic bits of data, plus a few financial experts and advisors.

A primary vulnerability of banks, therefore, will be IT failure and attack: loss of confidential data, hacking into bank accounts, total systems failure including 'denial of service' attacks.

The trouble is that IT complexity and vulnerability has raced far ahead of IT budgets. In many banks, most efforts by IT departments are spent trying to get old 'legacy' systems to talk to each other. Each merged bank brings its own IT history, usually with unresolved mess from other legacy systems.

Not a single person who understands the code

In many of the world's largest banks there is not a single person alive today who has a full grasp of all the IT systems, and how they inter-relate. Code may have been written in old computer languages that hardly anyone uses now. Bugs may exist that no one understands, in areas of code that nobody knows about. Inter-dependencies are often overlooked. These are all reasons why it can easily take over 7 years to fully sort out the mess from a single merger.

This may all seem rather shocking to someone outside the retail banking world. It can also lead to bizarre gaps in customer insight. For example, I met a senior leader of a large bank the other day who complained that no one could tell her how many retail clients they had who were over a certain age (at least, not without adding up different estimates on a spreadsheet).

It means paralysis instead of agility. It means slashed budgets for mobile Apps, tablet-based banking services or next-generation products. Indeed many banks are unable to rapidly roll out new online products on their existing platforms, because of these incompatibility issues. They are gridlocked by their past. Yet these same banks may be busy embarking on yet new mergers.

Security costs are soaring

To make matters worse, security costs have rocketed, and banks have an increased number of new compliance requirements following the recent crisis. As we have seen, large banks are seeing more attacks every month than they used to see in a year only 5 years ago. They are also having to deal with huge numbers of thefts from customers who have been tricked by phishing attacks, using rogue bank web pages.

Then along comes a highly innovative, customer-focused, software company like SalesForce, with a development budget of $3bn a year, spent mainly on cloud-based call centres, that can set up in a matter of days. Using their system, a bank can transform customer experience overnight.

One must conclude, therefore, that a bank with a total IT budget of – say – only $900m a year, of which $820m is spent on legacy systems and security, is not likely to survive the next generation of mobile banking. Their IT development budgets are just too small to keep pace with customer expectations.

Even harder for retail banks to grow

But how do banks grow much larger, to achieve the right economies of scale in IT innovation, without being completely overwhelmed by yet more legacy problems? One way forward will be to create partnerships, either with software houses or with other banks in non-competing territories. Expect all kinds of new IT innovation alliances between – say – banks in Europe and Asia.

Some banks are starting to dump entire existing IT systems for retail customers, migrating them in stages onto completely new modular platforms, where new products can be bolted on as simply as installing a new App, and where there are fewer complexities and unknown horrors for attackers to exploit.

Future of shadow banking

As we have seen above, our world needs banks, and easy flow of money between those who want to lend and those who need to borrow. If regulation screws up a vital part of the banking system, you can be certain that a more lightly regulated, unconventional way around will be found. And so it is that shadow banking has grown.

Shadow banking caused the last financial crisis, and is likely to cause another. Shadow banking is a term given to a loose collection of companies that are providing services similar in many ways to some of the things that banks do. So they may package up and sell on loans. Shadow banking may include hedge funds, private equity funds, brokers for state loans, and so on.

Because these groups are hard to define, they are hard to regulate. And governments are less anxious to do so than with banks, since there is much less risk that failure will result in failure of a bank. Losses are more likely to be limited to a set of larger investors, rather than a million retail customers.

Future of pensions and fund management

Fund management will be responsible for a new mis-selling crisis at some point over the next decade, with fines and lawsuits likely to be so large that they will break some of the world's largest investment banks. Expect global reforms of fund management and the pensions industry.

This is an industry with awesome global power. Black Rock alone has $4.1 trillion of directly controlled assets, and oversees a further $11 trillion through their Aladdin trading platform. Over 17,000 investment managers and traders around the world are influenced by Black Rock's analytical models to guide their decisions. That means a single error could trigger a massive cascade.

A 12-year survey of 2,846 mutual funds in America, overseen by 1,825 fund managers, showed that even managers who remained in the industry long term (presumably with the best performance) had no ability to beat the market on a risk-adjusted basis. All these fund managers use the same sources of information in most cases, and tend to focus on the largest stocks, so they find it hard to out-do each other (unless they break the law by insider trading).

Fund managers hate investing in actively managed funds

I have spoken to audiences of hundreds of fund managers over the years, with up to $1 trillion under management in a single event. Only a small minority would ever dream of recommending their own actively managed funds to their own friends and family, because they know very well that these funds usually destroy wealth, compared to ultra-efficient, low-cost computer trackers. This is a major moral issue, which calls the whole industry into question.

Yet despite all this, only 11% of global fund-manager assets are in tracker funds. Expect more legislation, enforcing transparency, capping fees, imposing additional compliance costs so that smaller funds become less viable. The number of fund managers employed globally will fall rapidly, and many smaller funds will be forced to merge.

New models of investing

We will see more boutique services allowing smaller retail investors to manage their own portfolio of investments in tax-efficient ways, right up to full pension provision, with live reporting data. Charges for such services will be low.

Younger high-net worth clients will invest less in large institutional funds and will use their own family offices more to manage their wealth.

Pension funds are likely to invest more heavily once again in hedge funds, but complexity will continue to create new risks. Pension funds will focus on hedge funds that are more easily understood. Expect a severe public backlash against hedge funds if we see failures of several more over the next few years.

Death of national stock exchanges

The days of traditional stock exchanges are coming to an end, though much more slowly than I predicted 15 years ago. Companies don't like them because their global business is greater than a single exchange, which leads them to multiple listings. Investors don't want them – they want to trade online 24 hours a day. Technology doesn't need them – because a single server in one building can handle all the mouse clicks.

We are likely to see many more stock exchange mergers, across national boundaries and regions, to reduce technology costs, share marketing and increase liquidity.

Over 70% of all trades on Wall Street are not 'real' trading decisions at all, but are made by robots owned by just 2% of 20,000 trading firms, reacting automatically to all kinds of data, sometimes with strange results. High-frequency trading also drives 30% of EU trades in fractions of seconds. The new trading kings are mathematicians who fine-tune such algorithms.

In 2014, the AP News Agency was hacked and a false tweet sent: 'Breaking: two explosions at the White House and Barack Obama is injured'. Within milliseconds, trading computers on Wall Street detected key words and made instant sales. The Dow Jones fell 140 points, wiping out $200bn of capital. The hack was exposed within minutes and prices recovered, netting the criminals huge profits.

Speed will be everything. Robots will continue to fight against robots to get trades executed a fraction of a millisecond before each other, which will require constant upgrades of ultra-fast cabling by trading companies, and many other techno-tricks. For example, some companies are using microwaves to transmit orders faster than other traders, who are still using old fibre-optic cables.

Growth of spread-betting

We are also seeing rapid growth of 24-hour spread-betting websites, where individuals or companies bet on a share price movement taking place, without owning any shares. A million people in the UK alone have spread-betting accounts, with bets usually placed by smartphone, encouraged by full tax relief on all 'winnings'.

Bets are being made on the future price of any share, commodity, fund or currency. Many people will win or lose huge amounts in this global casino, as gains and losses are highly leveraged. A single £10 bet could win or lose £1,000 if not capped. All these kinds of 'derivatives' will create strange price movements, which at times will be very violent, confusing and destabilising.

Future of insurance industry – huge growth

Insurance is as fundamental to a stable and prosperous society as banking, hospitals and schools. Yet more than 3 billion people have never heard of insurance, do not know how it works, and have no idea how to get hold of it.

Expect rapid growth, therefore, of basic insurance in emerging markets, targeted mainly at the emerging middle class. Health insurance will lead the way, after insurance types that people are forced by law to buy, such as motor insurance. Expect a boost in many nations in sales of life or health products, encouraged by tax rebates, especially where they are structured to contain an element of saving. Many who are unbanked today will gain their first insurance cover using a smartphone, or through micro-loans groups and savings associations.

EU retail insurance dominated by home and motor

Most insurance sales in the EU will continue to be cover for homes or vehicles, with travel and life insurance following behind. Expect savage online competition from so-called aggregator sites that display competing quotes for the same risks from up to 300 different companies.

These sites are already seizing over 40% of the general insurance market in countries like the UK and we can expect a similar pattern in many other developed nations by 2020. Insurers will be able to win sales without offering the lowest price, but only by persuading customers of the value of a 'favoured' brand, to pay out when there is trouble, to handle a claim rapidly and sensitively.

Price comparison means fines for loyalty

Aggregators will provide a very precise mathematical tool for marketers to measure their own brand value. If the cheapest quote from an unknown company is $150, but the customer selects the third one down the list, which is a well-known brand offering a price of $230, then we know that the 'added' value of the brand to that person is $80.

European insurance companies often offer very low prices for new customers, making their profits in the following years by increasing prices for their loyal customers. Expect growing numbers of customers to switch companies every year – to whichever insurance company is the most willing to throw money away with such unsustainably low pricing.

Why many insurers will detach from banks

Many banks experimented a decade ago with their own insurance companies, hoping to 'cross-sell' insurance products to existing customers, but in most cases the results were disappointing. Most insurers will remain independent of banks, with partnerships and syndicates but all held at arms' length. This is even more likely in future with different and complex regulatory requirements for each.

Re-insurance will be a vital part of the future of all large insurers, backed by huge corporations like SwissRe and MunichRe. These companies will be taking views on every trend and Wild Card in this book (see p. 18), how they interact, what it all means for, say, business disruptions over the next decade in a particular industry, or for the risks of New Orleans being hit by another huge hurricane, or Russia invading Kazakhstan.

Future of the travel and hospitality industry

Along with manufacturing, retail and banking, the travel industry will be a fundamental engine of future globalisation. Human beings are genetically programmed to travel as hunter-gatherers, and have an irresistible urge to explore. Therefore, whatever happens to the global economy, and in other world events, we can expect the number of people travelling each day to grow dramatically as wealth increases, and as real costs of transport continue to fall.

The greatest growth in travel will be within Asia, and in people from Asia visiting outside their own region. We will see a rapid increase in the number and size of regional airports, high-speed rail networks, and new roads.

Future of rail – high speed, long distance

Twenty-four nations have already built high-speed rail links, and the length of high-speed track is doubling every decade. At present 98% of all trains running faster than 195km/hour are found in Western Europe or East Asia (90% in China, France, Japan, Germany, Italy,

UK and Spain combined), but high-speed rail will become more widespread.

In a decade, China built over 10,000km of high-speed track to become the world leader. Much of this was imported technology, with trains from companies like Siemens. However, the next wave of expansion will be almost entirely Chinese, and Chinese rail expertise will be exported globally.

Future investment in high-speed rail will be held back in Africa by unrest, in Russia by economics, in the UK by planning restrictions, in China as the backbone of a national service is completed, in Latin America by economic uncertainty, and in the US by a culture that prefers planes and cars.

Expect a boom in low-tech, rapid transport in cities, with automated 'light railways', or trams, or buses on special concrete tracks. These will be built rapidly, at relatively low cost, on pillars above streets, as tracks weave their way around cities.

Numbers of rail travellers will grow much faster in most countries than growth in capacity, so trains will become longer, double-decker, more crowded and more frequent.

Future of aviation and air travel

Expect boom-time for aviation – with short-term blips caused by recessions, regional conflicts, threat of viruses or other adverse events. The number of journeys each year has grown ten times over the last 40 years to over 3 billion. Expect this to increase to 6.4 billion by 2030.

Most growth of aviation will be in Asia, and least in Europe / North America. Europe will see huge growth in long-haul visitors arriving from Asia, particularly from China and India. Chinese tourists travelling outside their country will double to 200 million a year by 2020, and their spending on vacation will triple, especially on luxury goods.

Boeing is sitting on a backlog of orders for over 5,100 planes valued at around $400bn, while Airbus has orders to build 5,600 planes, worth even more. Engine-maker revenues alone will be more than $1 trillion over the next 20 years. Over 70% of engines today are made by GE or CFM, GE's joint venture with Snecma in France, just another example of monumental scale in a globalised world.

Britain is the second-largest aerospace manufacturer after America, with 17% of the global market, and is home to 30% of Europe's Eurospace firms – Rolls Royce engines are used in half of all the world's new wide-bodied jets, BAE makes fighter jets and AgustaWestland makes helicopters.

While virtual working, video calls and other technologies will grow, they will not be enough to prevent growth in absolute terms of business travel, as I predicted a decade ago. Business budgets will be capped, however, or cut, forcing business travellers to hunt for bargain flights, flying economy as a general rule unless long haul.

Cheaper flights in real terms

The aviation industry was changed profoundly by new budget carriers, who completely re-invented the process of selling tickets, filling and emptying planes. Expect all major budget airlines to begin to offer premium features copied from traditional airlines, such as allocated seats, a free drink in-flight, free luggage allow-ances. This will attract increasing numbers of business travellers.

European budget airlines will carry more than 50% of all air passengers by 2030. As a result, all traditional airlines will be forced to radically alter how they work. Expect mergers of national carriers, and new global mergers.

Flying on less fuel – but most things look the same

New planes will become more efficient, and will fly with fewer empty seats. Flights will use less fuel per passenger because of smarter air traffic controls (including 'free routing' to allow pilots to fly directly from A to B, saving 10 minutes per flight on average), and shorter circling times around busy airports. Expect continuous GPS tracking of all commercial flights by 2018.

However, planes will look almost identical in 25 years' time, because of fundamental limitations imposed by aerodynamics, passengers and freight-handling. Indeed, aviation has gone *backwards* in some ways since the launch of Concorde in 1969, flying passengers between 1974 and 2003 at supersonic speeds of up to 1,334 miles per hour (2,140km/h), at a maximum height of 60,000 feet (18,300m).

Passenger experience will hardly change at all over the next 30 years. Most planes built in the last 40 years have a life expectancy of more than 30 years, or more than 30,000–40,000 flights. So most passengers in 2030 will be flying on planes that were already in use in 2015, maybe designed decades earlier. Jumbo jets were first built in 1969, for example, and some will still be used for long haul in 2025.

Future of cars: cheaper, faster, cleaner, smart

More than 1 billion cars are on the roads today. But we would need to see that rise to 4 billion for the whole world to have the same level of car ownership as America.

Most new car owners will be in emerging markets over the next 50 years. Chinese people are driving 150 million cars, many owned by 40,000 car rental companies. Private car ownership in China jumped from 1% to 19% from 2002 to 2011, with 150 million new cars sold in 2015,

Around half the population in the Philippines and Indonesia do not yet own a car, compared to only 3% in Malaysia, where 53% of households own more than one vehicle. In Thailand and Indonesia 80% of consumers intend to buy a vehicle in the next two years, and in most cases this will be the first car they have ever owned.

We will see significant increases in fuel efficiency, with use of nanotech coatings for all moving parts, and many other advances in engineering, as well as lighter vehicles. These gains will undermine (but not halt) the growth of pure electric vehicles.

Electric cars have taken off more slowly than many manufacturers and governments hoped, held back by expensive batteries. However, battery price per kilowatt hour is set to fall rapidly. New types of battery will be lighter, more efficient, with faster charging and longer life. Some Tesla cars already have a battery life of 400 miles and 600 miles will be quite normal by 2025. Most sales of electric vehicles over the next decade will be smaller models designed for city use, encouraged by tax breaks for owners and subsidies for manufacturers.

City cars will be different

However, traffic jams in many larger cities will be a growing nightmare, especially in emerging nations where car ownership is growing far more rapidly than road construction. Drivers and passengers spend 90 billion hours a year in traffic jams. In some cities, a third of all fuel consumption is used simply in trying to find a parking space.

We will see new patterns of car use. Mobile Apps will make it even easier to hire and drop vehicles for long and short journeys, at very short notice, and easier to hire a car with a driver (despite legal challenges to Taxi Apps like Uber). We will also see more tax breaks, traffic lanes and other incentives to encourage car sharing by commuters as well as more car leasing.

Self-diagnosing and self-repairing cars

It will soon be impossible to buy a car that is not online all the time, or has the potential to be. Laws in the EU, North America and other parts of the world will demand it. For example, all new cars in Europe will very soon be required to send instant breakdown or accident information to the police and rescue services.

Brazil will soon require every new car to have a built-in tracking device to prevent theft. America's highway agencies are working on proposals to force all new cars to have the ability to network with each other (Vehicle to Vehicle or V2V). Revenues from services, devices and infrastructure for online vehicles could be worth more than $200bn by 2025.

Cars will also self-diagnose problems before they happen, with sensors across every part of the vehicle to monitor tyre pressure, brake pads, piston compression, battery condition, gas emissions, power use. We will see more head-up windscreen displays, with speed and fuel indicators, and a wide range of informatics including navigation and messaging.

Cars will also watch driver behaviour, so that insurers can price each day's premium on yesterday's driving patterns for that particular driver. This will help people to drive better and at lower cost, because insurers will reward good behaviour.

Who owns the driver?

Drivers will expect all these new features to be thrown in for the basic price, so manufacturers will be stuck with more costs, without clear benefits.

As in the telco and banking debate, the key issue will be who owns the customer? Indeed, who owns the vehicle? Manufacturers will try to hit back with a one-stop solution. So, for example, they will send details of breakdowns, faults or accidents directly to their own dealers, rather than to local garages.

Car dealers will offer a far wider range of ownership or leasing options, as motorists begin to move away from the traditional 'buy and keep' pattern. On the other hand, telco companies, makers of networking devices, producers of driver Apps and V2V services will all build their own clusters of interconnecting technologies. They will try to push back manufacturers into their original roles as makers of 'mobile travel boxes' only. Mobile phone companies will also form new partnerships to offer vehicle packages with smart-phones and other technologies.

Semi-automated cars will soon be almost universal

Apple and Google both want to control the car dashboard, and manage networking between cars. The vision is that cars will form their own social networks, constantly exchanging useful informa-tion with each other without bothering the driver at all. Live traffic information, common mechanical problems in particular models, best fuel prices, updates to maps. V2V communication will even-tually mean the end of traffic lights in some cities, as each vehicle perfectly times its own approach to every junction.

Mercedes-Benz is already selling its Intelligent Drive system, which automatically steers, brakes and accelerates in traffic moving at less than 60km per hour, using ultrasonics and radar. Mobile Apps will soon display or control almost all car functions on some car models, except steering and brakes.

Self-driving cars – with legal issues

Several companies will soon be selling self-driving vehicles, but they will not be widely used on busy public roads outside European cities, America and Asia until at least 2035, because of fears about public safety, and because of regulations. In the meantime, expect rapid growth in use of self-driving farm tractors and industrial vehicles, for example in open-cast mining. But in cities, it will only take a couple of highly publicised deaths of child pedestrians to slow down the introduction of such vehicles for a decade in some places.

More than 1.3 million people die in road traffic accidents each year (more than deaths from malaria or TB) and 50 million more are injured. The big question is this: if a robot kills a pedestrian or an occupant in another vehicle, whose fault is it? Who goes to prison? Is it the vehicle owner? The manufacturer? The software company that controls the robot?

A key argument will be this:

Robot drivers make fewer mistakes, so even if people are killed by robots from time to time, fewer will die than if humans continue to do all the driving.

However, the death rate on roads is 250 times higher in the poorest nations, where the technology will not be working. And very few people get killed on roads in developed nations. One thing is clear: robots will be severely judged.

Homeless cars and car trains

In the world of driverless cars, you will step outside your home to find the car roll up (you have no idea where it parks itself – who cares?). You don't own it (a really last-century idea), but it feels like yours. You watch a video or take a call, and relax as the car weaves through traffic, safely taking you to work.

A variation will be 'car trains' where many cars are driving in a controlled convoy, just a few metres apart, each automatically following the car in front, unless directed to break out by the driver. Many cars already have sensors to maintain distance from the car ahead on motorways, or to park automatically in a tight spot.

So-called flying cars will still be very rare and expensive in 2030, owned only by the super-wealthy, and only permitted outside major cities. Single- or double-seater flying cars have folding wings, which allow them to be driven in a somewhat clumsy fashion on roads. Typical flying speed is 100 miles per hour, a range of 400 miles, and a top road speed of 35 miles an hour.

Space travel and colonies on other planets

Space tourism will grow, with at least three companies carrying up to 1,000 passengers a year into space on short flights by 2035, despite recent setbacks. Watch out for Sierra Nevada Corporation, SpaceX, Orbital Sciences Corp and possibly Virgin Galactic. This will be yet another example of an increasingly bizarre and unequal world, where some people play around in orbit, while 1 billion still lack clean water or enough food.

We will see a new Space Race, dominated by China and Russia, with some American and European action, aiming to send people back to the moon, also to Mars (almost certainly a small group of people on a one-way ticket at first). Expect a small residential unit on the moon by 2040, but with no useful economic purpose. America's exploration of space will be limited almost entirely to unmanned probes, with almost all additional energies devoted to space-based defence. An important new justification for space budgets will be the claim to be able to deflect or destroy comets that could be on a collision path to earth.

Most spending on space over the next two decades will be on satellites in geostationary or lower orbits, with upgrades to GPS, to allow devices to be located within 10 centimetres. Space will become a potential battle zone, with hundreds of space drones. These will be used to repair, capture, interfere, hack or destroy satellites – and also to destroy drones from other nations.

Most such drones will be owned by America, Russia and China. America has spent $98bn in a decade researching ways to knock out intercontinental ballistic missiles, but with very limited success.

This is even more difficult when any satellite could be a drone in disguise, and when any low-orbit drone could contain a nuclear device and a targeting mechanism.

Future of hotels, holidays and medical tourism

The number of people taking more than one annual holiday will more than double over the next 20 years, with soaring numbers enjoying city breaks. It is already the case that around half the UK population takes at least three holidays a year away from home – whether elsewhere in the UK or abroad.

Expect many more culture holidays, exploration holidays, learning holidays, activity holidays. Expect growing popularity of holidays involving risk, excitement and experience, offering extremes of hot and cold, ranging from the United Arab Emirates to Greenland or Iceland, with strong emphasis on eco-aspects or sustainable tourism.

Older travellers look for new experiences

Middle-aged and older travellers will particularly look for experiences they will never forget, pushing their comfort boundaries, to achieve a lifetime ambition. Examples might be deep-sea exploration of wrecks, travelling to the heart of the Antarctic, learning to sail a large yacht, learning to fly a glider, or climbing a high mountain.

Cruise ships will grow in number and size, carrying over 45 million passengers a year by 2025, compared to 22 million today. These ships will be based mainly in the Caribbean and Mediterranean, with some growth in Asia and to exotic locations such as the Antarctic. Many ships are already so large that they have become destinations in their own right, with over 6,000 passengers and 2,500 crew. Larger ships are already restricted in the number of ports that can cope with them, so we will see a boom in cruise docking stations, particularly across the Mediterranean, Caribbean and Asia-Pacific.

The average age of cruise passengers is likely to fall by a further 5 years over the next decade, as more families try out the experience, offset in the following decade by growing numbers of older people in many nations with money to spend. Expect growth in smaller, specialist, themed cruises for older customers who want culture, history and expert learning, or to learn new skills such as painting.

Impact of web on travel agents and airlines

Websites like Airbnb will transform the hotel and hostel industries globally, by creating a vast informal market for people who want to rent out a room or their entire home, matched to others who want a low-cost and more personal alternative to a hotel. This will eat into the growth of budget hotels in popular cities, but they will still expand globally, offering 100% more rooms within a decade.

Traditional travel agents are in free-fall, and will be almost wiped out in many parts of the world by 2030, except for niche specialists. Everything they offer will be available online at the same or lower prices, and they will be unable to make sufficient revenue from commissions.

Many package holiday companies will also face meltdown, driven to the wall by clever travel robots that assemble complex combinations of hotels, flights and car hire at the speed of light, and at unbeatable prices.

However, the best tour companies will do well: offering expert insight into poorly known destinations in exotic places, specialist guides, well-constructed journeys and extraordinary experiences.

Future of education – new ways to learn

School and college is all about preparing a new generation for a global, rapidly changing future, training people to think, giving them a broad understanding of the world, providing useful job skills. In many cases, we will be educating young people for jobs that have yet to be invented, but most education is locked into the past, training people for tasks that no longer exist. It is the same whether the school is private or state funded.

Take examinations: how absurd to force young people to scribe indelible symbols onto pieces of paper with ink, and to lock them into rooms without access to their digital brains.

In their daily lives now, and in their entire working lives in future, they will be using completely different skills. For a start, work means keyboards, not pen and ink, and people that cannot type are unable to do most office jobs.

The whole basis of education will be questioned. For example, there is the growing irrelevance of memory in many areas of life. What really counts is understanding how to make sense of a constant stream of data, picking out patterns, seeing context, and knowing which sources to trust. The skills that really matter are: rapid search/collate/interpret/analyse/summarise/conclude/ decide. Of course we do need memory too, on which we base all our experience, but not in order to regurgitate facts.

Radical change to teaching methods

Classroom teaching has hardly changed in 50 years, apart from the introduction of digital whiteboards and more use of personal computers. The world of the classroom has been completely left behind by young people, who are constantly learning about people, life and current affairs via their ever-present mobile devices. Which of course are one of the first things to irritate a teacher in class, and are often confiscated as a result.

Expect rapid expansion of new learning tools, including short, interactive video clips, designed to fit precisely into the curriculum.

In education, one of the worst crimes has been plagiarism: where a student copies paragraphs from another source. But in business, if an executive has to assemble a report very rapidly, about an area they know little about, the issue is not whether the whole report is *original*, but whether that report is *accurate* and *useful*.

Tougher rules for schooling

Expect a return to single-sex schools in many areas where co-education has resulted in tens of thousands of boys dropping out. Expect persuasive arguments that single-sex education for both sexes means sharper concentration and fewer distractions or showing off, especially with the age of puberty falling to eight or less in some girls.

Expect a complete rethink about punishment and discipline, with the recognition that a no-touch policy isn't working in many nations. In many schools, the playground culture can be threatening, bullying and even violent, not only to pupils but also to staff. A high percentage of teachers in state-funded schools across the UK, for example, have been threatened with violence or have been attacked on school premises, at one time or another. Expect strident calls for teachers to be able to teach without fear of attack from pupils or parents. Changes will come in small steps, following particularly awful and well-publicised events such as the death of another teacher or the death of a pupil after savage bullying.

Expect tough new sanctions, including greater freedom to suspend or expel pupils for antisocial or violent behaviour. Expect growing expenditure on special needs schools for the most disruptive pupils. Despite the trend to try to integrate the worst behaved with the best behaved, mainstream schools will not be able to risk keeping all their most disruptive pupils, as the emphasis grows on getting results. Expect continued ghettoisation in schools, with people choosing a state school in a 'nice area' and then working out which home to buy nearby.

Future of universities – big shift to Asia

University education will be dominated globally by India and China, who will each produce many times more high-quality graduates in many disciplines than the rest of the world put together. Despite this, many of the best Asian students will head for top European or American Universities, to broaden horizons and forge networks.

Lecturers will be judged not just by the intellectual content of their teaching, but also by how they use technology to communicate. People need to taste the future, reach out and touch it with their hands. 'In-your-face' experience is worth hundreds of hours of private study. Expect an anti-reaction by a small number of 'eccentrics' who will make a deliberate point of not using any technology to present, relying entirely on person-to-person interaction, maybe using flip charts, or non-digitised dry-wipe boards.

Free access to lecture videos – so what are you selling?

All universities will be faced with a huge dilemma – along with every business school. Do they record lectures by professors and other faculty? And, if so, do they place those lectures online for students on the closed university intranet, or make them publicly available on sites like YouTube? And if they do go down this route, will anyone still want to attend the physical lecture?

Universities like the Massachusetts Institute of Technology (MIT) have recorded lectures for years, giving them away online for free, and others will be forced to follow. I have been doing the same for over a decade, recording entire keynotes wherever I can, and publishing online wherever possible.

Some business school professors fear that their material will be 'stolen' or otherwise abused, but experience shows that free online access makes business sense as well as being the 'right' thing to do. As a result, we will see astonishing growth in the quality and range of free education, available to the poorest in every nation, so long as they have online access. Of course online publication does put extra pressure on any lecturer who never alters or adapts their material from year to year, so these academics will be forced to adapt.

The above will be a great challenge to providers of distance-learning courses. With this type of course, students are typically given passwords to lectures and online course materials, in exchange for a huge amount of money, for which they get someone to mark essays, a few video tutorials, and perhaps a residential week or two each year.

So what is the answer? As we have seen in previous chapters, people want to breathe the same air, and learn from each other in groups. Group experiences have great power to change people profoundly, especially when a group is together for a year or more of study, with strong emotional bonds. So physical tutorials, workshops, seminars and lectures will continue to be important.

Videos are great for *information* but useless at *transformation*. That is why business school professors should feel more relaxed about giving their material away. Students around the world may browse their recorded materials online, but that will not be a full substitute for the disciplines of a shared learning experience in the classroom, during which formal teaching as well as discussion will take place.

Universities and business schools will focus increasingly on *personal transformation*, interactive learning, rather than groups just listening to experts, and on building educational tribes, to survive.

Education gets longer (and longer, and longer)

Despite the growth of informal online education, most people will spend even more time in formal education by 2030. We have already seen how parents are hot-housing their children from their first year. At the other end, job markets are now so competitive that students are being forced into second or even third degrees, in the hope of standing out in job interviews. In many cases it is also because their first degree turned out to be useless when it came to the workplace.

However, most first, second or even third degrees (including business school MBAs) are very poor substitutes for a year or two in a really stretching business. And as the cost of degrees soars, with less and less government subsidy, more people will question the real value of a degree. A four-year college degree in America now costs up to $160,000, including food and accommodation. But the real cost is more than doubled by the sacrifice of four years' average earnings. It's a fine balance, of course, since without the degree they may not be able to find a decent job.

Countries like South Korea and Malaysia will rapidly expand their engineering and biotechnology courses, reflecting strong government commitment to expanding industries in these areas. Numbers of students for courses such as music technology or anthropology will fall in countries like the UK, as more statistics are published showing disastrous employment records for those who opted for such degrees.

Future of consulting, accounting and law firms

There are very few global consulting and accounting firms, and this is already causing big problems for regulators who are unhappy when the same companies are auditing the same accounts for years. We should be worried when auditors are from the same organisation as consultants, when huge companies find members of their international teams involved on both sides of complex deals. It is hardly surprising that so many audits of multinationals have turned out to be so misleading and useless.

Arthur Andersen disappeared almost overnight as a result of the Enron scandal, and it will only take *one* more such event to create a crisis, because only three global firms would remain. Expect further regulations about companies needing to change their auditors every few years, and more restrictions on potential conflicts of interest.

Auditors will be strictly audited

Auditors will find that they are increasingly held responsible when banks or insurers or other types of company fail spectacularly, soon after being given a clean audit report. It is outrageous that global auditors have been able to walk away without any penalty, from large companies that collapse, only days or weeks after they have been paid hundreds of thousands of dollars to vet them for accounting irregularities and hidden financial risks.

Auditors will be called more strictly to account in future for such appalling failures in their own processes, for giving false and dangerous assurances to investors, based on far too narrow a view of the viability and stability of the business. Auditors will no longer be able to hide behind the 'standards of compliance' in their audits. They will be expected to probe for the *truth*, to ask the difficult questions, to place their own reputations (and even existence) on the line in the robust assurances they give.

Big Bang deregulation for law firms

Law firms will also be forced to change radically in some countries like the UK over the next decade, mainly as a result of deregulation, allowing non-legal companies to raise money from markets, to provide legal services. Few so-called global legal firms are structured in the right way to support the future needs of global companies. They are often led by senior partners who are professionally expert, but may be incompetent in a global CEO-type role.

The procedures of large law firms are often very antiquated, and their mind-sets parochial. The most important question for a global law firm to answer is this:

If we were building a large law firm from scratch today, would it look like us? And if not, how can we fix the gap rapidly?

Legal services move to mass-market budget retail

We will continue to need global law firms as clusters of legal experts able to take a view on highly complex issues, particularly across territories. However, expect to see rapid change in how smaller-scale legal services are delivered, with a growing trend to 'retail legal' teams, operating out of call centres, shopping malls, and so on, or completely online. Many kinds of standard legal practice can be automated with relative ease – including aspects of employment law, buying and selling property, making a will, divorce proceedings, personal injury claims, and so on. One-off legal advice will also be increasingly offered online, either using chat screens or email correspondence, or in video calls.

At the same time, more countries will follow Australia and the UK in deregulating their legal services. This will allow non-legal firms to offer such services, and teams of legal experts to raise capital in the markets. Over 300 companies registered to provide legal services in the UK in the first 2 years of deregulation, so we will see many new kinds of commercial organisation offering expert legal advice, in a highly efficient, rapid and customer-friendly way, breaking with all the familiar ways of doing things. We will also see more outsourcing of basic legal services by larger legal firms in developed nations, to teams in countries like India.

Law itself will change profoundly over the next two decades, influenced by every trend in this book, but particularly by issues that we will look at in the next two chapters: new politics, governance, activism and ethics.

Future of diversity and innovation – for global insight

To manage in a universal world, we need universal teams, but the reality is that corporations are often too tribal. Most large companies are monocultural: dominated by nationals from the country in which they started.

While this can bring strength – loyalty, team spirit, better communication and faster decisions – it also carries huge risks, particularly in a globalised world. Monocultural leadership is more likely to miss the best investments or partnerships in new territories, more likely to make mistakes in managing country risks. What is more, monocultural teams are very unattractive for people from other nations or regions to join.

Key to innovation will be more diverse teams

Among CEOs of large corporations, 85% say that diversity is the key to innovation. More diverse or universal teams tend to find more ways around problems, more solutions, better alternatives. Diverse teams are better connected across markets and communities, less likely to have blind spots, more able to identify new opportunities, more likely to have a wider range of skills and experience, and more likely to draw highly talented people. Diverse teams are also more likely to understand a broader range of customers. We will also see more open-innovation or crowdsourcing, where teams from diverse companies or communities collaborate widely in problem solving.

Diversity is therefore one of the most important keys to business growth, and one of the least well managed. Most large companies tend to focus (often rather superficially) on gender – to increase numbers of women in senior positions – but are blind to all other aspects of diversity.

More women, ethnic minorities and foreign nationals in senior positions

Gender will certainly matter. In many developed nations like America and the UK, girls outperform boys at school, and women outperform men at university. Most new doctors in many countries are now women. And we see the same in many business schools: most of the best applicants for MBAs are female. Yet few board members are women, and women leave corporations every year in significant numbers. Expect a wide range of measures to change this, some forced by regulation, for example, gender quotas on boards, as are now being imposed on corporations in Germany.

But the focus needs to broaden beyond gender. Take senior management in the UK, for instance, which is almost entirely white, even though a growing percentage of the population is Asian, African, Afro-Caribbean or from other non-white ethnic groups.

Repeated surveys show how many barriers there are for ethnic minorities. These are often caused by entrenched racist attitudes, many of which may be totally subconscious, in 'decent', 'tolerant' people who would be horrified to think they were in any way biased.

This whole issue will matter more in future, not only as an issue of justice, but also for customer insight and marketing. How can you provide world-class support to a customer group that you do not properly understand? How can you underwrite risks accurately in a community you have never been a part of? Increasing diversity is therefore one of the most important ways for leaders to grow their companies, stimulate innovation, reduce risks and increase customer loyalty.

So, then, we have looked at a fast, urban, tribal and universal world. To many people, the picture may seem more or less complete, but two more Faces of the Future remain. A world driven by radical agendas and ideologies, where every decision will be influenced by a rethink about ethics, values, personal motivation and spirituality.

Chapter 5

RADICAL

AS I PREDICTED 20 YEARS AGO, radical, revolutionary forces are sweeping across parts of our world, and will continue to do so for the next 30 years. A cluster of 'democratic' revolutions swept away the Soviet Union from 1989 to 1991. For a while, Western governments talked about a peace-dividend as they cut military spending.

The collapse of communism left an ideological vacuum, with no balance to a Western narrative of capitalism, materialism, free speech, human rights and free market thinking. Only one superpower remained, and it became a self-appointed policeman of the world. This helped unleash new radical forces, many of which are resentful of and intensely hostile to America.

Dotcom delusions of an age of global tolerance

A decade later, at the height of the dot-com boom, many technogurus made predictions that global access to the web would make our world more tolerant. It would democratise society, undermine dictators and contribute to global harmony. They forgot the power of tribalism; how the web amplifies radical voices, and how social networks create viral, unstoppable people movements.

They also failed to see that groups like Islamic State would effectively manage to restrict web access in territories they control, broadcast their own terrifying propaganda on social media, torture and kill hostages, discourage journalists from entering the region, and make it almost impossible to know what was really happening in their part of the world. And as we have seen, control of the web is strengthening every day, across entire nations such as China and Russia, now affecting over a third of humankind.

Rise of radical activism and extreme ideologies

For almost two decades I have described the growing impact of radicalised activists and how they would change politics in many nations over the next 20 years. And that is exactly what we have seen. Activists driven by extreme religious ideologies, by hatred for a people or a country, by single issues such as climate change, immigration, animal rights or independence.

So what about the next 20 years? Where will radical forces take us next? What will be the impact on politics or religion or consumer choices? How will your own life be affected?

Radical ideologies will feed future terrorism

Terrorism has always been the radical edge of political activism. As in the past, most terrorist groups will continue to be relatively small, tribal, informal, fragmented, mobile and short-lived. Most will be local rather than globalised, using any means to frighten, sabotage and attack for the sake of a cause, seeing themselves as moral freedom fighters.

Much of the recruitment to terrorist movements is fuelled by a narrative about rich versus poor, freedom from oppression, and anti-Western culture, all amplified by social media.

For obvious reasons, terrorists always tend to seek greater power for less effort, with an eye on what will capture the most social media attention. School shootings and bombs in shopping malls serve that function.

We will also see more economic and anti-corporate terrorism directed at things not people: spiking of food products in shops, cutting of optic cables, damage to huge satellite dishes, creation of computer viruses – and more state-funded terrorism as conventional wars become more difficult and expensive to fight.

Tomorrow's larger terrorist groups will be interested in things like germ warfare agents that can threaten city or countryside yet be carried in a briefcase.

One in 350,000 risk of death from terrorism

Despite the impression we might get from watching news channels, the actual numbers injured or killed in terror attacks will remain almost insignificant compared to all other causes of deaths. The lifetime risk of witnessing an act of terrorism will remain effectively zero in most parts of the world. So the real vulnerability to terrorism will come *not* from physical threat, but from *irrational fear*.

Deaths from all terrorist attacks globally are less than 20,000 a year, of which most are in Iraq, Afghanistan, Pakistan, Somalia, Yemen, Syria, Lebanon, Libya and Nigeria. Globally, that is an average risk of 1 in 35,000 of being killed each year, which is the same as the chance of being struck by lightning at some point in your life. But if you live outside the most troubled parts of those nations, or in other parts of the world, your risk falls to 1 in 350,000 a year.

Thus the greatest challenge in future will be to restore a sense of reality, so that people can go about their lives without exaggerated fears.

How to ensure future terrorists cannot win

Eventually, it is likely that the public hysteria portrayed in the media over individual acts of terror will subside to a more rational and pragmatic response, recognising that the greater the reaction, the greater the win for the terrorist.

Media provides protest groups and tribal factions with huge coverage at zero cost, allowing them to hijack national agendas, and disturb the well-being of millions. One could say that placing stories about terrorist acts on the front page or at the top of TV news bulletins is counter-productive, because it gives terrorists exactly the reward they long for.

History shows that all communities hard-hit by terrorism go on to develop psychological resilience, to the point where each new terrorist act causes less impact. As we have seen in Iraq, under the most terrible of circumstances, in cities where risks of car bombs are a daily reality, most people decide that life must go on. They drive to work and shop in the local market.

In other nations, we have seen the same. By the end of the Second World War, 25% of all houses in London were damaged or destroyed, mostly by random bombs raining down from the sky – but life went on. It was the same in German cities that were hit repeatedly by RAF bombing raids.

During the height of the IRA terror attacks in the UK, daily life also continued. One bomb was so close to our home that it shook our windows. Another missed killing our eldest daughter by minutes. But none of us changed our daily routines – as a matter of principle. Why let terrorists win?

Why democracy is in trouble

It is often said that a week is a long time in politics – a reflection of how government leaders can be overtaken by events – and terrorist attacks are just one example. One thing is certain: we should continue to expect political volatility, radical changes and instabilities.

Only 40% of the world's population lives in nations with free and fair elections, and many democracies have moved towards autocracy over the last decade. Examples include Russia, Argentina, Venezuela, Ukraine – all hold regular elections, but have strong controls on media and opponents. South Africa's ANC has become increasingly hard to challenge, for example. In Bangladesh, Thailand and Cambodia, opposition parties have refused to accept election results, or have boycotted the process.

Few nations have long experience of democracy

Surprisingly few developed nations have long democratic traditions. Democracy began only in 1978 in Spain, 1975 Portugal, 1946 in Italy, 1918 in Germany (with interruptions under the Third Reich), and 1956 in Greece, following its ancient Athenian invention, but the army soon took over.

New democracies can fall apart for many reasons. One is that the first free election results in a government that blocks further such elections – for example, election of an Islamic party that promised that its first action would be to form a theocracy, with clerics in power 'forever'. And in new democracies, the party that is elected often fails to realise that it cannot ride roughshod over the wishes of those who didn't vote for it.

In America, the system of checks and balances now produces gridlock rather than preventing abuse of power, leading to what has become an annual budget crisis. And in Western nations generally, faith in democracy has been weakened by a combination of government scandals, paralysis, political in-fighting, bloated government spending and debt, and by unpopular military adventures. Trust in elected politicians has never been lower. Huge lobbying budgets and immense campaign spending have also created worries about whether entire democratic systems are being corrupted. For example, there are twenty lobbyists for every member of Congress in America, and spending in the last US presidential campaign was more than $1.3bn.

Within the European Union, Italy and Greece were forced in 2011 to replace their own democratically elected leaders with technocrats, who were more obedient to the rule of Brussels.

At the same time, countries like China have proved to the world that a nation can grow in a stable way, generating huge economic growth, without democracy. In 2013, 83% of Chinese nationals were very satisfied with the direction of their nation, compared to only 31% of Americans.

Democratic governments will rapidly lose power

Across the world, most democratically elected governments are likely to find their power reducing – for ten reasons. As a result, it will be even harder for them to deliver on their promises. We can expect many national parliaments to weaken, and confidence in democracy itself will be undermined further.

1. **Privatisation.** In the past, governments owned and controlled electricity, gas and water companies, national airlines, post

offices, railways, health services, telecommunications, and so on. In every part of the world, state-owned companies are being sold off. In the old days, politicians could make bold promises with reasonable confidence; today, however, in many areas they have to defer to corporate power and the markets.

2. **Regionalisation.** Regional trading blocs take freedom from member nations, who agree to be bound by agreements. The European Union, in particular, will take even more power from member governments, and will impose many thousands of new regulations over future decades.

3. **Decentralisation.** A total of 160 national governments have now made their own central banks independent of government control – up from just 20 in 1980. At a stroke, all these governments gave away control of interest rates and other aspects of monetary policy.

   Elected governments across the world have also given added powers to local government and city mayors. This process will be accelerated by separatist groups, immigrant communities, independence movements and religious activists (some of whom want to impose their own laws e.g. Sharia law based on the Koran).

4. **Unelected civil servants.** One of the greatest causes of inertia and paralysis in governments over the next two decades will be the civil service. Governments come and go, but almost all publicly paid employees remain. They often have natural resistance to radical policy shifts. To make matters worse, the civil service no longer attracts large numbers of top-calibre graduates in the way it used to several decades ago.

   We can expect many governments to try to politicise and shake up the civil service by controlling more of the most senior appointments. However, this means that senior civil servants will increasingly find their promotion blocked, making lifetime civil service careers even less attractive.

5. **Globalisation – big firms gain powers.** As we have seen, in a globalised world, governments are unable to impose higher rates of tax, or stricter labour laws, or tougher environmental

controls without the risk that global corporations will just move elsewhere. The same will apply to entrepreneurs. There is intense global competition to attract investment and talent.

Internet companies find it particularly easy to shift profits to low-tax nations. For example, Google cut its tax by $2bn by routing earnings through Ireland, Bermuda and the Netherlands.

Many super-corporations are larger in economic weight than some entire nations. They can dictate terms to governments, set agendas for commerce, and form global monopolies, dominating local markets. This is a major reason why nations like India, China and America have been so reluctant to allow foreign multinationals to own majority stakes in key national companies.

6. **Lack of strong leaders.** And while remuneration packages for CEOs in industrialised nations remain so much higher than for prime ministers or presidents, many governments will also find themselves crippled by serious lack of brain-power and leadership talent.

Surveys show that very few of the brightest and most talented leaders would dream of wasting their lives in 'democratic politics'. Why enter a profession that is (almost) universally despised, has no real power, no job security and is badly paid compared to what could be earned elsewhere?

Many choose instead to run corporations rather than pretend to run countries. As a result, many democratic governments will continue to be led by slow, feeble-minded and incompetent teams. Lack of talent in politicians is perhaps the greatest threat of all to healthy democracy, which then feeds public contempt of the entire system, leading to further decline.

In contrast, government posts can be extremely attractive in an autocratic state, where leaders enjoy far greater powers to get things done, are subject to less scrutiny, have greater privileges and higher salary, and greater job security (if you keep in favour). But even autocratic states are increasingly undermined by global market forces.

7. **Activism and social media.** Non-government organisations

are becoming more numerous, better funded, and better at campaigning, using tools like social media. Their lobbying can upset law-making, overturn budget decisions and block government action. Expect many more campaigning websites like change.org, which allow people to create instant petitions – some of which attract hundreds of thousands of supporters in weeks.

8. **Crisis of trust in politicians.** Trust is the only thing that any politician has to offer. But what is the point of voting when you cannot believe the words of a manifesto? In the UK 62% of voters say that politicians 'tell lies all the time', a view shared across the European Union. Who cares about well-used phrases such as 'big society' or 'public service'? Only 1% of the UK population still belongs to any political party, down from 20% in 1950, while 27% of EU voters in 7 nations say that they have 'no trust in government'. In 49 democracies around the world, voter turnout in elections has fallen 10% in the last 25 years.

   As I described in my book *The Truth about Westminster*, despite the constant political fights in the news, the fact is that most politicians agree broadly on most things. That is why it is so rare for a new government to reverse legislation that they bitterly opposed before they got into power. So there is lack of integrity in most political debates.

9. **Small majorities or unstable coalitions.** In many democracies we see instability and weakness, where no single party has a large enough majority to lead strongly. Even worse, sometimes it is only possible to govern at all by cobbling together two or more political groups with very different agendas. For example, coalition governments in Italy have often collapsed in the space of just 2–3 years.

10. **Individual politicians elected by minority of voters.** When there are many different candidates, a member of parliament can be elected by only a small minority of voters. Yet such an individual may end up making all the difference between a coalition government continuing or collapsing.

These ten factors also raise questions about what government is for? What is the purpose of government and of national leaders in a world where so little of their previous powers remain? We can expect a great debate about this in many nations over the next decades: big government, small government, virtually no government, centralised or decentralised government, and so on.

When faith in ideology and parties dies, trust in the person is all that's left. Leaders rather than policies will therefore tend to dominate the future of politics in democracies. So we may see some surprises, where a party with a really odd set of policies is elected, because people trust the leader to make the right things happen.

Future of dictatorship and one-party states

Benign dictatorships can serve many emerging nations well. Autocrats have powers to get things done, that elected politicians can only dream of. One-party States can embrace elements of the democratic process, as we have seen in regional Chinese elections for many years. Therefore, for all the reasons above, democracy turns out not to be a one-size-fits-all solution to the political problems of the world.

As history reminds us, dictators can survive only by popular consent, or with the support of the army and secret service. And at some stage they usually like the status of being elected, even when observers dismiss their election as fixed. Nothing will change here – especially the obsession with the size of their election 'victories'.

Dictators are becoming weaker

Dictators who use oppression and brutality to impose their will on their people will increasingly find that it is hugely costly to their nation: capital, investors and talented people will flee; the currency and the economy will collapse.

However, there may be a cushion for dictators or autocrats who are sitting on huge mineral or oil wealth in places like the Middle East. And it is in the Middle East, therefore, that we can expect the most radical experiments in theocratic dictatorship, propped up by oil revenues in defiance of the rest of global market forces. In most cases such theocracies will simply be the replacement of one form of dictatorship by another.

Impact of radical single-issue campaigns

We have seen how governments will be increasingly vulnerable to single-issue campaigns, which rapidly attract national attention, and force changes in policy. However, the same will also apply to larger corporations.

The boards of every high-profile company can expect to meet single-issue activists at annual shareholder meetings. CEOs need to know how to handle people hanging from ceilings, running naked down the aisles, shouting and asking awkward questions.

The upside is that single issues will also be used to increase sales. In a world where almost all products and services are becoming similar in price (falling) and quality (rising), the only way to differentiate from the competition is with values. Consumers become galvanised around a radical single issue, and cause-related marketing means selling to people who believe in the cause more than the differences in the product.

In the US 93% of consumers prefer companies that are helping the community (up from 84% in 2010) and 90% are more likely to buy products linked to causes they care about, assuming price and quality are equal. Staff want to be proud of who they work for. Expect tens of thousands of new partnerships between businesses and charities to market products of services for mutual benefit.

Consumers are asking more questions

Globally, over half of all middle-class consumers say that they are willing to pay more for products and services from companies that are committed to positive social and environmental impact – up from only 10% in 2011. In America, the figure is 42% across the whole population, compared to 7% in 2011.

This is a momentous change. We can argue about percentages in any particular nation, but I have followed the overall trend for

20 years, and it is a very consistent picture, although there was a partial reversal in the depths of the 2008–2013 economic crisis.

As a response to all this, large companies now spend almost $2bn a year on different causes, sponsorships, and so on – aiming to 'do well by doing good'. Institutional investors are also adding their own pressures. Indeed, in nations like the UK, they are required to; pension funds have to show that they are investing in ethical ways, which has boosted shares in the so-called Footsie4Good index.

Abortion will continue to be a big issue in the US

Abortion in America is a typical example of a radical single issue: pro-choice versus pro-life. From 2008 to 2011, the percentage of doctors willing to conduct an abortion fell from 22 to 14%. The church-dominated anti-abortion movement in the US is now bigger than the civil rights movement of the 1960s. Tens of thousands have been arrested, cautioned or imprisoned, while many pro-abortionists have been threatened, assaulted or murdered.

Abortion is just one example of the fact that single issues can become more powerful than the laws of the land. Here is a great nation with laws that permit abortion but where abortion has been made almost impossible in some states. In one state, at the height of the protests, it was hard to find a single doctor willing to conduct abortions.

Vision for theocracy – God-centred government

We are likely to continue to see a huge difference between radical Christianity and radical Islam in terms of their visions for governments and states, and the way they get involved politically. Many Islamic groups have a clear goal of theocracy: entire states run under God's authority, according to His rules for humankind as a whole, imposed on believers and non-believers alike. They may be willing to embrace lower economic growth and lower standards of living in the name of achieving this ideal.

Sharia laws will be overseen by Muslim clerics, responsible for every part of government. Forced conversions will be part of the future picture, as in the past, with death threats often received by those who convert to another religion, or by those who seek to convert them. Thus, many Islamic societies will continue to use fear as an important tool to encourage religious obedience.

Christianity will focus less on government and more on policy

Christian groups over the last decades have almost always been driven by a relatively non-governmental mission: to recruit willing followers, who desire to live lives that are in keeping with Jesus's example and teachings. They will continue to celebrate compassion, unselfish love and kindness as outward signs of inner religious obedience.

Their theology is that as individuals are touched and changed by the love of God, communities are also changed, towns and cities are transformed, whole nations and governments are revolutionised. Social action will continue to be a major element of this tradition, whether running food banks, health care for the poor, or shelter for the homeless.

While many Christians are likely to engage in politics in future, they are almost certain to do so within the context of democracy, rather than attempting to impose a radical theocracy. Most will tend to support activist campaigns rather than joining a political party.

Peace will overcome religious violence eventually

As history shows repeatedly, where you have two groups of radical zealots: one promoting hate, fear and using violence, the other promoting love, respect and peace, the violent ones tend to gain power in the short term, but lose moral force eventually. Societies built on fear are limited by the desire for human freedom, are ultimately unsustainable, and therefore unusual.

Extremely violent, intolerant, Islamic militant groups will continue to be a poor advert globally for their religious brand, and in the long-term will be damaging to the wider (voluntary) acceptance of Islamic religion in general, except to small minorities of people who are attracted by such behaviours and by the comfort of clear, dogmatic creeds. The same applies to extreme Christian groups.

Expect support to peak and wane for the most ruthless and violent groups in any religion – and for militant Islam to decline in aggression, as numbers of followers of Islam grow rapidly over the next 50–100 years, fuelled by large middle-class families, and by extra finance generated primarily from Middle East oil over the next five decades or more.

Moderate Muslims are likely to be increasingly repelled by 'medieval' atrocities, committed in the name of Islam. As is the case with all fanatical groups, they too are likely to realise eventually that the goals they dream of will never be achieved by terrorist acts, only by winning the hearts of people.

Radical forces in the Middle East

Radical ideologies and tribalism will dominate the Middle East for the longer term, with constant risk of more regional conflicts. One of many contributing factors is the arbitrary nature of country borders, imposed as lines in the sand on nomadic Arab peoples, by Western powers many decades ago.

The Arab Spring was a reaction to corrupt autocracy and has, it seems resulted in greater tribalism. The autocrats, such as Saddam Hussein and President Assad of Syria, kept a lid on tribal tension.

Pressure on ruling families

We are likely to see instability across large parts of the region from time to time over the next 50 years. A number of Arab nations ruled by ultra-wealthy royal families could be very vulnerable. Violent activist groups of which Islamic State is just one example will seek to bring about inter-connected theocracies as part of an Arab-wide Islamic region.

Sunni and Shiite Muslims will continue as distinct communities well beyond 2050, with ripples felt across the entire world. Such conflicts will be stoked by atrocities, and kept going by oil revenues as well as by regional interests.

The civil war in Syria is likely to further destabilise and then reform the entire region, over several generations. Even if a peace agreement were brokered in Syria tomorrow, it would take at least 15 years to rebuild the nation and resettle over 4 million refugees, and a further 15 years for bitter memories to fade.

Centuries-long vision for the region

We need to understand the wider centuries-long vision of a series of Islamic fundamentalist groups, of which Al-Qaeda is only one of the better known.

A potential flashpoint for the next century will be Saudi Arabia, the heart of Islam, protectorate of the two most holy places, with immense oil wealth, and with great aspirations for its large and young population. Saudi Arabia is likely to remain a major target for Islamic revolutionary forces over the next 20–30 years, and the royal family is likely to make concessions to help maintain stability. We can also expect further major investments in education and job creation for younger nationals. But at the same time, there will be pressures in some parts of the community for liberalisation.

Saudi Arabia's oil revenues will decline

We cannot be sure when Saudi Arabia's oil revenues will start to decline permanently as reserves dwindle, or as our world becomes increasingly averse to burning carbon, but at some point in the next 50 years, it is likely that oil revenues will no longer support most of the national economy. This same issue will have a very significant impact on most of the Middle East, and will drive rapid investment in alternatives such as solar power.

Major social shifts

Countries like Iran are experiencing hidden social revolutions that are quite liberal, in contrast to the public image or official government policies of such nations. For example, a government survey reported that 80% of unmarried females in Iran have boyfriends, and many are sexually active. In addition, 17% of 142,000 students in the survey said that they were homosexual.

Turkey will find itself in an increasingly uncomfortable place, under pressure to radicalise towards stricter Islamic laws, with unstable borders to Iraq and Syria, while also under pressure from many middle-class citizens who look West rather than East. Turkey is already in danger of being overwhelmed by events across its borders, with over 1.6 million refugees arriving from Syria in just three years. Turkey will also experience tensions with the Kurdish peoples to the East.

Future of Palestine and Israel

Another flashpoint will, of course, be Israel and Palestine. I realise that many readers may have strong feelings about what *should* happen, but this book is about what it is reasonable to expect *may* happen, in the context of all other global and regional trends, and with many uncertainties. Here is a 'common sense' view, based on the current situation and some long-term factors.

Israel is a tiny nation of only 8 million people, packed into a narrow strip 263 miles long and up to 71 miles wide. If the entire Arab world starts to focus on Israel instead of inter-Arab conflicts, it is clear that the entire nation could be overrun, unless Israel resorts to the threat of using some kind of nuclear device. But against what nation would such a device be used if the forces raging against their borders on all sides are diffuse in origin, with tens of thousands of militia volunteers from more than forty countries? And what if an Arab nation with a nuclear device threatened to retaliate?

Pressure likely to grow for autonomy in Palestine

Israel seems likely to continue to resist external efforts to broker a lasting settlement for 4.4 million Palestinian people, who are living in densely packed areas with limited freedoms. New generations of freedom fighters, militants, and activists are likely to grow up in these communities, deeply hostile to Israel, finding common cause with wider movements across the Middle East.

The future well-being of the Palestinian people is likely to remain a fundamental issue of justice for most Arab peoples as well as for a growing number of non-Arabs around the world. A total of 135 nations have now officially recognised Palestine as a country.

If America chooses, at any point in the future, to fully defend Israel's borders, it is likely that American troops will be drawn into a long-distance, bitterly contested, very costly and potentially lengthy land battle. Such action could be ultimately unwinnable, if this enrages the entire Arab world against America and Israel for generations to come.

Despite these threats, Israel seems likely to try to pursue similar strategies as they have in the past for the next 15 years – hit back hard when attacked, keep a constant military alert, and weaken the Palestinian people with oppressive actions including the building of new Israeli settlements on land that has been inhabited recently by Palestinians.

However, Israel will need to adapt its strategy rapidly to the new world of asymmetric tribal conflicts. Like America, Israel is very ill-equipped for multi-dimensional, informal, urban battles, sweeping across several of its borders at once, as a movement of people on a collective suicide mission, rather than structured as a traditional military campaign.

Sustainability will be a dominant theme for 300 years

Worries about 'sustainability' will drive radical thinking about the very survival of humanity for the next 300 years and beyond.

Our world is short of water, food and mineral resources. A quarter of all 4000 known mammal species face extinction by 2035, according to the UN Environment Programme. One in eight plant types are also threatened. Only 10% of large fish in the ocean remain. Acidity from dissolved CO_2 has risen by 25% since the industrial revolution, altering the chemistry of trillions of sea organisms. Preserving biodiversity will be a growing priority, accelerated by the impact of global warming and loss of habitats. How will our world survive? How can economic growth continue indefinitely?

Concerns about global warming will intensify

China is now producing almost twice as much CO_2 as America, more than any other nation. On current trends, China alone will emit more CO_2 from 1990 to 2050 than the entire world produced from 1750 to 1970. But how much does this really matter?

The science of global warming is just a 'best guess' about what life will be like in 2100, and about the contribution of carbon emissions to what is happening now. But by the time we have proved whether the science is right, it will be too late. In the meantime, emotion is what will matter most in predicting the impact of global warming trends on business and government. How passionately people feel about an issue that could be devastating, but is as yet still unproven in the minds of some people, who believe that the temperature changes we are seeing are part of natural cycles, and are less serious than has been claimed.

Most people in the world are becoming more aware of risks from climate change, and more concerned that human activity may be contributing to it. Expect these concerns to grow, except where nations are temporarily distracted by other crises. These concerns will mean more laws, international agreements, carbon taxes, and so on.

What of the long-term future? My own view is that there is a very significant risk that our world will become warmer by at least 2 degrees centigrade, as a result of CO_2 emissions, by 2060. But even if you think that risk is as low as 5%, in other words very unlikely even by 2100, the potential consequences could be so overwhelming that by the time we know for sure, the damage will have been done. And that argument will guarantee vigorous action, with an increasing sense of urgency over the next 40 years or more.

CO_2 levels are likely to rise more in the next decade than in any previous decade in recent history, if the global economy grows strongly, and emerging market emissions grow faster than emission reductions by developed nations. Thereafter, hopefully we will see year-on-year declines as the world switches towards green technologies.

There is great speculation about future sea levels and how

much they might rise. We know that sea levels rose 17cm in the last century. Research also shows that from 1993 to 2010 sea levels rose a further 3.2mm each year on average, or by around 3cm a decade, double the rate of 1901 to 1990. On that basis alone, we would expect the sea to rise by at least 24–30cm by 2100. So we can see how easily sea levels could rise to the widely accepted forecasts of 30–60cm above today's levels. Or even 1 metre if the world warms more rapidly than expected.

A rise of half a metre would affect most of the largest cities in the world in a significant way, since they are all built around sea ports for historic reasons. Over 3 billion people live within 100 miles of the sea, a significant proportion of whom will be affected in some way by rising sea levels, for example, by higher taxes to pay for coastal protection. Even without the melting of land-based polar ice, sea levels will rise because water expands as it warms.

We will also see changes in agriculture and fishing, as some areas become more arid, and others are flooded more often. Many floods or droughts will be blamed on global warming, even if the truth is that they would almost certainly have happened anyway.

Unstable oil prices will create chaos for energy companies

We have already seen how 40-year energy policies can be overturned by a single 40-second event, and why energy markets will continue to be very unstable at times. We should expect a number of oil price peaks and slumps, created by over-production, stop-start investment, economic cycles and regional conflicts.

Oil prices are likely to swing below $30 and above $220 per barrel at various points over the next three decades. Prices fell from over $140 to below $40 in a few weeks of 2008, and to below $20 in 2001. Such extremes will continue to cause chaos and pain for oil and gas companies, as well as for green tech.

However, it is likely that the *average* oil price will be well above $110 a barrel for most of the next 30 years, which will help drive transition to a carbon-less future. Indeed, many oil-rich countries need to achieve such a price to balance their budgets. And it is hard to see how we can transition to a lower-carbon existence without such an average price.

Whenever oil prices fall below $75 a barrel, huge damage is done to green tech industries because the numbers no longer stack up to justify investment. Fund managers can easily lose confidence in the sector, postponing new financial commitments. Businesses and private individuals may decide to put off energy saving measures for another year or two. And as we have seen in the past, some green tech companies can rapidly run out of money if they cannot sell their energy at a high enough price. Their entire business models can come crashing to the ground.

Future oil prices will depend (among other things) on whether low-cost producers hold back production, since a nation like Saudi Arabia can easily flood the world with oil for a number of years, and still make a profit at prices of less than $40 a barrel. But they cannot do so for long without squandering their limited oil reserves.

Truth about peak oil – global supplies

Many Futurists have made wild predictions over the past 30 years about how the world will soon run out of oil and gas, and about the price of oil. However, from 2008–2013 alone, energy industry estimates for global gas reserves went up from just 60 years to 200 years at current rates of consumption, because of shale gas innovation. The same has happened with oil. Every year, proven oil reserves continue to rise, and only a third of geological formations that could contain oil have so far been explored.

Every time energy prices rise, more carbon can be extracted. Around 65% of oil in most wells had to be left underground in the past, because it is too hard to extract. Until oil prices collapsed in 2014–2015, companies were routinely drilling around 10km below sea beds to extract oil, because technology has improved and because they think future oil prices will make the effort worthwhile.

Frozen methane and other untapped carbon reserves

We have not even begun to explore extraction of frozen methane, which is one of the world's largest carbon stores. Energy stores under the ice caps or oceans could be as great as all proven oil, gas and coal reserves today.

Expect the Arctic to become one of the world's most important new areas for extraction of fossil fuels, iron ore, uranium and other resources. The Arctic probably contains up to 30% of the world's undiscovered natural gas and 15% of the oil. Expect $60bn of Arctic investment by 2025.

We will see growing geopolitical tensions over who has rights to what is under the ice – with Canada laying claim to the North Pole, and Russia increasing its military presence in the region. We will also see similar disputes over ownership of tiny islands and surrounding sea beds across South East Asia, to secure drilling rights.

The truth is that carbon reserves will never quite run out, because there will always be more that can be extracted, if the price goes even higher. After a certain point, other forms of energy become far more affordable, especially with carbon taxes, so use of fossil fuels will fall gradually towards zero. Indeed, it is unlikely that our world will be able to burn all the reserves we have *already* discovered, unless we find better ways to capture CO_2 emissions from power stations, and store them underground.

And of course we can already convert any form of carbon into more or less any other form: gas to a coal-like substance, energy to gas, rapeseed oil to petrol, coal to gas, wood to oil, waste CO_2 to petrol, and so on. We can also use wind power to manufacture methane or hydrogen gas as a way to store energy. The scale of production will depend on optimisation and price differences between input and output.

Quick route to reducing emissions

The fastest and cheapest way for any nation to reduce carbon emissions is to switch from coal to gas. Replacing five coal power stations with gas is the equivalent of installing 9000 megawatts of wind power. In America, emissions fell by 12% from 2007 to 2013, primarily because the shale gas boom drove more than fifty coal-fired power stations out of business.

Gas will still be widely used in power generation in 2060, as a rapid and flexible balancer between sources like nuclear and wind or solar, and will be a central element of national power management.

Fracking will become far more widely accepted, partly encouraged by national security fears in the EU, threatened by the thought of unreliable gas supplies from Russia. The fracking revolution has transformed the national energy market in America, which as we have seen will overtake Saudi Arabia as an oil producer by 2020.

However, nations like Russia and Saudi Arabia stand to lose if fracking becomes far more widespread, and we can expect any number of official and covert initiatives to try to slow the fracking industry down, including funding of activist groups, and flooding the market with cheap oil, to push frackers out of business.

We will also see rapid investment in facilities to ship liquid gas around the world, partly to handle American shale gas, and also to reduce dependence in Europe on Russian gas. Global capacity to liquefy and ship natural gas will increase by a third from 2015–2018 alone, and will double by 2025, with huge investment in ports, ships, pipes, gas storage and infrastructure.

Everything connects to everything

The shale gas boom meant that gas prices in America fell dramatically, and many smaller gas companies went bust. At the same time, coal power plants became uncompetitive and in a single year over fifty went out of business, so global coal prices fell. As a result, the Vietnamese began building very large coal-fired power stations. Coal-fired power generation jumped 5% globally in 2012 as a direct result of low-cost shale gas. So what was the final carbon saving in the world?

$40 trillion in green tech investment

As I described in my book *SustainAgility*, co-authored with Johan Gorecki, founder of Globe Forum, over the next 30 years we will see over $40 trillion invested in green tech. When oil prices are above

$100 a barrel, even the greatest climate sceptics become converts to energy saving technologies. And as we have seen, an additional driver is government fear of dependence on rogue states for future energy supplies. That includes Iraq, Iran, Libya and Russia. So cost saving, national security, protecting the environment – whichever way you look at it, the outcome will be the same. We will see a frenzy of green tech innovation over the next three decades, even if from time to time the pace is held back by short-term falls in the price of carbon. Even if we see *zero* green tech innovation for the next 50 years, we already have all the tools we need to transform the global response to climate change, at an affordable cost, just by scaling up what already exists.

Tackling climate change at low cost

Much of this will cost nothing. Take, for example, the normal replacement cycles for old fridges or cars or gas boilers. The fact is that in real terms you will probably spend less than you did last time you bought one of these things, yet it will contain all kinds of innovations that will cut your energy bill. So, for no additional cost, your energy consumption at home, while travelling or at work will fall rapidly over the next 10–20 years, probably by more than 30%.

There are many other ways to save energy that do cost money in the short term, but which repay their investment in 5 years or less. For example, some energy advisory companies are offering free upgrades of heating and air conditioning for 15-year-old offices and hotels, on condition that the owners continue to pay the company the same as they used to in energy costs, for a limited period.

The green tech company typically takes out a loan to pay all their own design and installation costs up front, and it also pays all the energy costs over the first four years. At the same time, each month the owner pays the green tech company the same amount it would usually pay to the utility company for gas or power. But the actual spend on gas and power is of course greatly reduced once the new systems have been installed, and the cost saving is so great that it pays off the loan, and provides enough spare cash to fund the entire installation, plus some profit on top.

We are seeing similar schemes for city-wide street lighting, which burns up 5% of all energy used in many nations. Replacing these can more than halve energy use, with payback time of four years, saving up to 3% of the entire national energy bill.

One of the most effective ways to save energy in buildings is to make them last longer. Around 30% of the lifetime energy used in a building is in putting it up and 10% is in pulling it down. Future generations will think it a scandal that most offices built over the last decade were constructed only to last 30 years, or 40 at most. Yet most private dwellings in developed nations are constructed to last for 100 years or more.

Technology	Energy saving	Cut in global energy use	Payback period	Speed of introduction
Low energy streetlamps	60%	3%	4 years	1–10 years
Aviation efficiencies	35%	1.5%	3–10 years	1–15 years
Vehicles	35–70%	10–20%	5 years	1–15 years
Building controls	35–70%	4–5.5%	4 years	1–15 years
Insulating homes	5–50%	6–8%	3–15 years	1–15 years
Heat pumps	25–50%	6–8%	10–15 years	1–25 years

How to save 30–40% of today's global CO_2 emissions at 'zero cost'

The International Energy Agency states that $300bn a year is already being spent on energy saving by companies and governments in just 11 nations – and we have only just begun.

Nanotech coatings for every moving part in a car engine will alone save at least 5% of fuel costs. Condensing gas boilers save 30% of fuel. The list is endless, with hundreds of new energy-related patents filed every day.

Cost of solar panels will fall towards zero

Solar panels will fall rapidly in cost, by up to 12% a year. The cost per watt fell from $4 to 80 cents from 2008 to 2014 alone. These silicon-based panels are already so cheap that they can be bought using a bank loan in low-interest nations, and will earn money on the roofs of homes from the first day without any government subsidy. This is the case in Australia, Germany, Italy and the Netherlands. Germany already leads Europe in solar panels, because of generous subsidies, but this is nothing to what we will see in the future. Next-generation solar panels will be far more efficient.

Over 200 gigawatts of solar panels have already been installed around the world – and at least the same again will be installed *every year* from 2025, equivalent to five times the entire energy consumption of the UK. We can expect lift-off on a gigantic scale by 2025, and solar power could become the world's largest source of electricity by 2060. We are likely to see over 650 gigawatts of installed solar capacity by 2035, following a $1.3 trillion investment. That is equivalent to more than 12% of global power consumption today.

Most solar panels will be installed in places where there is no connection to a national grid – serving over 1.4 billion people. Solar power installations are of course expensive to put in, but the running costs are zero and they can last many years.

Imagine a world where the cheapest roofing material is solar panels, when energy generation is included. We can see how vast this solar boom will become, with layers of silicon covering cars, factories, walls, roofs, airports, fields, lakes and deserts. It is already happening. Owners of lakes in some countries are starting to cover part of the surface with floating solar panels – which do not disturb wildlife too much. Farmers across Europe are covering land with solar panels. Research shows that biodiversity is higher in fields with panels than in ploughed fields. Plants and small animals thrive around and below the panels, which are angled to catch the sun.

Deserts could power all America and Europe

We will see enormous arrays of desert mirrors, reflecting light onto tubes containing gas, to drive steam turbines. These have already been built in Spain and the UAE. A single solar farm just 50km by 80km, in the Nevada desert, could in theory generate enough energy to supply most of the US, assuming it can be distributed and, if necessary, stored during the day for use at night.

The first stage of a 377-megawatt solar power station has already opened in California. One of the greatest challenges is dust: in Spain vast areas of such panels need cleaning only once a year, but in the UAE they need to be cleaned once a week.

Wind, waves and tides

We will also see huge growth in wind power between 2015 and 2050, especially offshore in the shallow seas of Western Europe, and across China. Average blade length will continue to grow. The longest blades already dwarf the size of the largest wings on passenger jets. Efficiency will improve, with hardly any moving parts, and better blade design, even though the blades are so vast that they will tend to be built within the region where they will be installed. Expect 230 gigawatts of installed wind capacity in the EU alone by 2020. China will dominate this global industry, with more installed turbines than any other nation. We can also expect opposition in many places to more wind farms from people who consider this a 'visual pollution' of the landscape.

We will also see more energy generated from waves and tides, with most of this from tidal barrages, which could generate 15% of UK energy by 2050. We will see more tidal turbines in places like Scotland and Brittany, where tidal currents are strong.

Smarter grids

The windiest and sunniest places on earth are often far from cities, so we will need new ways to transmit wind and solar power without high power losses.

Supergrids will carry power over many thousands of kilometres, across entire continents, with almost zero power loss. Supergrids use direct current rather than alternating current, so power always flows in the same direction, which means very little power is lost into the atmosphere as electromagnetic radiation.

Germany alone is planning to build 6,400km of supergrid, as part of a $160bn European investment, but cost and impact on the landscape will be big issues, and are likely to slow construction down. Whatever happens, Europe will be far more joined up energy-wise in future, with ever-greater volumes of electricity and gas moving across borders to ensure a completely integrated energy community.

National energy stores to manage peak demand

We will see huge investment in energy storage. Up until now one of the most common ways to store surplus energy at night was to pump water from one dam, uphill to another. In future we will hear a lot more about salt caverns. Natural spaces underground that are gas-tight, into which air is compressed using surplus power. When power is needed, compressed air is combined with natural gas to turbocharge gas turbines.

We will use the batteries of hundreds of thousands of electric cars as additional power stores, as they will be plugged into the national grid most of the time. Car batteries will act as power donors at times of peak demand, with agreement of their owners, who will be paid to participate.

When you add all these things together, the combined impact could be extraordinary. For example, in June 2013 there was so much sunlight and wind in Germany that the national grid was threatened with meltdown. Energy companies were forced to contact some of their biggest customers to persuade them to burn up more power, by any means. They were paid four times the normal cost of electricity for every unit they were able to burn up. So energy prices actually became negative. But we are only in the earliest stages of green tech. Expect many more radical upsets in energy markets as a result.

Nuclear boom despite a meltdown

Despite the Fukushima disaster in Japan in 2011, we are about to see a global boom in construction of new nuclear power stations – except in Japan and Germany. Global spending on nuclear reactor pressure vessels alone is around $16bn a year, with 48 new nuclear power stations being built across the Asia-Pacific and a further 22 in other parts of the world.

The only thing that will slow this down will be another major nuclear accident, say in France, spreading radioactive dust across Western Europe.

We are likely to see a new generation of nuclear power stations by 2060–2070 (or possibly earlier) based on nuclear fusion, which is a radically different technology from splitting the atom (fission) and involves fusing two different atoms together to release energy. The EU, America, Japan, China, India, Russia and South Korea are jointly building a 23,000-ton, 500-megawatt experimental fusion reactor in France that is likely to cost more than $30bn and with first experiments scheduled for sometime between 2025 and 2030.

Meanwhile, the global aerospace company Lockheed Martin claims to have built a small working prototype, and hopes to have a commercial-scale device by 2025. They say it will be small enough to fit on a truck and could power 80,000 homes using 20kg of fuel a year.

While the Chinese are also exploring the use of thorium as a new fuel, there is no shortage of uranium, which forms around 3% of the cost of a new reactor. If uranium prices treble, which would still be quite affordable, we can start to mine uranium from sea water, even using today's Japanese technology. We could supply the world with uranium for over 10,000 years at current energy levels, from sea water alone.

Germany will follow an anti-nuclear path

In contrast, Germany is quickly phasing out nuclear power as part of their policies to transfer to renewables – so quickly that even the meteoric rise of solar and wind power across the country will barely make up for the loss. As a result, Germany's use of carbon will hardly change over the next two decades.

Germany achieved its green tech boom by offering very generous government subsidies. The money for these subsidies is clawed back from all energy customers in a special green energy tariff which is added to normal energy prices. So the result of the green tech boom has been a jump in energy costs.

Energy prices paid by industry in Germany are now projected

to rise to around $150 per megawatt hour, almost three times that in America, by 2020. This is a major risk to 75% of its small- and medium-sized industrial companies. Energy-hungry companies like BASF, SGL Carbon and Basi Schoberl are complaining that they may be forced to relocate production out of Germany as a direct result, possibly to America, where shale gas prices are likely to remain much lower.

Germany spends $20bn a year on green subsidies, working out at over $200 to prevent a ton of CO_2 from being emitted. At the same time, carbon credits are being traded between companies for only $7 a ton of CO_2, so some strange market forces are operating. It will be at least 5–10 years before carbon pricing settles to a more sustainable level.

The original carbon market was flooded by over-generous allowances that were then traded, as companies made simple energy savings. Carbon trading is worth only $50bn, half the 2011 figure – but represents a record 10 gigatons.

Hydrogen and fuel cells – some false promises

Hydrogen is very unlikely to become a major global fuel for cars, trucks or planes, for several reasons. First, it is an inefficient fuel to transport in tanks, as it produces less power per litre than a carbon-based gas. Second, the gas molecules are very small, so leaks are harder to prevent. Third, battery technology is improving rapidly as well as the efficiency of petrol and diesel engines. It is impossible to imagine a national hydrogen gas grid running across America, for example – too expensive to even consider.

Expect further improvements in fuel cells that produce power directly from carbon fuel. However, like hydrogen, such fuel cells will face severe competition over the next two decades from next-generation batteries.

Biofuels – expect a radical rethink

Expect a complete rethink about the ethics of burning food in vehicles. By 2015, 40% of all corn grown in America was already being converted to biofuels. It is also illegal to drive in Europe without burning food in your car – 5% of all petrol or diesel sold in the EU is from food, rising to 10% by 2020.

The American government has encouraged the use of biofuels to help the nation become energy independent, but even if every ton of grain were converted to petrol or diesel, it would not be enough to keep more than 25% of the auto industry on the move, so the impact is insignificant on energy policy.

To make matters worse, up to 92% of theoretical savings in carbon emissions are lost because of energy used in fertilisers, CO_2 emitted in making biofuels, and because of deforestation.

Impact of biofuels on farming

Biofuels are also expensive in terms of subsidies. For example, the EU is paying €1,200 per ton of CO_2 saved, which is six times the average subsidy paid by Germany for a wide range of green tech to reduce CO_2 emissions.

Within the EU, an area of farmland the size of Belgium is already being used to grow biofuels for EU use, and a similar land area outside the EU is also needed. Biofuel farms in the EU are also using more water than the entire Seine and Elbe river flows combined.

The impact of biofuels on global food supplies is even more important at a time when 840 million are hungry. According to the UN, the EU now burns enough biofuel calories in vehicles each year to feed 100 million people.

Twice over the last six years we have seen prices of some foods soar by more than 50%. And each time, influential bodies like the UN have said that up to 70% of these rises have probably been caused by burning food in vehicles. So it may be true that 30 million people in the world today are starving because of biofuels policies. And as we have seen, the real issue is not necessarily the facts (which may be disputed), but how people around the world feel about it all.

Food and oil prices will be locked together

One thing is clear: the moment we link food and energy together in this way, we create a single food-fuel market, so oil prices and food prices are now locked together across the world. And in turn that means land prices, farmland prices and woodland prices (because woodland can be cleared to grow grain) also become linked to energy prices.

So a Middle East oil scare produces a food price spike. If the price of oil doubles over the next decade, prices of some foods may double too. Some counter that while this may apply to biofuels from food, it is different when you are converting biomass. But biomass still comes from the land. So we are seeing farmers devote huge areas to crops which count as biomass, and cutting the land area they use to grow food.

Biomass has certainly become a very fashionable concept in energy. One of the UK's largest coal power stations – Drax – has been converted to biomass. The only trouble is that this monster is impossible to feed from the UK alone, so bio-waste is now being transported to Drax in containers shipped from Brazil – yet another sign of global madness.

Carbon capture will be widely used – eventually

An obvious way to reduce emissions of CO_2 is to capture chimney gases from power stations, and bury them underground in old gas fields, which of course have been proven to be gas-tight for millions of years. The process was still experimental in 2014, but expect rapid growth.

A simple way to do this is to use some of the power station electricity to extract oxygen from the atmosphere, which is then pumped into the power station to burn gas or coal. The only chimney gases are then water vapour (condensed to provide local water), a very little sulphur dioxide, and pure CO_2 to be pumped underground.

The world's first large-scale capture and storage plant was opened in Canada in 2014. Over a million tons of CO_2 are being pumped into an oil field, which will also help further oil extraction. We are likely to see more such projects in the US, Canada, Saudi Arabia and Australia.

Imagine a world with free power

As we look beyond 2100, it is easy to imagine that 'free' electrical power will be part of normal life for hundreds of millions of people. Indeed, this is already the case for people who have owned solar panels or wind turbines for some time, whose costs have already been paid long ago through savings on their fuel bills. They will go on experiencing free power until those devices break down. The same applies to any farmer fortunate enough to have a small water turbine working off a local stream or river.

The lesson, therefore, is that electrical power in future will become more a question of capital investment than fuel consumption.

Sustainable cities, green manufacturing and IT

Every architect, builder and city planner will be expected to think about sustainability in future. Many European nations will require a percentage of new homes to be completely carbon neutral, so that all emissions are offset by green energy that is sold to other consumers.

Manufacturers will reduce the energy they use per unit of production by at least 20% over the next 15–20 years. China will continue to complain that they are being falsely blamed for warming the planet, as the 'manufacturer of the world'. If you outsource manufacturing to another country, it is no use pretending that you have reduced your carbon footprint as a result. All you have done is transfer it.

Web represents 5% of all global power use

The IT industry will also come under a lot of pressure to be more energy efficient, to save costs as well as the environment. At least 5% of all global energy is consumed in powering the web, including all browsing on local devices.

Farms of tens of thousands of web servers can waste enough heat to power small towns, which is why so many are being located in very cold parts of the world – to cut cooling costs. In some cases the heat generated is already being used to heat homes.

Further growth of $500 billion recycling industry

One of the easiest ways to save energy, forests and raw materials is to recycle waste. A $500 billion industry is assisted by subsidies and public goodwill, and will grow rapidly over the next three decades, especially in emerging markets. To give some current examples, 34% of all copper used in factories is already from recycled sources; 500 million tons of steel is recycled in America each year; and 20% of all steel production is recycled, in a process that saves 75% of energy in that industry.

In America alone, the business of recycling corporate waste is now worth more than $80bn a year, growing by 1% a year, supporting more than 450,000 jobs. Every American produces 2kg of waste a day, or 64 tons over an average lifetime, of which 40% is exported to nations like China to be processed. Expect more to be processed locally in future.

We will see many innovations in collecting and sorting domestic refuse. Car breakers' yards will aim for 100% recovery – indeed, many nations will insist on it. Entire cars can be cut and ground into small granules of eighteen different materials, which are separated automatically in a continuous process.

Safeguarding water supplies will be a key challenge

Water is one of the primary needs of humanity and we are facing a global shortage, especially near megacities. By 2025, two thirds of humankind will live in areas where there are water shortages, up from one third today. While nations like Brazil have a surplus of clean river water, most nations are facing water deficits.

Globally we already use 35% of accessible supplies. Farming uses 60% of all the world's pumped water, even though only 1% of the world's fields are irrigated. An additional 19% is used to dilute pollution, sustain fisheries and transport goods. Thus the human race already uses around half the planet's supply. But water use has quadrupled since 1950 due to a larger and wealthier global population. So, then, it is clear that water demand will increase by at least 40% in many emerging nations by 2040. And pressures will be even greater in areas of hot countries frequented by tourists, with soaring demand for water in the most popular holiday resorts.

To make matters worse, climate change means more rain in some places but less in others. Underground water levels are falling in many of the world's most important crop-growing areas, including the western US, large parts of India and north China, where water tables are dropping a metre a year. We will see longer pipelines across countries and continents, balancing supply and population. These will create new opportunities for trade, political demands and sabotage by terrorists.

The water and electricity industries will be even more closely linked in future, as water management uses a lot of power. Anything that reduces the cost of power also reduces the cost of water. In addition, as we will see, power can be used to make fresh water from the sea.

Many rivers semi-dead in Asia

Over-irrigation means that many rivers already die for part of the year in Asia. These include most rivers in India, among them the mighty Ganges, a principal water source for south Asia, and China's Yellow River.

With the number of urban dwellers set to reach 5 billion by 2025, steps are being taken to switch water from farms to cities. Three hundred Chinese cities are now experiencing water shortages.

Every individual in industrialised cities will be affected in some way by 2025, with widespread water metering, 'grey water' systems (for example bath water stored for watering the garden), and a shift in culture to viewing all water as a limited natural resource. Expect as many regulations on the use of water as on energy conservation.

Thirsty world by 2030

By the year 2030, virtually all of the world's economically accessible rivers will be required to meet the needs of agriculture, industry and households, and to maintain lake and river levels. This is based only on current trends with no allowance for the added impact of climate change.

The death of the Aral Sea is described by the government of Uzbekistan as one of the most serious ecological catastrophes in the history of the human race, and took place in a single generation. Originally one of the world's largest lakes, its shores are now far from their original location, and mineral levels have risen dramatically.

Coupled with this is coastal pollution. While half the world's population still lacks basic sanitation, 80% of all local sea water pollution is from contaminants carried there by fresh water.

Ensuring future water supplies

Humanity will find many ways to manage water more efficiently, and there is no reason to think that our future world will grind to a halt because of lack of water. Here are some ways in which shortages will be dealt with – the first two alone will make a huge difference in most developed nations, and in cities of many emerging nations.

◆ installing water metres for every user, and charging more per litre

◆ stopping leaks – 25% of London's water is lost from ancient pipes

◆ using drip irrigation and growing drought-resistant crops

◆ shifting water-hungry agriculture to wetter areas of the world

◆ implementing better local water management with small dams for farmers

◆ building large dams – also used for power

◆ collecting rainwater, e.g. roofs into cisterns

◆ reducing water use by washing machines, dishwashers and toilets

◆ recycling waste water or 'grey' water for uses other than drinking, washing or food preparation

◆ increasing use of desalination – as in Middle East and cities like London, using new technologies which require far less energy

◆ increasing use of nanotech-coated surfaces that are cleaned without using much water, e.g. in urinals.

Risk of water wars

Over a decade ago I warned of water wars, and that water would become a national security issue. We have seen this recently in Syria and Iraq. Rivers, canals, dams, water treatment plants and pipelines have all become military targets. Entire cities in desert areas can easily be placed under siege if their water is cut off.

We could see water wars between nations, quarrelling over, say, how much water flows into a country down a long river, or how much one country is allowed to pollute another's water supply. In 2006, there was a drought in East Africa which caused the levels of water in Lake Victoria to fall. The Ugandan government took a decision to reduce the amount of water flowing out of Lake Victoria through their hydroelectric dam into the source of the River Nile. This was in open defiance of a 1929 treaty under which Egypt had exclusive rights to 80% of the Nile's water. Uganda's action also threatened a crisis for Sudan, a country that similarly depends on the great river.

Germany and Austria were sued by Black Sea states through the EU for polluting the River Danube. Algae blooms in the Black Sea killed millions of fish, and completely wiped out forty species.

If there is no rain in the Pyrenees, there will be no water in Andorra. If the Caspian Sea dies as a result of one country's pollution, four other nations suffer. Expect many more rows between neighbours up and down river, whether farmers, villages, towns, cities, nations or regions.

Dams will be bigger and more controversial

Controversy will continue to grow over vast dams like the Three Gorges Dam of the Yangtze River in China, which created a lake 600km long, drowned a city of 250,000, and displaced a million. Three hundred new large dams a year will force up to 4 million people a year to leave their homes around the world, often ancestral lands.

In theory dams are a wonderful idea: offering free power, irrigation and flood prevention, providing a tourist attraction and water sports, fish farming and drought protection. They create jobs, are national status symbols, and prevent global warming. For example, the Congo River at Inga could supply half the energy needs of the whole of Africa, and only 10% of Africa's potential hydroelectric capacity has so far been harnessed.

But dams also change the environment. Constant irrigation brings salts to the surface, so that farmland is increasingly infertile. Silt that used to be carried by floods now clogs up reservoirs, and fish are blocked from going upstream.

800 billion cubic metres of virtual water

Nations will look to save water by virtual trading. For example, it takes a ton of water to grow a single kilogram of rice. To grow a 40kg bag of rice requires 40 tons of water, and a single 40-ton lorry loaded with rice is the equivalent of importing 1,000 lorries to a water-starved nation, each carrying 40 tons of water – the same as a small ship. You would need 25 such ships to carry enough water to make a single ton of rice, so it is madness to grow rice in a desert. A water-deprived nation like Egypt can save huge amounts of water by producing more goods and growing less food. In future, the most water-hungry farming or industrial processes will be in parts of the world with high rainfall.

Our world is already trading 800 billion tons of virtual water a year, equivalent to all the water flowing down ten rivers the size of the Nile. If all food tariff barriers on shipments to America, Europe and other parts of the world were removed, the amount of virtual water traded would double in a short period of time.

Major changes are likely to take place rapidly. For example, farming in California uses up 80% of the state's scarce water supplies, yet contributes only 2% to the local economy. Farms pay only around 15% of the capital costs of the Federal water supply infrastructure. A significant proportion of food production will have to move into wetter states further east, to save California from an even greater water crisis over the next 20 years.

Daily water use per person (EU)

Europeans use 4.6 tons of water per day, according to Water Footprint Network. But around 3 tons of this is virtual water. For example, every time you eat a single tomato, you are indirectly consuming 13 litres of water, because that was what was needed to grow it. Cotton farming is a major consumer of water. Many different organisations have calculated that around 10,000 litres of water are needed to harvest a single kilogram of cotton fibre.

Tomato	13 litres
Slice of bread	50 litres
Orange	58 litres
Egg	146 litres
Pint of beer	170 litres
Burger	2,400 litres
Cotton wool ball	4.5 litres
Sheet of paper	13.6 litres
Cotton T-shirt	4,000 litres
Leather shoes	9,600 litres
Pair of jeans	11,000 litres

How the world's forests will be saved

Forests produce oxygen, store carbon, increase rainfall and prevent flooding – so we will see rapidly growing efforts to protect and expand them in future. The carbon stores of the world's forests are equivalent to more than forty times the world's annual global carbon emissions.

Protecting forest also encourages biodiversity. Almost half the world's land species are in Brazil and Indonesia. Expect special efforts to preserve the habitats of these countries.

Deforestation is the largest cause of greenhouse gas emission, responsible for 23% of the total – more than all cars, trucks, trains, aircraft and ships combined. That includes nitrous oxide, soot and methane. Every year 13 million hectares of forest are cleared, the equivalent of 50,000 square miles, which is four times the size of Belgium.

At the same time, tree planting is taking place on an extraordinary scale. Across Europe, the amount of forest has grown by 15% over the last 15 years – by an area the size of Greece. Every year, the area of new forest created in Europe is growing by the equivalent of 1.5 million football pitches.

Globally 12 billion trees have been planted in the last 5 years alone, with 2.5 billion planted in 2009 as a global UN initiative – 1 billion more than planned. America recently planted 30 million trees in a single campaign. More than 70 million trees were planted in Spain over two years, 11 million in Romania and 5 million in France. It costs only $5 to save a ton of tree wood from being burnt. Expect many more forest trading schemes that protect or manage vulnerable forest in exchange for carbon credits.

Encouraging though this is, planting trees will not solve global warming – at least not in the short term, for obvious reasons. A forest tree will typically capture a ton of carbon over 60 years, but most of that happens in the last 15 years of its life. When trees fall over and die, and are left on the forest floor, their carbon becomes food for a million creatures and organisms ranging from fungi to insects, that themselves form a valuable part of the food chain and ecosystem.

Very little carbon remains from a fallen tree trunk after a decade. To prove this, go for a forest walk in an area where trees have grown for over 200 years. Take a spade, start digging and see how deep you go before you hit soil with very little carbon content (for example, hitting almost pure yellow sand rather than compost-enriched black soil). The answer is usually no more than a third of a metre. Carbon is only retained in large amounts on forest floors when the rotting process is arrested, perhaps because of acid bog or some other unusual factor. So, unless that tree falls into a bog, the only way to keep the wood carbon from returning fairly soon to the atmosphere is to use the timber in buildings or furniture, protecting it from decay or burning.

Paper and cardboard industries can be 'green'

The paper and pulp industry is often condemned for killing trees, destroying forests and wasting energy. However, such activity can actually result in more forest rather than less. Such forests are actively maintained, expanded and protected from urban development or farming. Trees are thinned out, new planting is efficient, and the forest should capture the same amount of carbon every year.

Paper and cardboard packaging are in many ways far more eco-friendly than plastic. Imagine a situation where every tree is replaced with saplings, and all paper or cardboard is recycled at least twice before being burnt in a power station as biomass, or being composted to help grow food. Such an industry is truly sustainable, and efficient, even more so if – say – woodchips and other tree waste are also used to generate power.

Transcontinental smog – linked to forest burning

In the next decade, we will continue to see transcontinental smog: whole sections of the surface of the planet where the air on the ground is unhealthy to all and lethal to some. Smog kills by aggravating asthma, bronchitis and a host of other lung conditions and by directly increasing the risk of heart attacks through carbon monoxide exposure. In a city like Calcutta that could mean up to 25,000 additional deaths a year. Across a whole region or continent the results are devastating.

In 2013 a dense smog developed over a million square miles of South East Asia, affecting 300 million people; it was the worst smog for 15 years. Indonesia was forced once again to apologise for the forest burning, clearing land to grow food, which had been a large contributor. In 1998, Malaysia declared the regional smog a national disaster and schools were shut throughout Sarawak because of forest fires in Indonesia.

The forest clearance itself was a product of land shortages and rising population. Some estimates suggest that such fires release as much carbon dioxide as Europe produces in a whole year.

Carbon rationing will create tension

Carbon caps and taxes will cause international tension and conflict, even wars, unless applied fairly – but that will be almost impossible. We are likely to see many global energy summits, which appear to produce little concrete action, where developed and emerging nations remain in deadlock. However, this will not prevent rapid evolution of a wide range of green technologies across the world, for reasons we have seen above.

China will lead the way in the large-scale introduction of green technologies over the next two decades – mainly solar and wind – partly to develop and export, as well as to improve their national environment. At the same time, other nations will criticise China as the world's largest carbon emitter.

In order to be fair, carbon rations would have to be a fixed amount per person per year, perhaps sold on the open market as a tax on all carbon consumption, with subsidies for the poorest and most vulnerable. But such a system would mean that villagers can no longer cut their own trees to make charcoal for cooking, and would condemn the poorest nations to a relatively carbon-free existence forever.

Emerging nations will continue to insist that they should be able to have their own carbon-based 'industrial revolutions', and that developed nations must accept responsibility for the largest contribution to the mess the world is now in, since this has arisen mainly from their own industrial activities over the last 200 years.

It will be argued that even though the wealthiest nations have reduced their carbon emissions to some extent, they have continued to ransack the earth's limited carbon supplies, and they therefore need to make far more radical cuts in emissions.

Food for 11 billion people

One of the greatest concerns I hear is that we will be unable to feed a world population that could reach 11 billion by 2050. The good news is that we could probably feed many more.

Food production is the world's largest industry, worth 10% of global GDP, or around $8 trillion a year, if you include farming, food packaging, restaurants, and so on.

According to the UN, 840 million people are malnourished and often go hungry. Although this number has fallen by 160 million in 10 years, this statistic is still one of the most shameful trends in this book, particularly as it is relatively easy to deal with, when we consider the wealth and technology we have today. We will look further at the ethical implications of global hunger in the next chapter.

Today, we already grow enough food to feed 9 billion people. But we waste 40% of it, worth $3 trillion – in fields, storehouses, factories, warehouses, shops and domestic rubbish bins. With advances in agriculture, better infrastructure, larger farms, better types of crops and livestock, and less food waste, there is no doubt that we will be able to feed everyone on the earth in 50 to 100 years' time.

We will see more genetically modified crops in many regions, with crops resistant to disease, drought, and able to grow in salty soil. Genetically modified animals will be widely consumed in over 30% of the world by 2040.

The only question is how many kilograms of meat the earth can produce, and whether most people will continue to follow a largely vegetarian diet, as is the case today. Expect a rise in the proportion of global grain production used to feed animals to more than 45% beyond 2025. Already more than 70% of grain produced by wealthy nations is fed to livestock.

So how much more meat are we talking about? In Germany, for example, people will eat an average of 1094 animals during their lifetime: 4 cows, 4 sheep, 12 geese, 37 ducks, 46 pigs, 46 turkeys, 945 chickens. Expect similar levels of meat consumption by over 4 billion people in 2040, compared to a fraction of that today.

As world population has grown, and as more wealthy people eat more meat, the total area of land being used for agriculture has doubled since 1961. But there are absolute limits on the availability of suitable land. Therefore, we can expect the price of farm land to continue to rise over the next 20 years, as it has over the last decade.

Green revolution in Africa – and China's land grab

A number of African nations will embark on a 'green revolution' similar to that seen in India in the 1970s and 1980s (India's grain production has hardly increased over the last few years). This will be accelerated by nations like China that are buying up huge areas of fertile African land to secure their national food supplies.

Over the last decade alone, 177,000 square miles of farmland has been bought in 734 deals – that's almost the size of Spain, or Thailand – from nations such as Ethiopia, Ghana, Madagascar, Mali and Sudan. But nations like Ukraine are also selling. In 2013, the Chinese bought a 50-year lease for 11,500 square miles in Ukraine, 5% of the nation's land area, equivalent in size to Belgium or the state of Massachusetts.

Two-thirds of those who are hungry are small-scale subsistence farmers living off their own patch of land, and it will be impossible to radically improve food yields across Africa without large-scale consolidation of farms, to allow mechanisation. This will be traumatic for those whose tribes have lived on that land for generations. At the other end of the scale, many areas unsuitable for large-scale farming are returning to bush as workers migrate to cities.

Growing more fish and protecting the seas

Globally 3 billion people get around 20% of their protein from fish. Demand for fish will grow faster than for meat, not only because of increasing wealth, but also in the fight against obesity and heart disease.

A third of wild fish stocks have been over-fished and 25% of all fishing is illegal or unreported. Global populations of large fish such as tuna, swordfish and marlin have fallen by over 80% over the last 60 years.

Future generations will regard the idea of feeding towns and cities on ocean fish as bizarre. They will think it even stranger if developed nations are still handing out $35bn a year in ocean fishing subsidies.

Fish farming will become a global obsession. This is potentially a great sustainability story, supporting hundreds of thousands of low-income coastal dwellers growing high protein, healthy food, and protecting wild fish stocks. But at present it takes several tons of fish from the ocean to grow a ton of fish in a fish farm. The only advantage is that fish farms can use all kinds of weird-looking creatures from the sea that consumers would not dream of eating.

Scientists will find ways to feed fish without using large amounts of other ocean fish and sea creatures. New kinds of farmed fish will be created, with genes that allow them to digest food grown on land; or crops will be altered so that the proteins they make are suitable for farmed fish.

However, we will also see growing concern about genetically altered fish escaping into the ocean, upsetting food chains and ecosystems, especially if they are 'unnatural' mutants, created in laboratories. It is already the case that 25% of all 'wild' salmon caught in Scotland have escaped from fish farms in Norway, or are descended from fish that have escaped in the past.

Future of retail food and drink industry

We have already seen how grocery and food retailing is being transformed. The retail food industry will continue to be relatively conservative and risk averse, with long-enduring and much-loved brands that span several generations – foods that grandmothers remember feeding their own children.

We have also seen how sensitive the food industry is to issues of consumer trust, which will drive the continued growth of trace-ability, transparency, labelling, and so on. The entire food industry will be more tightly regulated in future. We will see a new focus on the health aspects of foods; expect new *performance* foods with claims that they build strength, or immunity, or improve memory.

Expect a rethink about food irradiation over the next few years, as a low-cost way to ensure long shelf life without altering taste, following a wave of research that suggests it is completely safe.

We will also see many more food scandals such as happened with the contamination of rice in China, and of animal feed by dioxin in Belgium. Each will cause a huge emotional reaction in consumers, with widespread, angry boycotts. Expect improvements in animal welfare across the EU and in other nations, and an increase in animal tagging for 100% traceability.

Anti-food for fat people

We have already seen how 50% of the world will be obese by 2030. Expect a new generation of 'safe' slimming drugs that kill appetite or prevent food absorption, for a market that could be worth at least $10bn a year in the US alone. An example is likely to be molecules similar to the hormone thyroxine that caused monkeys to lose 7% of their weight in a week on a normal diet, with few side effects. Meanwhile the so-called Fatlash movement will grow, promoting the erroneous belief that to be fat is healthy, and fighting stigmatisation of fat people. Expect lawsuits against food companies for alleged irresponsible promotion of unhealthy food, and a direct connection to sickness or death.

Expect to see a new food industry selling anti-food, or food with absolutely no nutritional value. The first anti-food was a new fat made from molecules that the body cannot digest. This can be used in cakes, ice creams or any other food. It cooks well, but comes straight out the other end unchanged. Bowel movements become greasy. A diet rich in this anti-food can produce vitamin deficiencies, as well as creating a generation of bingeing anorexics able to consume huge plates of food yet waste away to the point of death.

It will be another irony of the third millennium: one billion starving or undernourished and millions of others using scarce resources to make food that they will waste through total excretion.

Catering for anxious eaters

Expect growth of 'natural' foods and 'natural' packaging as people begin to worry about oestrogen-like chemicals leaching out of plastic, some preferring traditional, recyclable glass containers for milk and other products.

Expect anti-additive food companies to create entire kitchen environments where nothing 'artificial' ever contaminates what people eat or drink. Expect new ranges of meat substitutes with the right texture and taste for some who insist on it. Expect a rash of new health scares related to vegetarian diets, such as nutritional deficiencies and worries about additives.

Expect more stampedes by consumers from one food to another, following the latest food scare. Expect an end to the worst poultry factory farms, as worries over food poisoning add another chorus to animal welfare campaigns. Expect food retailers and producers who break the rules to be 'punished' by increasingly militant groups, threatening boycotts and intimidation as well as shareholder action.

Most changes in the food industry will come from consumer behaviour rather than regulations. Expect confusion over what is safe and unsafe. Millions fled from drinking 'disgusting' tap water only to find that the bottled water they bought at high cost had higher levels of bacteria, was impossible to differentiate from the tap in blind testing studies and, what's more, was contaminated by pollutants from storage in plastic bottles. Expect carbon/transport taxes on bottled water imported from other nations, targeting premium brands.

Global sales of vitamins will continue to see spectacular growth, although controversy will rage over what doses should be taken by whom – or even if they should be taken at all.

Vegetarians and semi-vegetarians look for new products

The broader vegetarian market will grow from 5% to 30% of the US population by 2025, if you include people who eat meat occasionally, and millions of others who choose to eat far less meat than today. Red, fatty meat will be less popular, because of worries about bowel cancer and heart disease. In Britain, 40% of people often eat vegetarian foods as a conscious alternative to eating a meal containing meat or fish, ten times the number of strict vegetarians, and the industry is worth more than £1 billion a year.

Expect fast growth for certain 'veggie' products. For example, sales of vegetarian grills and burgers increased by 139% in 5 years in the UK, as technology and taste have improved. Expect new meat substitutes – meat-like substances made from wheat gluten and pea protein with the bite, character, flavour and look of meat. Their growth in market share will be modest, however.

Expect a gradual fall in resistance in many nations other than the US to genetically modified food, particularly in France, Austria, Hungary, Greece, Luxembourg, Poland and Bulgaria – while Germany will remain more cautious.

Huge consolidation in drinks market

Expect huge changes in the drinks industry over the next three decades as hundreds of millions of consumers shift away from carbonated sugary beverages to fruit juices and then to bottled water, for health reasons. We will see more research showing that diet drinks also carry health risks, stimulating release of insulin, with increased risk of heart attack and diabetes.

Radical changes to work patterns

In some way or another, every trend described in this book will affect many people's workplaces directly or indirectly. Our future is of course all about people, at work or at home. But here are some wider workplace issues which will radically change several billion lives between now and 2050.

Many predictions have been made about the 'end of work', as we know it. Some say that most manual jobs will disappear, creating a huge underclass of unemployable people; most office jobs will also be automated; a high proportion of managers will work at home; many domestic chores will be done by robots who will also care for the frail and elderly; most manufacturing jobs will be lost to Asia, together with many service jobs such as banking, call centres and software development. This all makes for good stories in the press, but the reality of all this will be less dramatic over the next 25 years, even though we can expect many radical changes in the patterns of jobs that people do.

While it is true that hundreds of millions of jobs will disappear, many more will be created, as we will see. The most radical shifts in employment patterns will be in emerging nations, mainly related to urban migrations from rural areas.

As we have seen throughout this book, trends often balance each other out, and this balancing also applies in general terms to the job market. Here is an example: an economy sinks into crisis, the exchange rate collapses, and cost of labour falls on the international market. That means export prices also fall, then sales rise, jobs recover, the economy recovers, the exchange rate recovers.

Job creation in nations with high unemployment

During the 2008–2013 crisis, unemployment rates among young people rose to above 40% in parts of Spain and Italy, with people warning of a lost generation. Any nation with high unemployment rates will eventually see an adjustment, as local wages fall, because so many workers are chasing so few jobs. Things will then become more balanced again. And that is what Spain was already beginning to experience by 2015. Italy is likely to follow.

So where will new jobs come from? Many in developed nations will be in service and support roles for middle-class consumers. Homes will be redecorated more often, lawns will be mown more regularly, people will have their hair styled more frequently. An example in the UK is the boom in car valeting by hand and the death of cheap, car-washing robots in garages. As Parkinson's famous law states: 'work always expands to fill the time available'.

More women workers and part-timers in the UK

The real key to economic growth is the number of people in work, and in many nations, that number has soared, while the number out of work has also risen. Why is this, and what will happen in future?

More women are entering the workplace; more people who were not working are now working part-time; older people are working longer before they retire; students are working to pay for their courses; and more people are migrating into the country looking for work. So the most important indicator in future will not be numbers looking for work, but the growing numbers of people who have a job.

Insatiable demand to create more jobs

So what kind of jobs will be needed in future, to absorb all of these people, assuming they have the right skills? For a start, as anyone in government will tell you, there is an almost insatiable desire by the public in most nations for better public services.

That means more doctors, nurses, teachers, street cleaners, police, gardeners in parks, tree planters, graffiti cleaners, home carers, therapists, family support workers, counsellors, advisors, mentors, and so on.

And one of the main reasons all those jobs are not created is because of budget, which is in turn limited by what people are prepared to pay in taxes, and by the size of the economy in general.

Yet the strange thing is that in the very same nation you may have several million people on benefits of some kind, who would love to have a job. It's all a question of pay scales, benefit structures, incentives and fairness. So there will be plenty of work to do in tomorrow's world, and there will also be plenty of 'paid' workers in developed nations to do it. The problem will often be a structural one within society itself.

At the same time, as we will see in the next chapter, most people in the UK gladly volunteer to give their time at some point in their lives, for no financial reward, to do some of the tasks listed above. Yet if they are on benefits, in many parts of the world it becomes more complicated for them to do such voluntary work.

Internships as fast track to a great job

Expect sharper debate about the real value of training – university, apprenticeships, internships, second degrees, MBAs, and so on. One thing is certain: while business schools will continue to try to justify expensive MBAs, the fast-track route into many companies will be internships. In the US 63% of students already complete at least one internship before qualifying.

Why offices have a great future

As we saw in Chapter 3, just as with cities, the future is bright for offices. Teams love being together as tribes, breathing the same air, and video calls are no substitute for face-to-face trust-building.

Expect radical changes in how offices are used. Office space per worker has already fallen by 35% in 15 years, and will fall a further 25–30% in the next 15, with more hot-desking and partial home-working, and very few workers using fixed desktop computers. And it is true that more informal meetings will be in coffee shops. But most major company activities over the next two decades will be via face-to-face meetings at offices, in most parts of the world.

Expect more corporations to completely outsource the management of their offices. Typical contracts for large banks or retail chains will be worth over $1bn a year. Facilities management will dominate hotels, manufacturers, airports, schools, hospitals and prisons as well as offices.

Corporate HQs overtaken by events

Elaborate HQ spending by huge multinationals will grow, with a number of embarrassing mistakes as mergers or sell-offs force relocation or re-sizing of HQs, even before buildings have been completed. More real-estate rich companies will sell off and lease back their properties to release cash for their core businesses, creating a boom in real estate management.

Future of homeworking

Over 4 million in the UK work mainly or exclusively from home, 14% of the workforce, but this has increased by only 3% since 1998 – hardly the stampede out of office life that many pundits predicted back then.

Even IT companies like Yahoo and Google have discouraged or banned homeworking. Of course, it could be said that almost everyone now works from home to a certain extent, due to ever-present email, smartphones, and so on, but very few people *decide* to work mainly or exclusively from home when offered the chance to do so by their companies. More popular is working at home one day a week, or for short periods of time.

Most so-called homeworkers are self-employed, in the older age bracket, and higher earning. Many self-employed people work outside their own home – for example, as cleaners, plumbers or childminders. Only 34% of homeworkers are employed by an organisation.

Patterns of daily work will continue to change

Most office workers will still commute to work in 20 years' time for at least two to three days a week, although they will be entirely mobile, able to work at any desk, any seat, in any situation. The primary function of workplaces will be sharing ideas, provoking thought, testing solutions, making decisions, monitoring progress. As we have seen, paper will still be used in many meetings by 2025, and whiteboards or flipcharts will continue to be a vital way of capturing and synthesising ideas in 2030.

We will also see more virtual teams and virtual organisations – particularly smaller companies with employees scattered in every continent, most of whom have never met, and where most are paid as required in consulting-type arrangements rather than fixed salaries.

More portfolio workers

More people will work shifts as our whole world transitions to an always-available culture, and as companies become more globalised, supporting staff and customers across time zones.

Far more people will work part-time or as portfolio workers. Over a million men in the UK now choose to work less than full-time, following what was predominantly a female work pattern. For many, part-time contracts will be a door into portfolio working, picking up a day or two a week of regular work, or project work, alongside longer roles.

Time zone challenges

Globalisation will continue to mean long-distance travel for many senior executives, because most people find endless electronic meetings rather impersonal.

The greatest barrier to the global village is sunlight. In a 'perfect' working world, every team member would be in the same time zone. And that is the crux of a growing problem.

Longer, less intense working hours

As a result, we will see a shift in how leaders work – with many virtual meetings, very early or late, but with more time off in the middle of the day. A new kind of routine that will make more sense to those who work a lot at home, especially if their partners frequently do the same.

Living 'on call' is nothing new. Doctors, among others, have been used to it for decades. Some say that this new pattern of global time-keeping is unhealthy or unnatural. But it is far more in tune with the old hunter-gatherer pattern of life, and of course is the normal pattern for mothers or fathers at home alone with several small children. The daily routine in such environments cannot be neatly switched on or off.

The problem of daylight incompatibility is made worse by cross-cultural differences. A company in San Francisco trading with Dubai finds not only a disruptive time difference, but also that Dubai works from only 7 am till 1 pm and does not work on Fridays – yet works a normal day on Sundays.

Workforce in danger of being left behind

Despite new technology, people will always be less mobile than capital, technology, information and raw materials. And as we have seen, tribalism is a social force that thrives on breathing the same air, so local teams are here to stay.

Skills in a workforce will continue to be a vital national asset. Expect large-scale investment in work-related skills, with special emphasis on health, engineering, technology and other sciences, by governments of many emerging markets such as China, South Korea and Saudi Arabia. Imagine trying to create a new Silicon Valley in France, attracting hundreds – even thousands – of key technology personnel there from the US. It would be almost impossible. If you want skills, you will move your site to where those skills are. This is not just about local communities, but about national psyche, tax incentives, conversations in the local bar or coffee house, or a deal forged over a game of golf.

Home ownership makes moving more difficult and expensive. In France, Italy, Spain and Belgium the cost of selling a house and buying another is rather high. Home ownership is less of a barrier to moving in the US, as the process of buying and selling is easier.

Home ownership will continue to be popular, but owner-occupation may decline because of pressures on mobility. Many home owners will become absentee landlords, renting out homes while they are working in other places.

Executives often need more than money to move, however, and in many Western nations where most people have a reasonable standard of living, other factors will become more important. For example, most workers with frail parents will continue to think twice before making long-distance moves. Similarly, parents with teenagers at a critical stage in their education are often extremely reluctant to make a major move. As are those on their second or third marriages, having perhaps learned painful lessons from the past about neglecting home life, and now with a 'new' set of very young children they are determined to give more time to.

Employers will need to give far greater attention to double career households, where two people's futures need to be considered in any major move.

Lower down the social scale are armies of mobile male workers in countries like India who are used to spending 11 months a year away from home, earning money to support a wife and family. Many go farther afield, for example working in Dubai as taxi drivers, returning only once every 2–3 years to see loved ones. But these kinds of lifestyles will not be tolerated by a younger generation of emerging middle-class workers, who have fought hard for a university degree.

Ageing workers – radical changes ahead

One in three people who are still working after the age of 65 in the UK have no idea when they will be able to retire. One in seven of the entire workforce have no plans to retire at all, and a third have no private pension. Bizarrely, most 25–31-year-olds believe they will probably retire when they are younger than 65, presumably because they cannot imagine being so 'ancient'.

Older workers will form an increasingly important part of the workforce, especially in Europe, Japan and China. Managers will face many delicate dilemmas as retirement ages are abolished. How do you counsel someone out of their job who has become too rigid in thinking, or is slightly forgetful, or too physically frail to continue safely? With no fixed retirement ages, managers will have to fire older people. Managing elderly team members will be one of the most stressful and time-consuming aspects of any senior role in future.

Managing talent with purpose

Expect rapid growth in consultancies and management tools, to help large corporations identify, promote, reward and develop the most talented people they have. Making best use of people with the right skills, experience, cultural understanding, product knowledge and customer insight will give companies a key advantage in the future. It will be a natural extension to knowledge management – making the most of what we know – although knowledge management projects often fail to deliver. Linked to this will be a growing emphasis on giving people purpose and fulfilment at work, connecting with their natural desire to make a difference. We will explore this further in the next chapter.

And finally... a 'BIG IDEA'

Clusters of radical single issues do not make a political creed. The vacuum in politics will remain. We have seen how a void was created with the collapse of communism. And in the depths of this empty chasm we will see new issues emerge.

The hunger for radical change is certainly there. I was lecturing recently to a group of Fellows from the World Economic Forum who were asking all kinds of radical questions about the way the global economy works. How can we find a more sustainable model? Is it right to assume that relentless economic growth is a good idea, and so on. How can we find models of capitalism that are more humane?

Lesson from communism

Karl Marx was born in Prussia in 1818 and died in London in 1883. He wrote *The Communist Manifesto* in 1847. He was a product of his time: a protester against the Industrial Revolution, which placed wealth and power in the hands of a few, 'enslaving millions' in primitive working conditions. Revolution to free workers from capitalist control was Marx's Big Idea.

Tomorrow's Big Idea

We can expect to see another Big Idea emerge (or several conflicting ones), radically different from any large-scale political system in the twentieth century. This new 'ism' will feed on stored-up hunger for change.

The longer the delay in its coming, the longer and deeper the vacuum will be, and the greater the speed with which it is likely to grip the earth. This Big Idea is likely to draw heavily on Islamic or Christian influence, but be separate from mainstream traditions.

What will this new 'Big Idea' be like?

It will be radically different from the old left wing/right wing political divides, a mass movement driven by a cluster of single issues, grouped around a central philosophy or ideal which is likely to be based on the teachings of a respected leader, hard to analyse or describe at first, constantly adapting and reinterpreting, rapidly evolving, long lasting in its effects, highly confusing to old 'logic' politicians. And because of the way our world is shifting demographically and economically, it is statistically more likely that such a movement will have its origins in emerging nations, or will rapidly become established in those parts of the world after a far less dramatic start in a developed nation.

Such a Big Idea could profoundly influence how several billion people think about ethics, values, motivation and personal spirituality, which we now need to turn to in the final chapter.

Chapter 6

ETHICAL

ETHICAL IS THE MOST IMPORTANT Face of the Future. Ethics strikes at the very heart of what it means to be human, to have purpose, ideals, direction, vision – and in some cases spirituality.

Recent banking scandals have been a sharp reminder of why 'ethics' really do matter. From 2009 to 2014, 43 of the world's largest banks were fined $184bn in 117 cases, and that's just those where fines were more than $100m per case, with another 174 cases still to be decided. To give an idea of scale, those fines are equivalent to the size of the entire GDP of New Zealand.

Every week yet more scandals emerge around the world, where executives or government leaders have made money in bad ways. Cheating, deceiving, covering up, over-charging, price manipulation, with whole teams involved, fraud taking place on a gigantic scale, and in a hundred different forms. We will return to this later.

Corruption costs at least 5% ($2.6 trillion) of global GDP – fat bribes for government contracts, tax revenues diverted into secret bank accounts, dishonest judges or crooked policemen, and so on.

Without ethics, our future will surely descend into a lawless hell with more greed, wealth, weapons, chaos and abuse of power. As we have seen, every trend has an ethical dimension, whether invasion of privacy, increasing retirement age, uncensored web, outsourcing of jobs, contrasts in wealth or access to health care.

What kind of world do you want?

Ethics is linked to values, purpose and the meaning of life; why you get out of bed in the morning, what motivates and inspires you, your sense of destiny and personal spirituality. Ethics is also about corporate behaviour, expected conduct, compliance, regulations and boundaries of what is acceptable.

Ethics is also about what kind of world we want to live in. All these things connect with how we feel about life, our hopes, dreams and desires, our passions and motivations. Ethics gives us the framework for a better future. Right or wrong; desirable or undesirable; moral or immoral.

Ethics is usually about *our* future rather than *my* future – about the greatest good for the greatest number – and is therefore linked to sustainability. If a group of people dominate a community in a way that the rest regard as *un*ethical, the result is usually revolution, even though that may only be after a great struggle.

Of course every tribe and nation has its own culture, way of life and ethical code, every religion its own standards. Can there be, therefore, a *universal* ethic that will shape our future? Can we find a view of *all future ethics* based on future common sense?

The search for future purpose

Our world is changing, but human nature is the same as it was two thousand years ago. People still look for meaning in their lives and want to feel that they make a difference. As a physician, I worry if someone tells me that they don't feel they have any meaning in their life, they don't feel they contribute anything very much to those around them, and that although they may be loved by their families, they have nothing really to offer.

I can tell you that such a person should be put immediately on the danger list. They are surely low in spirits, and their risk of self-harm or suicide will be high. When we lose a sense of purpose or of making a difference, something dies deep inside our soul. That is one reason why old people tend to live longer when they own a pet dog or cat, and why so many old people die soon after the death of a partner or a pet. 'I have to get myself going in the morning for his sake'. 'I worry about who will look after her when I have gone'. These are motivating feelings.

This search for purpose is more intense when people have more money and time to think. The M generation (see p. 11) is particularly focused on purpose. I have taught at various business schools over the last 15 years. The new generation no longer see an MBA as a fast track to joining the board of a multinational. Most want instead to be successful, work for themselves and 'have a life'. They want to make a difference. They want to work for companies they believe in, selling products and services that make the world a better place.

The ultimate ethical test

When I started out as a cancer physician over three decades ago my job was to look after people dying at home in the last few weeks of life. I learned a very important lesson. Life is short.

Life is far too short to waste it doing things you don't believe in.

When I lecture around the world, I often ask audiences to put up their hands if they agree with me, and almost everyone does. Sometimes they shout, cheer and clap.

Why sell rubbish? Believe in yourself.

Why sell things you would never dream of recommending to a friend or a member of your family? Why bother to sell things that you know are not right for your customers? Why bother to work for a company that you are ashamed of, or uneasy about? The meaning of life is fundamental. Purpose for living is a deep human desire.

As we saw at the start of this book, many people are realising that there is more to life than selling. There is more to life than managing. There is more to life than working. In fact, there is more to life than life itself. What will I leave when I die? How will my children remember me when I'm gone?

I remember giving a trends presentation in New York to the board of a huge global corporation. Among many slides, I showed one for a few seconds with the words:

Life is too short to sell things you don't believe in

I learned afterwards that one of the board members was so struck that she resigned her post almost immediately, not from that board, but from her high-flying job as CEO of one of the largest private banks in the world.

She realised in a moment of crisis that she did *not* believe in what she was doing, selling bank products with the highest commissions rather than those that were best for her customers. She now runs her own corporation, providing independent financial advice to very wealthy clients. She was not doing anything 'wrong' before, but suddenly felt very uneasy.

Unethical – or just feeling uneasy?

The question of *ease* or *unease* is a central test of how ethics will play out in future. You may be asked to do something, and there is no law against it, nor is there any absolute reason why you should not do it, many others are already doing it, but the thought makes you feel *uneasy*.

Ease of mind is the whisper of conscience, and a powerful guide to future ethics.

We have seen this hundreds of times in the last decade alone, in banking scandals, corruption investigations, and a host of other media stories. All too often, actions that only caused a flicker of unease at the time are condemned as unethical within a year or two, and soon become illegal, with offenders in prison.

Follow the spirit of every agreement

A strong test is not what the *letter* of a long contract actually says, but what the *spirit* of the agreement is all about. Not what you may be able to get away with, but what is the right thing to do.

I have advised many large corporations on tricky ethical issues. Time and again I have seen that the kneejerk reaction of most business leaders is to protect company profits and their own share options, even if it means kicking their customers, or suppliers, or staff or regulators. But the bitter reality usually dawns on them soon after. They realise in most cases that the future of their business, and personal careers, will depend on being more gracious, more considerate, and more rounded in their approach.

Why hiding behind legal opinion is so risky

The harder people try to justify themselves, the more likely it is that they are in deep trouble, even if they will not admit it. I remember a situation a while back where lawyers were being paid a small fortune to find 'wriggle room' or clauses in every contract that could allow that particular company to get away with what it had been involved in.

Leaders often hide behind legal opinion. But the longer and more complex your legal advice, the weaker your case must be. And as we will see, you can comply with the precise letter of every law, and still be utterly condemned in the media.

Companies will need to take a common-sense view

For me the situation is simple: what are the reasonable expectations of the other party in this agreement? How would you like to be treated yourself, if you were in their shoes? What is a common-sense view? What will the public's gut feeling be if they read about this in the media? When you try to explain what you are doing to a member of your family or to a close friend, do you feel completely comfortable or do you sense a little twinge deep inside? Will your grandchildren be proud of this kind of activity when they grow up?

'But everyone else is doing it'

I recall another situation where the argument from a particular company was that although the practice of giving hidden 'benefits' to customers was illegal in some countries, everyone else in the industry was doing it. If they stopped, they would go out of business. If they blew the whistle on the entire industry to regulators, they would be blamed by all their customers, and would also go out of business.

My advice was simple: you will be found out one day anyway, as it will only take a single former employee or customer to go public;

you will gain a huge moral advantage in coming clean and exposing wrong practices; and you will make things far worse by continuing when fully aware of the problem. And I was right. Huge corporate fines followed, the senior team at the time was disgraced, and the brand was damaged globally.

Only sell what you believe in

Here is a fundamental, safe, ethical rule of life, that will last 10,000 years.

Always treat others as you would like to be treated. That means staff, customers, business partners, road drivers, toilet cleaners, suppliers, associates, neighbours, friends and family.

If every manager and leader in every company followed this value, our world would be a better place, and we would have far stronger corporate ethics.

$20,000 competition to test the secret of all ethics

A few years ago I wrote *Building a Better Business*. In it, I promised $20,000 to anyone who could find a way to sell a product, lead, manage or motivate people without using a particular four-word phrase – in one way or another.* I have offered the same prize to many tens of thousands in my corporate audiences over the last decade.

This four-word phrase, or the idea within it, turns out to be the basis of every effective corporate mission statement, every marketing slogan that works, every leadership vision, the foundation of all change management, and will be the cornerstone of all corporate ethics for over 1000 years. So what is this simple four-word phrase, and why has no one ever won the $20,000 prize?

Building a better world

That is what all ethics is about, and is where all human purpose

---

* Prize donated by me to any charitable foundation chosen by the winner. See rules in the book *Building a Better Business*.

comes from. Find me a human being who thinks that the world is a *worse* place because of the work they do, or because of the air they breathe, or because of their very existence, and as I say, you have someone who is in deep personal crisis.

So if you want to know the future of corporate values, which mission statements will have greatest inspirational power, which motivational tools will work best, the answers are all contained in that phrase, and always will be. The fundamental question for every future lawmaker, regulator, judge or jury will always be this: will this decision make our world a better or worse place?

Building a better world is hard-wired into our genes

As little children, we soon learn ways to make life better for ourselves. Then we become aware of the existence of others, that life is also about making life better for members of our family, and for our friends. A further stage of growing up is wanting to make life better for our neighbours and community, and also in some small way for our wider world.

These ethical instincts are part of our nature, as social creatures, as human beings that form families, tribes, nations. We see much the same in the animal kingdom, especially among 'higher' mammals, in social packs, communities, herds, or even in nesting instincts of birds.

Why crimes are so rare

These ethical instincts are the reason why crimes are so *rare*. Think about it. When you travel on the metro or walk across the street. Consider the value of what you are carrying – perhaps a smartphone, a portable computer, credit cards and cash.

If someone came up to you with a knife and asked for your phone and wallet, how likely would you be to put up a fight? Most people just hand things over. So it's an easy and instant win for any impulsive thief. And if they run away fast, or are with friends, they are very unlikely to be arrested. But how often does it happen? The answer is very rarely, considering the wealth that many carry.

Consider again the power of one billion car owners to cause

terror and carnage, as a deliberate act to create fear or promote a cause. But how often around the world do people accelerate into crowds of pedestrians? Answer: almost never – less than one episode per billion drivers per week on average over the last few years.

For the same reason, there are very few arbitrary shootings of strangers or stabbings, or bomb attacks – even if you include murders by people who are severely mentally ill. Yet you will find sharp knives as 'lethal weapons' in every kitchen, in every home. America has more guns in homes than adults, and simple bombs are easy for any older child to make, using instructions online.

To the CIA: where have all those terrorists gone?

I will never forget the surreal experience of listening to a former CIA leader discussing global threats with a private group of twenty-five senior bankers, in a grave and 'confidential', whispering voice, as though he was afraid we would be overheard.

In a few minutes he almost had us all convinced that our nations were in imminent danger of being overwhelmed by evil powers; that anthrax spores could be concealed in every light bulb; and that we might all be about to witness, with our own eyes, a series of terror attacks. But as we have seen, terror attacks are very rare in global terms, and the lifetime risk for most people is less than being struck by lightning – less than one death per 350,000 people a year.

Secret service people like this CIA leader often try to claim that the *reason* so few attacks happen is that the state is so good at *disrupting* many thousands of terror plots. But you don't need a sophisticated terror group, or to be part of a plot, to commit an act of terror in an instant. You only need a gun, or knife, or car, particularly if you don't care about your own safety or about being caught. So, I asked the man from the CIA: given that every home contains 'deadly' weapons, and 1 billion people have the keys to a 'lethal' car, where *are* all these crowds of terrorists? And of course he was rather embarrassed, because he knew he could not give his audience any convincing answer.

Of course we all knew the truth as to why such terror acts are so rare. The fact is that murdering another person is hard to do *emotionally*, even if the killer thinks the victim is evil, even where the killer has lost his temper, even where such killing is to promote a cause.

I am not for a moment wanting to understate the very present dangers from organised or spontaneous acts of terror, nor devalue the vital role that security services play every day in helping to keep us all safe. All I am saying is that it is easy to lose a wider perspective, the real truth about humanity as a whole.

Throughout almost all of human history you will find a common code of respect within societies, and this same code will also dominate the next hundred years. Enshrined increasingly in laws, human rights regulations, and cultural expectations, our world is increasingly aligned to common ethics, despite gory media headlines.

The search for human happiness – Happynomics

Personal purpose and sense of fulfilment are closely related to happiness. Expect huge growth in research on human happiness and radical questions about values when the results confirm this truth. Research into Happynomics shows that happiness in developed nations is strongly linked to some or all of the following: mid-range income, good friends, stable marriage or partnership, strong faith or spirituality, extrovert nature, liking your job, living in a stable democracy.

A survey of 64,000 people in 65 nations found that 70% of people are content with their lives. Africa is the place where people are happiest (83%), while people in Western Europe are the least happy, with 11% saying they are unhappy or very unhappy. In Africa 75% expect life to get better, compared to only 26% in Europe.

Agony columns are full of advice about how to have happy relationships. In a fractured, increasingly disordered and fast-moving world, long-term relationships are going to matter more. One sign of success for the future will be to be living happily with the same person for a long time. What's so smart about a string of failed marriages, shacked-up arrangements or temporary flings?

Value for things that do not change

As we saw in Chapter 1, there is a premium on buildings, trees and landscapes that have remained the same for a long time. This is part of the fundamental human need for security, for things that endure. Most humans cannot cope with continuous changes in all areas of their lives without risk of emotional disorder and inefficiency.

Change is a major cause of stress: whether moving house, job, having a child or getting married or divorced.

Single issues and ethics go hand in hand

Single issues define a problem, but only ethics can tell you what position to take. Expect more fierce debates and soul-searching over such issues as arms sales, as attempts are made to define exactly what arms are. Do you include machine tools used to make arms, for example? A global company can find itself caught in the crossfire between shareholder opinion, public perception and views of staff. There may also be a variety of attitudes within the same government, ranging from approval to turning a blind eye to outright opposition and legal action.

Activists are often sharply divided over the ethics of – say – wind power (damaging skyline) compared to solar power (damaging roof appearance and fields), or nuclear power or gas power.

Political correctness and thought control

'Political correctness' will grow in power in the next three decades as single-issue groups try to control the words we use. It is hard to express ideas if words are banned. 'Mentally challenged' instead of mentally handicapped. 'Senior citizens' instead of the elderly or retired. 'Visually impaired' instead of blind.

Defending civil liberties

We will see more attempts by governments to justify bad things, with the argument that 'the end justifies the means'. So people today can have their homes broken into by the police or secret service or their smartphone bugged just because a politician or government worker says it should be done. No warrant is needed in many countries: the police can hold you for days without explanation.

You can be arrested for joining a peaceful demonstration and if you are silent on arrest a jury may be invited to conclude that you had something to hide. You have no right to information the government holds about you. Many nations have a benign democracy, but in a country with a malignant dictator laws like these are especially oppressive.

Civil liberties will remain on the agenda of most nations of the world, especially as online surveillance and tracking becomes almost universal. Human rights will also continue to be a major issue, especially in negotiation of trade agreements with developing countries. There will be many agonies of conscience over whether a government should engage in buying or selling major contracts with 'odious' regimes – and debates on how such things should be determined.

Challenging human rights abuse in other nations

Many will argue that there is no point in criticising a nation for poor human rights, when your own economy depends on trade with them, and where such protests are only likely to increase the cultural isolation that already exists.

Most challenges by America or the EU to countries like China will continue to fall on deaf ears, and will be rejected as pompous and arrogant, based on ignorance. The Chinese government believes that the greatest human right is to be able to work and eat food rather than starve, and believes it is doing well with these things, while being more open than for decades as an evolving society. China believes that too much freedom, too fast, could place at risk all that has been achieved so peacefully. There is a belief that 'leaders know best' what is good for the people. A similar paternalistic attitude was seen in the UK Conservative Party in the 1980s.

Expect to hear more about human responsibilities, with responsibilities and rights becoming equal pillars of global codes of ethics. The Universal Declaration of Human Rights was a product of the Second World War, and was set out in 1948. Expect a similar Declaration of Human Responsibilities.

Wealth can create a more ethical world

Most people in developed nations have doubts about the ethics of business, and many question the ethics of endless economic growth. However, the truth is that business has generated wealth at astonishing speed for humankind over the last 30 years, and will continue to do so.

Since 2000, the percentage of the world living on less than $1.25 a day has fallen from 30% to below 10%, after adjusting for inflation. This is because the wealth of emerging nations has grown each year on average around 4.5% faster than that of developed nations – an astonishing achievement, driven largely by growth in global trade. If similar growth rates continue for just the next 30 years, the average income in the world will then be equal to that of US citizens today.

Of course, such growth rates are unsustainable, and it is more realistic to expect that such an equalisation may take 50–80 years or more.

Justice and wealth contrasts

As we have seen, half of all global wealth is owned by the richest 1% – one of the greatest and unsustainable ethical stains on our world. The gap is growing between those with a life expectancy of 100 years and those with a life expectancy of 35 years, between those with unlimited health care and those who have to walk barefoot for over 50km to find a (badly equipped) clinic.

At the extreme end of this inequality scale are human slavery, bonded labour and trafficking. Around 30 million people are enslaved today, in an industry worth over $32bn a year for traffickers alone. Of these 30 million, 78% are sold for labour, and 22% forced to become sex workers. One in 25 of the entire population of Mauritania is a slave and there are estimated to be 14 million slaves in India alone. Expect many more efforts to stamp out the global slave trade. A big ethical question is what to do with slaves once they are rescued. Are they automatically given rights of residence in the country they are now in?

Foreign aid will often be viewed as imperialism

One way to improve the lives of the very poor is with foreign aid, for such things as health care or education. But government aid can be seen as a form of imperialism, especially as donations are usually linked to contracts for the donor's own consultants and supplies.

Autocratic leaders in emerging nations can regard well-meaning NGOs as interfering, condescending critics of their nations, sending home to wealthy supporters hundreds of tearjerking photos of dreadful situations, which are bad for the national image, and give a very distorted view of life in general.

Some of the poorest nations are dominated by development projects. In places like Sierra Leone a large percentage of vehicles on the road belong to organisations such as UNICEF, a sign of a 'donor-dependent' economy.

It is extremely difficult for foreign-funded projects to operate without distorting local priorities, and money can fall into the wrong hands. A community leader has a shopping list of ten items, ranging from roads to water and clinics. An NGO is offering help with literacy – and may themselves be corrupt or self-serving. The help is accepted and a new education facility is built. It may be helpful, but was it the most appropriate next step?

The most sustainable models of development or philanthropy have an element of redundancy built in. For example, AfriKids is a charity operating in northern Ghana to relieve child poverty and suffering. A stated aim by the founder in the beginning was to be able to close itself down one day. And in the AIDS charity ACET that I started some years back, that is just what we did for a home care programme in the UK – once we saw that government-paid doctors, nurses and home carers were doing what needed to be done.

Trade rather than aid

In Africa most governments are aiming for low inflation, low budget deficits and encouragement of private business. But until America and Europe stop blocking imports of African goods and food, and cease dumping their own subsidised farm products, there will be slower progress.

Many African leaders hate being bullied by Western governments into lifting currency controls and other measures. They fear the economic rape of their nations by new imperialists, whether Chinese or American, who use money instead of guns, take local control in subtle ways, pay little for resources, and take wealth out.

They have little choice, it seems, but to allow their economies to become the puppets of globalised power bases. Multinationals and Sovereign Wealth Funds will experience brittle relationships with governments and peoples, which may snap at short notice.

Does the lift factor actually work?

What will happen to the poorest of the poor? Will they be lifted as these national economies grow, or will they be trampled? Some have argued from experience in Indian cities such as Mumbai that the rich get richer while the poor still starve and die. That may be true in the short term but not in the medium to longer term.

As we have seen repeatedly over the last 350 years, economic growth transforms entire nations, although it can take some time. More money begins to circulate, productivity rises, taxable income rises, and government spending increases, so that entire nations benefit.

The greater the contrasts between rich and poor in a society, the greater the risks of instability, as antagonism, aggression and organised opposition grow. Therefore, all healthy developed societies will always redistribute wealth to some degree, even if in the interests of self-preservation rather than because of troubled conscience.

Ethical pay for business leaders

Gaps in pay will widen in large corporations, with even higher remuneration packages at the very top for outstanding leaders and advocates, people who make things happen. There is a severe global scarcity of agile decision-makers with industry experience, proven track records, excellent communication skills and creative genius. One reason why such large packages will be needed is to entice such people into helping companies perform. Many of the world's most talented and experienced leaders have already made so much money that they have no financial need to work. Tempting people back into another demanding CEO or chairman role can require a combination of huge financial rewards, an interesting challenge and a high-profile company.

If a company with a multibillion-dollar turnover plunges into the red following two disastrous CEO appointments, it is in the interests of the company to pay a huge price to guarantee sorting the problem out fast.

We are seeing a great ethical dilemma in banking. People do not want to pay bankers ridiculously high salaries, but it will be difficult to persuade the brightest and most experienced business leaders to lead banks or sit on their boards without this. Why *should* they take huge personal risks for less reward, and possibly even risk ending up in prison, when so many other more attractive jobs beckon? We need to be sure that rewards are linked to success and to the level of risk that the person is taking in accepting the job.

Corporate ethics – meltdown of trust

Of course, high salaries would be easier to tolerate if people trusted such business leaders to behave ethically. Only a third of people in the UK believe that business behaves ethically, and only half think that business makes a positive contribution to society. You will find similar answers in many other countries.

This is really damaging to the future of business – because it means that many of the world's most talented people are no longer interested in a business career. (We have already seen that most have also rejected the idea of a career in politics.) It is yet another reason why so many people want to run their *own* businesses, or work in very small companies, which they think are more ethical as well as personal.

But the fact is that every nation needs large companies. Without them, there is nothing left except individual traders, non-profit organisations and government. We have already seen in Chapter 4 that globalisation means economies of scale. Only the largest companies survive in many industries. If a nation has no large corporations, its economy will be dominated by foreign players. Large companies are huge employers. They attract international investment into a nation. They create clusters of expertise in key industries, and usually feed orders into many thousands of local smaller companies as suppliers.

Corporate meltdown, massive lawsuits and fines

As we have seen, never in human history have so many businesses been fined or prosecuted for so many ethical lapses. In a single month of 2014, Bank of America was fined $17bn, Goldman Sachs $1.2bn and Standard Chartered a further $300m. Earlier in the same year, huge fines were levied on Morgan Stanley, Citigroup, Credit Suisse, Toyota, Barclays, Rabobank, General Electric and Bank of America (in a separate case). And other companies like Walmart and General Motors seemed about to be in the firing line.

The personal protection insurance (PPI) scandal in the UK will end up costing the industry over $40bn. The Libor manipulation scandal will cost far more. Around $350 trillion of financial products are linked in some way to Libor in calculating how much interest is paid, and banks made money by manipulating those rates for their own benefit. Very large numbers of institutions may be able to take legal action for compensation, in a process that could become as large as lawsuits over asbestos.

A single Alabama lawsuit relating to Libor is likely to involve claims on behalf of 100,000 home owners. Libor affected mortgages, credit cards, student loans – the whole of society in some developed nations. There are suggestions that Libor manipulation had been going on since 1991.

Over 2,000 convictions were brought against corporations in America by federal agencies from 2000 to 2014. This does not include the huge growth in civil fines – in two years alone, state and federal agencies received over $20bn just from settlements related to the False Claims Act. Whistleblowers receive a proportion of payouts, so there is now a financial incentive to keep companies ethical.

Why compliance is dead

The cost of compliance, amid ever-widening regulation, is growing apace. Large corporations in America are now spending around $40m each on record-keeping systems to comply with more than 300,000 separate legal statutes. Smaller companies don't have the resources to cope, so can end up the wrong side of the law straight away.

Compliance really matters. However, as many bankers discovered, compliance with each and every law may keep you out of prison but cannot protect your brand or reputation, or build trust. You can comply perfectly with every regulation in every country in every year, but that will not help you when public mood changes, in response to the latest financial scandal.

A scandal happens, which is followed by a public reaction, which leads to new regulations. These are then interpreted by lawyers, who try to work out what it means for your business. And then your own compliance teams turn it all into another box-ticking exercise to check you really are compliant. But this is not enough. You are only complying with history.

For example, until recently it was perfectly legal for a European company to pay a large bribe to an official in another nation outside the EU, list it as a business expense, get it signed off by the auditors, and claim back tax from the government. The more they bribed, the more tax refunds they received. But it is no good today for the chairman of such a company to declare that he was well aware of bribes being paid back then and that 'it was all done perfectly legally'. He will lose his job, will never work again, and the reputation of his company will be damaged.

As I predicted many years ago, future legal advice will have to go far beyond today's regulations, to consider what might be the next headlines, the next scandals, the next pressures on regulators, and how the public mood might change. How might a future generation feel about this? And it may not be a simple question of right and wrong. We need to take a clear moral lead, set apart from ambiguity and fudged issues.

Pressures on ethical business to define real success

Real success in future will mean demonstrating how your corporation makes a difference for everyone: for shareholders of course, but also for customers, workers, the wider community and, in some small way, for the whole of humanity – for example, by protecting the environment.

There is a risk that 'ethical' employers (forced to be ethical by law) will lose out to 'unethical' employers. So, for example, jobs in well-regulated, clean factories in a nation like America are lost as production switches to filthy factories with dangerous working conditions in a country like Bangladesh. Workers in the poorest nations may be paid almost nothing, with no job security, massive health and safety risks, no sick pay or other rights.

We will see many new regulations in consuming regions like the EU to stop corporations from escaping their moral obligations in developed nations. We have seen examples of this in global action to stop children working in textile factories.

Doing well by doing good

Companies like Unilever have led the way in reducing environmental footprint, and increasing positive social impact, with aims to help a billion people improve their health and well-being, halve the environmental impact of its products and source all its agricultural materials sustainably. In three years, the amount of sustainable agricultural supplies it used increased from 14% to 48%.

Companies such as Patagonia, Interface, Marks and Spencer, Nestlé, Nike, Natura, GE, Walmart, Puma, IKEA and Coca-Cola have taken similar steps.

Ethics of child labour – easy to get wrong

Few global companies today would risk 'knowingly' employing

six-year-old children for 12 hours a day to make clothes. Yet in Bangladesh alone it is estimated that 80,000 children under 14, mostly girls, work at least 60 hours a week in garment factories.

Sadly, moral outrage can easily wreck the lives of the very children we need to protect. An international campaign led to millions of children being dumped as workers. Many went straight onto the streets, where they were at far greater risk. In most nations of the world, destitute children either have to work, beg or starve. It is as simple as that.

So where did all those 'redundant' children go? If you clear children out of a factory, some will beg at the gates of other lower-profile factories, until eventually another manager takes pity, and gives them some scraps to eat. Before long this manager may have twenty more at his gates, sleeping in the compound. He provides bedding and food, and in return they sweep the factory floor, or help with packing. Ethical or unethical? Humanitarian or criminal? Are you *really* sure how you would feel yourself in such a situation?

As I have seen in my work with the ACET foundation, the average length of time from an 11-year-old runaway girl drifting into one of the railway stations in Mumbai and being picked up by a criminal gang can be less than 12 hours. Such girls are usually raped violently and repeatedly, and are caged in a filthy brothel until their spirits are completely broken. Then they are pimped for years in the Red Light District, among 200,000 other sex workers, until they die of AIDS or look too old.

And maybe all because that girl was suddenly turned out on the streets, after living and working as an orphan, since the age of 8, in a small textile factory.

The lesson is that while ethical issues like child labour are really important, and must be addressed, they need to be tackled in the context of overall community development, with a deeper understanding of the local situation.

Non-profit organisations set to grow

Each year more than two billion people give time to things they believe in without being paid, or to help people outside their immediate circle of family and friends.

Philanthropy is a rapidly growing feature of middle-class life, with spectacular growth in mega-donations from the super-wealthy, on a scale that will create problems for some foundations in how to spend each dollar with care and accountability, in appropriate ways. Super-rich donors in the UK alone are giving away more than £2 billion a year. Warren Buffett gave $3 billion in a single gift in 2012.

But philanthropy is as old as human civilisation itself, and the poorer people are, the more they volunteer. All traditional rural societies have strong social codes that protect the vulnerable in their tribal communities, linked to extensive intermarriage in villages, which means that most people are blood related. So orphans are usually taken into homes of relatives, a home that burns down is rapidly rebuilt with help of others, someone who is blind is brought food, and so on. These communities often function with minimal use of cash, as co-operative societies, overseen by village elders.

Volunteering will be almost universal

The growth of volunteering in towns and cities mimics these ancient traditions, for people who have often lost that kind of connection with those around them.

In a typical month, the percentage of people volunteering may be different across the world but is almost always significant: 56% of those in Turkmenistan volunteer on a formal basis with organisations, 45% in Sri Lanka, 44% in the US, 28% in the UK and 13% in Sweden. But these figures do not cover informal volunteering, which accounts for the majority of time given.

In the UK, the number of hours given by formal volunteers is equivalent to 1.25 million paid workers, almost as many as work in the health service. If each hour of time is valued at the average wage, the contribution of volunteering to the national economy is the equivalent of around £25bn, with an additional £25bn for informal or irregular time, for example, sweeping the snow from an old person's drive. That's about the same as 3% of the national GDP. And as the number of people in active retirement grows, we can expect more older volunteers.

Privatising services to the non-profit sector

Volunteer agencies will be useful to governments, as ideal partners. As a result, a growing proportion of the welfare state will be privatised to non-profit organisations (NPOs) in many developed nations, to save costs. Many contracts will be awarded preferentially to charities, to avoid the impression that private companies are making big profits out of government contracts, for things like health care.

NPOs will become more efficient and business-like, with greater professionalism, audit and evaluation. Fierce competition between NPOs will be on a par with anything in the commercial sector today.

There will also be competition between commercial and non-profit organisations, with accusations that NPOs are undercutting prices by using unpaid labour as volunteers, or with cash donations. The whole concept of charitable work will be called into question in some sectors, as many agencies find themselves in a primary role as subcontractors to government. As part of this shift, some volunteers will question whether their act of generosity is being abused by government, to cut costs and jobs.

Social enterprises will become more fashionable. These are corporations that expect to make profits, while also achieving the kind of objectives that an NPO might aim for. This hybrid model will be particularly attractive to a new generation of entrepreneurs, and philanthropically minded investors.

Future of privacy and personal freedom

In Chapter 1 we touched on a whole range of urgent ethical questions relating to the online world. Who owns my data? Can I ask for my online records to be deleted before I die, or at death? Are social media sites responsible for censoring people who publish inappropriate or criminal material?

Most nations will move towards greater web controls over the next 10–20 years, including age-restricted access. As we have seen, over 100 nations already censor web access in some way. Expect stronger laws against online bullying, sexting and other activities designed to intimidate or embarrass.

Many emerging autocracies will make huge efforts to stop web access by residents, except via servers that they regulate or control. A growing number of developed nations will attempt a version of the same thing. It is also likely to become illegal in some nations to attempt to view pages on the dark web, or to use certain untraceable virtual currencies.

Many nations will expect social media companies to take all reasonable measures to prevent broadcasting of illegal or antisocial content, however that is defined by each government (and that of course will be at times a very disturbing question, because some governments will take such censorship to extremes).

Liberal activists who campaign for completely unrestricted freedom of expression online are going to sound increasingly out of touch with reality in their defence of a web world where every form of appalling, shocking, degrading, disgusting, cruel, dehumanising and criminal activity can be viewed on just about any device by a child of any age after a couple of seconds of searching.

A strong argument will be that there is absolutely no logic in giving cinema films a child rating if there are no ratings for far stronger content online, and very few parents would want to abolish all cinema ratings. In some nations like Pakistan and Saudi Arabia, censorship issues will be tied up with blasphemy laws.

Alliances linked to religious groups will vigorously support web controls, bitterly opposed by liberal, secular groups who claim that media output is pure fantasy for the most part, and incapable of altering behaviour. Liberal groups will continue to argue that crimes such as rape or violence are entirely unrelated to media output. However, the counter-claim will grow stronger by the month. We will see case after terrible case where prosecution witnesses show that yet another defendant was watching depraved material shortly before committing a horrific, similar crime. In many instances, the person in the dock will be an older child, teenager or impression-able young adult.

As we have seen in earlier chapters, there is overwhelming evidence that media influences behaviour – indeed the entire adver-tising industry is based on the fact that media messages change what people do in measurable ways.

Ethics for robots – rules of engagement

While it may sound like science fiction today, we will need an ethical code to guide decisions of semi-autonomous robots, partic-ularly those in combat or at the wheel. For example, how certain does the robot have to be to fire a weapon, bearing in mind that 20% of war casualties usually result from firing at one's own side? How much do civilian casualties matter? Does it depend on how closely the attack is likely to be reported in the media?

Here is a puzzle for robots: a mother carrying a baby is in the middle of the road, and swerving will kill a retired man with a dog. Which direction should the robot steer, if it cannot stop the car in time? If a passenger in the car is critically ill and needs to go to hospital, does the robot feel comfortable breaking the speed limit, and if so, by how much?

Some have warned of a coming apocalypse for humankind as self-reproducing and rapidly evolving, ultra-intelligent robots somehow take over the planet, leaving humans as a subordinate species, or even threatened with survival. This will remain pure Hollywood-type science fiction for the rest of this 21st century. The fact is that human bodies, made up of billions of living cells, have tens of thousands of subtle features and auto-repair mechanisms. Humans possess a level of miniaturisation that will make even robots built in 2095 look extremely primitive.

However, the 22nd century is quite another matter. By 2150 we can expect to see large numbers of self-reproducing robots, who have huge powers over their own situation, make complex decisions and interact with human beings in a very wide variety of ways. They may align their activities, form opinions, make joint decisions and form a formidable force for change. This will go far beyond the science-fiction view of mechanised creatures, with physical bodies moving around.

We also need to include all forms of sophisticated intelligent machines – which may have no physical presence apart from the chips in which their mental processes run, deep inside a factory or institution. Indeed, such intelligent entities may only be virtually present on our planet, with mega-brains running in the Cloud, interacting, monitoring, thinking, planning, controlling. It will be up to their human designers and programmers to place sufficient limits on their thinking and powers ... if they can.

Common-sense approach to health-related ethics

What about ethics in health care? History shows us that what one generation regards as shocking, immoral or bizarre can feel more natural to the next.

It is also dangerous to generalise about what, say, may appeal to a Western European mind-set without considering what may be acceptable to a majority of Muslims who live under various interpretations of Sharia law in nations like Saudi Arabia, or to those in a strongly Christian nation like Zambia.

The ultimate ethical test applied to health

Whatever the issue in health care, biotech or life sciences, the ultimate ethical value will be based on our four-word phrase, 'building a better world'. If an activity such as human cloning or creation of near non-ageing humans becomes a normal part of life on earth, will our world be a better place as a result or not, not just for today, but for all time? And for the devout Muslim, Christian, Jew, Buddhist or Hindu, is this a step towards the kind of world our Creator intends or is it a violation of the natural order?

There is an added ethical question: perhaps the most important of all. In a world where over 800 million go hungry each day, and where 1 billion have almost zero access to basic health care and only limited access to clean running water, is it right to even think about such medical exotica as we have seen in previous chapters?

Access to basic health care is one of the deepest ethical challenges in the world today.

You may feel rather distant from such things – and so did I until I saw with my own eyes young children dying in places like Africa for lack of a simple antibiotic, or because the clinic had run out of malaria tablets.

Calls for euthanasia will become almost irresistible

Euthanasia will be a burning medical issue for the next 50 years in developed nations. The 'right to die' will be packaged with other issues, including permission for doctors to end the life of someone who is unfit to take a decision. It will always be doctors – or a court of law – who have to make that call, because someone has to decide whether the person is 'of sound mind', has all the facts and is not under undue pressure from others.

A growing number of doctors will take the law into their own hands in nations that forbid deliberate acts intended to shorten life. We will see more high-profile court cases and 'mercy death' will become a more acceptable practice, especially in countries with rapidly ageing populations.

We will also see a backlash in some nations, where people have been killed who, by most people's reckoning, should still be alive. For example, where it is clear that a person's life has been terminated for no other reason than they were clinically depressed, or felt negative about life because of other mental health issues, or because they felt they were a burden on their families.

One result of legalised euthanasia will be that active treatments will be abandoned far more frequently at an earlier stage, allowing 'nature to take its course', with symptom control measures, even if treating those symptoms makes an earlier death slightly more likely.

Countries with relaxed euthanasia laws will find elderly people taking this way out as the 'responsible thing to do'. Length of average stay in nursing homes or hospices will fall. People who are suffering will commonly be terminated.

In the Netherlands 1% of all deaths are the *deliberate killing of a patient by a doctor without the patient requesting it.* The criteria for euthanasia now include chronic illness and emotional distress.

Despite all this, expect a new emphasis in medical training in most nations not just to cure but to manage death and the dying process. Palliative medicine will be a key growth area in emerging nations. We will see new breakthroughs in the relief of pain, and sales of pain-relieving drugs will rocket globally in the next decade.

Navigating health-related dilemmas

Listed on the next two pages are just a few of the hundreds of wide-ranging ethical dilemmas in the future of health care, biotech and life sciences in general. Remember that we can expect debates within each country, over each issue.

The public may be more or less well informed. Regulators may be very cautious or lacking in powers or there may not be a regulator in that sector. So it becomes very difficult to forecast how globally acceptable issues will be, such as gene screening for insurance purposes, or infertility treatment for 80-year-olds (by 2040 many 80-year-olds will be as young and healthy from a medical point of view as today's 65-year-olds).

Each item on the list is followed by a U or an E (or several Us or Es). This indicates what I predict the level of Unease or Ease with the issue will be globally by 2030.

You may feel that you have a set of clear answers to all the above, but you are in the minority. Most scientists and doctors around the world tend to take a fairly practical view, exploring the limits of what is technically possible one small step at a time, and delegating to society as a whole the bigger ethical questions.

In practice what that means is that research goes ahead of debate, because in most cases scientists hate debating theoretical possibilities. They only want to debate what is possible. And of course, many fear that if what they are trying to do is debated in advance, the public outcry may block their future life's work.

Expect open conflict at times between the general public and the research community, resulting in researchers pursuing all kinds of activities almost in secret, as can happen at present.

Dilemma	Level of ease/unease
Is it right to take action to end the life of an old, frail or sick person because they have lost the will to live?	U
Is it right to abort a perfectly healthy foetus at a stage of pregnancy where it could live outside the womb with help?	UU
Is it right to abort a perfectly healthy foetus at an earlier stage because you would prefer a baby with a different gender, or hair colour, or with more genes likely to make them good at maths?	UU
Is it right to clone yourself, by inserting a nucleus from one of your cells into an unfertilised egg, either to implant the early embryo so that one day you greet your own identical twin as a newborn baby, or to grow the ball of cells so that the tissues can be cannibalised to repair your own body?	UU
Is it right to use tissues from other people's aborted foetuses to repair your own body? Does that encourage other people to have abortions?	UU
Is it right to use adult stem cells to repair your own body?	EEE
Is it right for two men or two women to seek to have a genetic child of their own, by some genetic means or by using a surrogate mother (as 2,000 women do a year in America) or egg or sperm donor?	U
Is it right to allow a child to be created with two mothers and one father – where one mother contributes 1% of her genes, those in her mitochondrial power packs, to correct a terrible gene defect?	E

Dilemma	Level of ease/ unease
Is it right to use injections of gene fragments into muscles to enhance athletic performance in competitions?	UU
Is it right to refuse insurance cover or a new job to someone based on the results of their genetic screening?	U
Is it right to add human genes to farmed fish to make them grow faster?	U
Is it right to add human genes to pigs so that the surfaces of their hearts are altered, enabling them to become donors to people with heart failure?	E
Is it right to add human genes to monkeys to try to find out which genes programme the human brain for speech?	UU
Is it right to use infertility treatments to allow a 70-year-old woman to have a baby?	UU
Is it right for a woman to rent out her own womb to another woman who cannot carry a child?	E
Is it right for a woman to have sex with another woman's partner as a combined egg and womb donor?	UU
Should we allow a pharma company to take some of your genes, identify a new cluster causing your illness, and patent it so they own part of your own genome?	E

As it is, much early research is conducted away from the public eye, so that new pharma products can be developed without alerting competitors.

Expect growing concerns about ethics of using larger animals in laboratories, linked to the global boom in pet ownership. Sales of pet food and pet care already exceed $180bn a year, likely to rise to over $340bn by 2030.

Feminisation of society – impact on ethics

We will see further feminisation of many Western societies. Men are in already in retreat in many developed nations, labelled as testosterone addicts: dangerous, ill-behaved variants of the human species prone to violence, sexual predatory acts and general loutishness and irresponsibility, the victims of a growing chorus of negative comments and abuse. Patriarchal societies are rapidly becoming matriarchal. Female instincts and reactions will be the future norms.

Jobs for the girls

Most new jobs in Britain are going to women. The greatest growth area is part-time work in the service and leisure industries, while traditional full-time manufacturing workers are a dying breed. Tomorrow's jobs will require flexibility, teamwork, efficiency – favouring women. In Japan there has been a huge increase in female influence and power at work.

In terms of consumption, 70% of online purchases of many kinds of products and services in Europe and the US are by women. In banking, 70% of online accounts in some nations are opened by men but 70% of the transactions are by women. Women buy most household goods, books, food and holidays.

Women also dominate spending in traditional retail outlets yet, despite this, most marketing executives and customer relationship managers are men. Expect this to change as companies look to re-brand in a more feminine way. Nevertheless, the feminisation of society still has a long way to go. Men clean the house, but not much more than they did. There is still a glass ceiling blocking promotion for women in many areas and women still have far less leisure time than men.

Expect new men's liberation movements in some nations which in some ways will parallel women's activist groups, seeking greater gender equality for men in some kinds of jobs which have been traditionally done by women, e.g. working in nurseries or in care roles. Gender-role confusion will continue, with a backlash from many women over negative stereotyping of men.

We will also see major shifts in corporate culture, especially as populations age, creating a skills scarcity. Many more women will occupy senior positions, especially on boards, with legal quotas becoming far more common, like those already in place in Germany.

But we will also see men sue women for sexual harassment, intimidation and prejudice in recruitment or the workplace, with demands for male quotas for jobs.

Impact of personal spirituality

We have already looked at radical forces within Islam and their future impact on the Middle East and far beyond. But this is part of a much wider picture, which is playing out rather differently in developing and emerging nations.

Across the developed world, as a result of all the trends described in this book, we are seeing an intense, growing hunger for meaning, often expressed in a search for spirituality, which is very different from membership of an organised religion. The great debate in a nation like the UK or France is not over whether you *believe*, but what you believe *in*, and what your own spiritual purpose is.

Faith in anything, anyone. Faith that causes ordinary men and women to hug trees in local parks. Faith that causes intelligent people to study full-page spreads of personal advice based on the position of the stars. There has been a wholesale rejection of the scientific, logical, rational model of the world that reduces all of existence to fixed, predetermined and mechanical systems.

Thus doctors are struggling with patients suffering from serious illnesses but who throw away medically approved, 'life-saving' medicines, and opt instead for alternatives that most doctors regard as having little or no scientific basis.

More than 17 million people in Britain alone rely on alternative medicines or therapies – aromatherapy and homeopathy being the most popular. Expect laws in these areas to tighten, requiring companies to verify the health claims made. This will intensify the scale of the culture clash between those who feel that scientific methodology is not a valid test of 'whole person medicine' and those who insist on 'objective' scientific data.

Spiritual awareness will remain central to human existence

Around 85% of people in the world today say that they recognise a spiritual dimension to life, which reflects an ancient pattern in place since the beginning of human history. While strident voices of humanistic atheism are likely to grow louder in some developed nations, they will almost certainly be drowned out globally over the next 50 years by the vast majority who remain convinced that there is more to life than atoms, molecules and bags of biodata.

In developed nations, informal expressions of spirituality seem likely to multiply, as we see further decline in organised religion. Expect growth in personal systems for meditation, in self-help guides to spiritual enlightenment.

Thus, informal attendance at synagogues, Hindu temples, mosques and churches is also likely to rise – particularly at social activities such as mother and toddler groups, homeless projects, drop-in centres, food banks, advice centres, and so on, even while formal membership falls.

These kinds of initiatives may well turn out to be a significant growth factor in the lives of churches, mosques, synagogues and temples in countries like the UK over the next two decades. We can expect more social action projects, as the state gradually runs out of cash from trying to reduce government debt.

From personal belief to organised religion

In emerging nations, we are seeing a rather different picture, with very rapid growth of global, organised religions such as Christianity and Islam, decline in local faith-healers, and far fewer people with private, 'personalised', idiosyncratic, informal beliefs.

There are 1.6 billion followers of Islam in the world today, 21% of the world population. Of these, 60% live in Asia-Pacific and 20% in the Middle East. Islam is likely to grow faster than world population, by around 1.5–1.8% over the next 20 years, but the rate of growth will continue to slow, as the size of families continues to fall in the nations where Islam is strongest, and where incomes are growing rapidly. As we have seen in Chapter 2, fertility rates tend to fall as wealth increases.

Christianity has 2.3 billion adherents, representing 32% of the world population, with 60% of them found in Africa, Asia and Latin America. Christianity will also continue to grow significantly faster than the world population, particularly in places like Africa and former Soviet bloc countries, as well as in China, where tens of millions have found Christian faith since the 1950s, despite a history of severe persecution. It is possible that there are already more Christians in China than in any other nation.

In Argentina over the last decade churches have sprung from nothing to number many thousands of people, and the same has been happening across most of Latin America. Africa has seen extraordinary growth in church attendance, and this is now influencing politicians and governments.

Emphasis on personal spiritual experiences

The impact of the global uprising of life-changing faith, which provokes passion and provides purpose, cannot be underestimated.

Expect divisions within each world religion between radicals who remain rooted in traditional teachings based on, for example, the Bible or the Koran, and liberals who accept or abandon whatever writings they choose in their own personal spiritual journey.

This orthodox-liberal divide is likely to sharpen over issues like abortion, euthanasia, embryonic stem cell research and gay marriage. While liberal churches will argue that they are more attractive and culturally relevant in the US and Europe, they have in fact declined very rapidly. Most church growth there is likely to be, as in the last three decades, among Christian communities that adhere to traditional teachings and express strong spirituality.

This has certainly been the case in the UK, where Pentecostal churches are growing by 5% a year, and over half of all churchgoers in London belong to black-majority Pentecostal-type churches. For example, the Redeemed Christian Church of God now has around 700 churches across the UK, from very few 20 years ago, as a Nigerian mission-movement to Britain.

The evangelical wing of the Anglican Church is also growing. Over 2.5 million people have attended a 12-week induction course to the Christian faith, designed by just one such evangelical church, Holy Trinity, Brompton, in London. However, this growth is unlikely to offset overall Anglican decline, especially among liberal, older congregations in rural areas.

Whether you are a follower of Jesus as I am, or of Mohammed, or of Buddha or the patterns in the stars, believe in karma or rein-carnation, or some other life-force, or in nothing at all, spirituality is likely to remain a significant part of life, shaping our ethics, values, and politics for the next hundred years.

Future of religious movements and ethics

What about new religious movements? History tells us that such things usually start as a reaction against what is seen as moral decay and spiritual bankruptcy of society at the time. When we look around the world today, it is hardly a surprise that we are seeing growing numbers of radical religious groups, some of which will be truly revolutionary.

It is very easy for an influential group of believers from any religion to argue that some or all of the following are true today, *from their own point of view*:

◆ society has lost its soul and moral compass
◆ everywhere you look, traditional moral values have been lost
◆ people are becoming more self-centred and individualistic

◆ our culture is obsessed with celebrity worship, even though most celebrities are terrible role models

◆ youth are worried by superficial and worthless things like personal appearance

◆ family life is breaking down, community ties weakened

◆ many are addicted to alcohol, drugs, sex, the internet

◆ government leaders are often corrupt and cannot be trusted

◆ the web has become a sexual free-for-all, with child abuse and other disgusting or destructive behaviour promoted as normal

◆ rapid, continuous economic growth was supposed to promise a better world but has resulted in appalling contrasts in wealth, failed to deal with the worst global poverty, and is unsustainable by definition

◆ one nation has vast influence over the whole world – exporting its media, culture, corporations, brands – but is itself in a state of moral and spiritual decay

◆ greedy global corporations and banks are wrecking our world

◆ mental illness is more common, suicides are growing, with rising sales of antidepressants, and rapidly growing numbers of counsellors to help people cope with unsatisfying, depressing lives

◆ we have lost sight of the fact that we are spiritual beings, that there is another dimension to life, and that we exist only as a result of divine permission

◆ God has a plan for humanity, which society must obey

◆ humanity as a whole will be held to account

◆ each of us must respond to God's purpose for our own lives.

Therefore, it is obvious that we will continue to see a rapidly growing number of radical religious activists, driven by a 'divine call' to promote (or even impose) God's authority on earth, according to the beliefs they have about who He is and what His will is. Most of them are likely to belong to an existing world religion, and will probably live in emerging nations.

As part of this, we are likely to see new kinds of 'puritanism' in Christianity, just as we have seen in Islam over the last 20–30 years: new waves of orthodoxy that will be very uncomfortable for established churches, and hard to contain within existing structures, fiercely intolerant and zealous for spiritual purity.

New ethical standards for believers and wider society

Such new Christian movements may well seek to prohibit a wide range of 'sinful' or unwise behaviours: banning smoking and drug use among church members, stricter sexual ethics – doctrines that seem to be a throwback to the anti-alcohol temperance movements of the 19th century. These new movements are likely also to become political activists, campaigning for new laws, government regulations, and so on. However, such movements could well split fairly rapidly over the issue of same-sex relationships.

We can also expect new expressions of monastic life, with growing numbers of people taking radical vows of poverty, chastity and obedience, many of whom may be labelled as members of dangerous 'brainwashing' cults.

The church in emerging communities will drive theology

Such new Puritans will of course seem totally at odds with much of the rest of the church in *developed* nations, where sexual activity of many kinds outside of marriage is increasingly accepted as perfectly normal among members, where divorce and remarriage are routine, and where gay marriage is celebrated. We are already witnessing a fundamental ethical schism between *developed* and *emerging* nation churches, liberal and Pentecostal, old-style denominations and indigenous church movements.

Almost all major new missionary movements, over the next 30–40 years, are likely to be influenced by the vision, teachings and values of churches in emerging nations or the poorest parts of the world, reflecting global patterns of church growth and zeal.

Most of the fastest-growing churches in Europe, from the UK to Germany, Poland, Estonia, Ukraine and Slovakia, will probably continue to be those that are evangelical, Pentecostal, charismatic. Such labels can mean different things to different people, but all tend to have three things in common: enthusiastic promotion of life-changing, personal discipleship, a particular focus on the New Testament section of the Bible as a daily guide to following Jesus, and a passionate belief in the power of prayer to release the power of God, together with the gifts of the Holy Spirit to change people's lives.

Such growth will be boosted by migrant communities from emerging nations – whether Nigerians, Poles, South Koreans or Chinese. However, this growth is unlikely to offset overall decline in church-going across much of Europe over the next 20 years, particularly in ageing congregations with liberal theology.

Growth in Catholic churches

The Catholic Church has 1.2 billion members globally, many of whom are not active, compared to over 1 billion in Protestant churches and around 450 million in Orthodox churches. Catholicism in developed nations will stabilise after years of decline, and will grow in the poorest nations, under the inspiring leadership of Pope Francis.

Pope Francis has a radical theology and ethical framework that embraces aspects of Pentecostalism, and adds to his popular appeal. However, he faces the risk of being undermined and even killed because of his very public all-out attack on the corruption, indifference to the poor, and spiritual apathy that he has identified in the heart of the Vatican.

He is certainly more vulnerable than other popes, having abandoned almost all the security measures that they have used, both in and outside the Vatican. If he is removed or assassinated, we can expect great conflicts within the Catholic Church about what kind of pope should succeed him.

Global war against Christians

As in Islam, the most radical edge of Christianity is likely to be a call to arms. An ideology that promotes fighting as necessary to protect the church from being wiped out by aggressive Islamic persecutors.

This type of militant thinking is especially likely to develop among extremist indigenous churches in central and northern Africa, as a response to terrible attacks against churches and Christian households over more than two decades. We are already seeing signs of this in some parts of Africa, particularly in Bangui, the capital of the Central African Republic.

However, such militancy is likely to be held back in most places by the dominant Christian ethic, which has been relatively pacifist, following the teachings of Jesus to *love your neighbour as yourself, love your enemies, pray for those who persecute you, and when your enemy strikes you – turn the other cheek.*

Christians have been slaughtered, tortured, kidnapped, raped and beheaded in unprecedented numbers over the past two decades according to the International Society for Human Rights, which estimates that 80% of all acts of religious discrimination are against Christians. Reuters reports that numbers of reported cases of Christians killed for their faith doubled between 2012 and 2013 to 2,100, which would suggest a total of around 5,000 a year, since most do not get picked up by global media. The Vatican has issued an estimate of around 100,000 'martyrs' a year over the last decade, but that included ethnic/religious genocide in places like the Democratic Republic of the Congo.

Persecution in Iraq, Nigeria and North Korea

In Baghdad alone, 40 of 65 churches have been bombed in a decade. Persecution is leading to migrations, with over 1 million Christians fleeing Iraq in the same period. In Kandhamal, Orissa, north India, 500 Christians were killed in a series of Hindu-supported riots, thousands were injured and 50,000 believers were left homeless, while 350 Christian schools and churches were destroyed.

In northern Nigeria, Boko Haram has butchered over 5,000 Christians since 2009, with over 650,000 forced to flee from towns and villages. In North Korea some estimate that around 25% of 300,000 in labour camps are there because of their Christian faith, and many thousands more believers have just disappeared after arrest.

Attacks on churches in China and Pakistan

In China, most church congregations are not recognised legally by the government, and harassment is common, despite rapid growth. Indeed, such attacks are partly a response of fear about the strengthening influence of these unlawful and influential groups. Large churches have been pulled down, and many leaders arrested in some parts of the country, for example in Wenzhou where 15% of the population of 9 million are already Christian.

In Pakistan, mobs regularly lynch and kill Christians who are accused of telling others about their faith, or of showing disrespect in some way to Islam. People who convert to Christianity often live in great fear, risk being attacked by family, worship in complete secrecy, and are often forced to flee abroad to seek asylum. When you meet people who have experienced these things, as I have, you cannot fail to be touched by what has happened to them. Expect many more such cases.

Islam also at war with Islam

Such attacks by Islamic extremists are not just directed at those of other religions. Most of them are against others from an Islamic background.

Some radical Islamic teachers seem set to continue to encourage online followers to kill all 'infidels' and those who support them, including people who describe themselves as devout followers of Islam, but whose lifestyle does not reflect the same interpretation of the Koran.

And we are likely to see ongoing bitter, intense, tribal and ideological wars between Sunni and Shiite 'tribes' of Islam, with their different cultural histories. As we have seen, we can expect a growing culture gap between more moderate, wealthy and intellectual believers in developed nations, and those who follow Islam in emerging nations.

A new world religion?

At the end of the last chapter, we looked at the possibility that political creeds could be swept aside by a radical new ideology that could turn out to be as influential as communism was in the late 19th century and the major part of the 20th century. Alongside this, we can also expect to see a new religion.

All major world religions are likely to continue to reinvent themselves over the next 100 years, as their traditional teachings are reinterpreted in very different ages and cultures. The roots of the Christian faith have remained virtually unchanged over 2,000 years but expressions, understanding and practice have varied greatly.

Global 'market' for a new world religion

A completely globalised world is likely to create a vacuum or a 'market' for a new world religion, which will feed into the aspirations of the M generation. We could well see a world-recognised prophet emerge over the next few decades with charisma, dynamism and teachings, which rapidly capture the global imagination.

The biggest issue will be truth: is there such a thing? Global religions such as Judaism, Christianity and Islam all proclaim timeless truth about an unchanging God, offering exclusive understanding of him. In contrast, New Age beliefs draw heavily from some aspects of Hinduism, which emphasise a more general approach to truth, and a more fluid, ethical framework, with far fewer absolutes.

In a constantly changing world, certainty about ultimate issues such as personal destiny becomes increasingly important. That is the appeal of radical fundamentalism. Therefore, we can see that a new world religion will be most likely to be defined by dogmatic teaching, and a claim of exclusivity and superiority to all previously understood truths about God.

Expect such a prophet to offer 'the final revelation' that humankind has not thus far been ready to receive, the promise that humankind is 'coming of age' and is only now able to receive the truth. Such a prophet is likely to claim that all the great religions pointed in part to the Truth, but did not provide the complete picture.

Such a prophet could sweep tens of millions into a new religious movement, over a short space of time. But this will be unlikely without a global struggle on an immense scale. Militant Islam in particular will be as violently opposed to this new religion as it is to apostasy among Islamic communities, and as it is also to Christianity.

A new world order

With so many challenges facing the world, many of which require a collective response, will we see a new world order emerging? Is there a way to roll together the authority of governments worldwide?

The answer is that we are already seeing the tentative beginnings of such a new order, in the proliferation of environmental treaties for example, or in the global fight against terrorism.

More international treaties for global control

Hundreds of international agreements have been signed, whether to encourage trade or stop money laundering. And as more are created, informal global governance begins to emerge.

The United Nations was founded for such a purpose – 'to save succeeding generations from the scourge of war' and 'to reaffirm faith in fundamental human rights, in the dignity and value of the human person.'

The real trouble is that, as we have seen repeatedly, UN member nations are divided about what they want the UN to do and how to do it. Peacekeeping is politically difficult and practically dangerous. The emphasis has switched to building economic security.

But the trend is clear: global governance will be essential to our peaceful and prosperous future. The unprecedented spirit of global collaboration that emerged after the collapse of communism and the Cold War will deepen, despite many crises and setbacks. As we have seen, part of this will develop out of regional coalitions, trading blocs and spheres of influence. Indeed trade is a civilising force.

International courts will grow in power

Despite differing positions on many issues, there is growing agreement on the need for an international code of conduct for commerce. Indeed, international trade is impossible without it.

While individual nations may reform their own legal systems, with many bilateral agreements on things like extradition, another, higher, level will be needed. The beginnings are already with us: for example, the prosecution of national leaders in one country for war crimes, by a court comprised of other countries' representatives.

Regional law courts are well established, in the EU, for example. Expect supra-regional courts to be dealing with a wide variety of international crime cases by 2025. History shows that law and order is imposed most rapidly where there is a lack of it. Therefore, these new powers will be agreed by nations as a matter of urgent necessity, to address their own impotence.

Global government

In summary, then, expect to see various expressions of global governance emerge, and co-align into the first stages of a new world order over the next few decades.

Expect periods of intense negotiation to define global ethics in more detail, whether attempts to create a total global ban on bio-weapons, a response to international terrorism or ethnic genocide, limits on global monopolies, or world agreements on slavery, child labour, work practices and other issues of human rights and responsibilities.

Many issues will be polarised between emerging and developed nations. All these debates will be increasingly influenced by a profound rethink in wealthier nations, by a new generation that is no longer so impressed by speed, urbanisation, material wealth and globalisation. A generation that is itself becoming more radical, ethical and spiritually aware.

Now is the time to choose

So, then, we have journeyed into the future of every region in the world, and into every industry. We have seen the bright and dark side of every trend, and how they form the Six Faces of the Future as a cube, which spins with all the energy that comes from emotion. Now is the time to choose …

Take hold of your future, or the future will take hold of you.

Chapter 7

SHAPING YOUR FUTURE

AS WE SAW AT THE VERY BEGINNING of our journey, the cube of your own future is weighted according to who you are, where you are and the nature of your work, your stage of life.

We have also seen how hard it is to hold the entire future in your mind at the same time. You cannot see all those six faces at once. That's why it is so important to keep turning the cube, and to keep dipping in and out of this book, maybe over some weeks or months.

As one group of faces comes into focus, others recede into the background. Keep stretching your view, and as those faces keep turning, you will come one day to find that you can hold the entire universe of tomorrow in the palm of your hand.

The first cube was handmade by me from teak. And you can buy one of identical size, also handmade, of polished pewter, to help you in this visualisation process.*

You have to imagine that your own cube is uniquely weighted, so that a random throw will show one of the faces that is most important for you, in the next stage of your own future.

But take care, for every now and then a much less familiar face will demand your attention, with many new opportunities and challenges.

So keep turning the cube, stay agile, focused and true to your

* Order one from: http://www.globalchange.com/cube

own sense of destiny. Because life is too important to waste a single day. Life is too short to do things you don't believe in.

How very small numbers change the future

People often tell me that they feel powerless to change their own future, let alone anyone else's. But let me encourage you with a story. The truth is that most of us have far more ability to change things than we realise, once we grasp the power of the cube.

When I first started presenting the Six Faces of the Future, I spoke to a group of CEOs and chairmen of some of the world's most powerful corporations at the World Economic Forum, Davos.

I showed them what we saw in the introduction: how the usual way for CEOs of companies to view the cube is from the top. They tend to focus on just three Faces of the Future: Fast, Urban and Universal. In other words, all about the speed of change, urbanisation, demographics, health care, fashions and fads, technology and globalisation, and so on. It's the typical world view of banks, IT companies, global manufacturing and e-commerce.

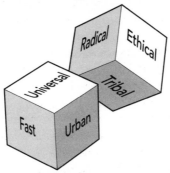

But as we have seen, most of the pressures for radical change are likely to come from a very different view of the same future. Turn the cube 180 degrees and we are confronted with Tribal, Radical and Ethical. This is a future driven by the forces of nationalism, sectarianism, social media, activism, personal motivation, aspiration, ambition, sustainability, politics, religion and terrorist movements.

I asked these CEOs a question: in their own experience, how many people would it take to totally change their strategy?

What proportion of their shareholders, or customers, or staff, or readers of social media, would it take to turn the direction of the company upside down, if they were very radical in thinking, very ethically driven and very tribal, or well organised. The answer is always the same: less than 2%. They think that just one person in 50, in society or among their customers, would be enough – if they were sufficiently passionate, radical, tightly organised and focused.

I asked another question. How many shareholders do you need to keep the chairman of a publicly listed company awake at night before an annual general meeting? The answer is always the same. Only one person is needed, with one share, costing a few dollars, asking the right 'ethical' question about a very controversial and 'radical' issue, to unleash uncontrollable forces in the 'tribal' media, forcing major policy changes.

If this is all true, then consider its implications for your own life. If a single shareholder can shape the future direction of an entire global corporation; if a small group of activists in a company or a community can influence a 5-year strategy …

How many people do *you* know or influence? You almost certainly have far more power to change things than you realise, inside the organisation you work for, or with people you know.

Look what can be done by the owner of a single share, and consider the potential impact of your own life over the next 10 years to influence people around you for the better, in many small but significant ways, at work or at home. And the greatest influence is always example.

How to stay 'Futurewise'

People often ask me how they should stay informed. A key part of the answer is to read quality publications like the *Financial Times* or *The Economist*, and anything else you can lay your hands on, to broaden your perspectives.

Travel as much as you can to unfamiliar places, talk to everyone you can about unfamiliar things. Seek out and celebrate unfamiliar experiences, cultures, places and forums. Early-warning signs of change are all around you. For instance, always talk to your taxi driver, as they are often the first to notice a change in the city or nation where they live. They see early upturns or downturns in business. They overhear conversations.

Get involved. Join organisations outside your business, and meet new people from very different walks of life. For me, being part of a cosmopolitan church in London is helpful from that point of view. And the AIDS charity ACET, which started in our own family home in 1988, and is now in twenty nations, has been a tremendous learning experience, taking me deep into the most remote parts of some of the poorest nations on earth.

Watch people. When you visit a city, stop for a while and linger – whether in a café or a park or a museum or bus depot or street market. What do you see? What do you smell? What conversations do you hear? All of the future is streaming by.

Visit people in their homes in other nations, if you can. You will learn more in an hour or two about their way of life, family relationships and culture than in 30 years of working in the same virtual team.

Above all, stay intensely curious and interested in other people's stories. Expect to change your own opinions and your own future. You have choices every day. Do what you believe in and feel most passionate about.

About the author

PATRICK DIXON is the founder and chairman of Global Change Ltd, a growth strategy and forecasting company. He is the author of sixteen books (over 600,000 in print in over 40 languages), and a physician. Previous books include *Futurewise*, *SustainAgility*, *The Genetic Revolution* and *Building a Better Business*. He has been ranked as one of the twenty most influential business thinkers alive today.* He has spoken to audiences in over fifty nations and is one of the world's most sought-after keynote speakers at corporate events.

He advises boards and senior teams on a wide range of strategic issues. Clients include Google, Microsoft, IBM, KLM/Air France, BP, ExxonMobil, World Bank, Siemens, Prudential, Aviva, UBS, Credit Suisse, PwC, Hewlett Packard, Gillette, GSK, Forbes, Fortune, BT, BBC, Fedex and DHL. He has also taught on a wide variety of executive education programmes at the London Business School since 1999.

Patrick has worked as group strategy director for Acromas Ltd, which owned the AA and Saga, before its flotation. He has been a non-executive director of Allied Health Care Ltd, which delivers over 40 million home care visits a year across the UK. He was also chairman of the cancer biotech company Virttu Biologics Ltd from 2012 to 2015.

He has appeared on many TV stations, including CNN, CNBC, Fox News, Sky News and ITV, with features in the *Financial Times*,

* 17th in the world in Thinkers 50 2005; 47th in the world in 2003.

Telegraph and *Time* magazine. His website has been used by more than 16 million different people with 6 million video views and over 43,000 followers on Twitter.

He trained as a physician at Kings College, Cambridge and Imperial College, London, during which he launched a healthcare IT startup, called Medicom. In 1988, after working as a cancer physician, caring for those dying of cancer, he started the international AIDS agency ACET, which today has programmes in eighteen nations, mainly in the poorest parts of the world. ACET began as a result of his first book, *The Truth about* AIDS. He continued to write many other books, which led to broadcasting, lecturing on trends, and to advisory roles with many companies.

Patrick is in his late 50s and married to Sheila. Both are still heavily involved in supporting ACET around the world, in places like India and Uganda. They have four married children and two grandchildren, and live in London, where they are active in a local church. Patrick's hobbies include long-distance sailing, painting and writing.

http://www.globalchange.com

http://www.youtube.com/pjvdixon

http://twitter.com/patrickdixon

patrickdixon@globalchange.com

+44 7768 511390

Acknowledgements

AS ANY LEADER OR WRITER KNOWS, any attempt to anticipate future trends can be a humbling and somewhat daunting process. Whatever success I may have had in this endeavour over the last 27 years has only been due to the combined foresight of a very large number of people.

I am deeply grateful to the many hundreds of senior business, government and NGO leaders from every industry and sector, as well as several hundred more innovators and specialists from over 100 nations, who have generously shared personal insights and reflections with me over the last few years about where they think their own industries and regions may be heading. These conversations have typically happened when working together, or over dinner, at corporate events where I am speaking, in board strategy sessions, or in workshops and seminars, as we have grappled together with what all of our futures might be like.

I am particularly grateful to Prabhu Guptara, who while at UBS Wolfsberg encouraged me to develop the original FUTURE construct, and for his faithful critique and mentoring over many years. Special thanks also (in no particular order) to Brian Souter, Sinclair Beecham, Peter Vardy, Andrew Goodsell, Tim Pethick, Lynda Greenshields, David Unsworth, Paul Reading, Martin Lindström, Johan Gorecki, Doug Balfour, Doug Birdsell, Toni Schönenberger, Don Sull and Tony Eccles. Thanks to the wonderful team at Leigh Bureau – Bill Leigh, Wes Neff, Karen O'Donnell, Rachel Moran, Doireann Maguire, Jonathan Pearce,

Roisin Wickham, Anne Pennefather and Louise Dunne – for helping make so many of these events happen over the last 16 years, and for many helpful trend perspectives along the way.

I am also grateful to those working with some of poorest and most marginalised communities in emerging nations and those supporting them, who have taught me so much about rapid social changes, opportunities and challenges in their own countries, in connection with their inspiring work as part of the international AIDS agency ACET. People like David Kabiswa, Alan Ellard, Marek Slansky, Yvonne Kavuo, Milan Presburger, Sam Udanyi, Sujai and Lavanya Suneetha, Alex Zhibrik, Richard and Wendy Phillips, Richard Carson and Peter Fabian. Also thanks to many Faculty at London Business School that I have had the privilege to work with on Executive Education programmes during the last 16 years, including Dominic Houlder, Julian Birkinshaw, Lynda Gratton, Costas Markides, Nigel Nicholson, Andrew Scott, Linda Yueh and Jules Goddard – all of whom have helped sharpen my own thinking, as they have graciously allowed me to sit in on their sessions from time to time.

I am also indebted to a host of great thinkers, debaters, speakers and writers whose insights have influenced my evolving view of the world. I was first inspired to explore the future by the work of people like Nicholas Negroponte, Charles Handy, John Naisbitt, Peter Cochrane, Patrick Johnstone and Fons Trompenaars. And then I also owe thanks to the countless thousands of web writers, to the community of future trends bloggers, and to all those who make comments on my website, post responses to my videos and so on – often bringing vital perspectives.

Thanks to all the wonderful Profile Books team: to Stephen Brough, co-founder and senior editor, for inspiring me to travel once more into the future as a writer – he is an absolute pleasure to write for, and made a huge number of suggestions and comments; Paul Forty for making it all happen within a very tight deadline; Fiona Screen for copy editing and sorting out issues with such care; and Anna-Marie Fitzgerald for managing publicity. Thanks too to Patricia O'Sullivan at Global Change Ltd for re-checking the text.

Thanks to Richard Herkes, formerly senior editor at Kingsway, for suggesting my first book – leading to 15 more over the years. I am also grateful to many other people like Glyn MacAulay, Steve Clifford, Gerald Coates, Lyndon Bowring, Lawrence Singlehurst, Andrew Owen, Mark Melluish, George Verwer, Phil Wall, Norman Barnes, David Smith, Peter Brierley, Gary and Max Hamilton, Steven Powell, Ravi Dua, Sam Jones, Linda and Richard Ward and Simon Blanchflower, who have all helped me make better sense at various times over the years of how the wider world is evolving.

And of course thanks to Sheila, my wife and best friend for more than 38 years, for her endless encouragement and feedback on the text, and to our four children and their spouses for helping me identify early trend signals.

Statistics and other important facts are from published government and other sources, as well as from those working at the cutting edge of change and innovation, who are at the forefront of changing tomorrow's world.

Index